ACCLAIM FOR

Leah Hager Cohen's

TRAIN GO SORRY

"With skillful storytelling [and] understated passion . . .
Leah Hager Cohen presents readers with an intimate look at
the new politics of deafness. . . . Deaf culture, her book
suggests, is a culture of closeness that is worth saving."
—*Washington Post*

"Part autobiography, part proud polemic on behalf of 'deaf
culture,' part history of the deaf-education movement, part
case studies at the Lexington School. . . . With passion and
historical perspective . . . Cohen has a reporter's eye for
detail and a gift for the sharply illuminating phrase."
—*Cleveland Plain Dealer*

"Cohen's writing is precise; she is an acute observer of
details, of moods and subtle shifts in power."
—*New York* magazine

"A powerfully and poignantly rendered account of a quite
special instance of the struggle for understanding. We all
try to learn about the world from one another—but this
book tells us how some of us do so against tremendous
odds, yet with notable and touching success."
—Robert Coles

Leah Hager Cohen

TRAIN GO SORRY

Leah Hager Cohen earned a B.A. in fiction writing at Hampshire College and an M. S. from the Columbia University Graduate School of Journalism. She currently lives in Somerville, Massachusetts.

TRAIN GO SORRY

Leah Hager Cohen

TRAIN
GO
SORRY

Inside a Deaf World

VINTAGE BOOKS

A Division of Random House, Inc.   New York

FIRST VINTAGE BOOKS EDITION, MAY 1995

Photograph on p. xiv courtesy of Sue Cohen.

Library of Congress Cataloging-in-Publication Data
Cohen, Leah Hager
Train go sorry : inside a deaf world / Leah Hager Cohen.
— 1st Vintage Books ed.
p. cm
Originally published: Boston : Houghton Mifflin, 1994.
ISBN 0-679-76165-9
1. Lexington School for the Deaf.
2. Lexington School for the Deaf—Students.
3. Deaf—New York (N.Y.)—Means of communication.
4. Deaf—New York (N.Y.)—Social conditions. I. Title.
HV2561.N72N35 1995
305.9'0872—dc20 94-23501
CIP

Manufactured in the United States of America
30 29 28 27 26 25 24 23

To
Mary B. Romig,
105 Albemarle Street,
and her wooden box

Author's Note

There exists no practical written system for American Sign Language. Throughout this book I have used italics to represent signed communication transposed into English. The transpositions are my own; I have done my best to make them faithful to the signer's original meaning, emotion, and register. Italics appear every time sign language was part of the mode of communication, regardless of whether the signer used pure ASL, signs rendered in English word order and supported by spoken English, or anything in between.

During most of the research for this book, I assumed the role of an observer, remaining outside the action. Occasionally I felt compelled to step in as an interpreter. The interpreters' code of ethics prevents me from reporting any of the information I had access to in that role; for this reason, I refrained from interpreting as much as possible.

TRAIN GO SORRY

"This Court for the Deaf"
Faye and Sam Cohen, Washington Baths, 1934

Oscar reading to a group of students in our Lexington
apartment in 1969. My sister, Reba, and I are in white dresses.

Reba, my brother, Andy, and I on the steps
outside Lexington, 1973

Sofia and Irina Normatov,
Lexington classes of 1993 and 2001

James Taylor, Lexington class of 1992

1

Coming into the Language

That our family's home was a school for the deaf did not seem in any way extraordinary to Reba, Andy, and me. Lexington School for the Deaf was simply where we came from. Our apartment was on the third floor of the southern wing of the building, above the nursery school and adjacent to the boys' dormitory. The walls and doors, incidental separations between our living space and the rest of the building, were routinely disregarded. Our father might be called away from the table in the middle of dinner; we children often played down the hall with kids from the dorm. It wasn't until Reba, my older sister, proved at age six to be a sleepwalker — discovered one night riding the elevator in her pajamas — that our parents even thought to install a proper lock on the front door.

We lived at the school, in Queens, New York, because our parents worked there. Our mother taught nursery school; our father was the director of child care. But their involvement extended far beyond their jobs. They put out *The Afterschooler*, a newsletter about residential life. They hosted holiday parties, cranking our stereo so that vibrations thrummed through everyone's rib cage. They built a snack bar in the basement for the high school kids, using giant electrical spools for tables. They invited people from all parts of the Lexington community to have dinner at our apartment, from student teachers to administrators, from alumni to people on the maintenance staff.

They seemed intimate with the very marrow of the school, and tended it with infinite care. Our mother painted giant murals that hung on the first floor: reproductions of famous children's book characters, altered slightly so that a hearing aid nestled in each one's ear. And our father extinguished a fire in the basement one night, pulling on jeans in response to the alarms that simultaneously clanged and sent pulsing red beams along the corridors.

Our parents knew every inch of Lexington, every passageway. In his rear pocket, our father carried a dense batch of keys. Yellow and snaggle-toothed in their neat leather holder, they pivoted forth to open any door. When he was summoned away from us — to hold a child who was out of control, or to interpret *Miranda* rights for police who were arresting a student, or to transport a blender from the kitchen so that the dorm kids could complete a cooking project — our mother would guide us on small adventures. She would take us to the pool for evening swims, afterward changing us into our sleepers in the locker room. She took us to the auditorium for movies, special screenings of subtitled prints that were shown in the days before closed captioning. She took us to watch the Lexington Blue Jays play softball out on the field, and when we got bored she taught us to weave crowns from the white clover that dotted the sidelines. On hot days she equipped us with paintbrushes and saucepans of water so that we could "paint" the patio that led to the playground. Once, on the Fourth of July, she led us up to the roof, where we ate green ice cream and watched fireworks flash around the dark grid of the neighborhood.

Lexington was our red-brick castle, our seven-acre kingdom. My sister and brother and I pedaled our tricycles up and down the hallways, over the tan-and-cream bands of buffed linoleum. Later, on summer evenings, we learned to ride two-wheelers in the narrow strip of parking lot. Our books were stamped out from the school library; we picked up the mail from our slot amid the faculty boxes in the general office. Once we helped plant corn and tomatoes beyond the northern wall of the auditorium. We even ran the proverbial lemonade stand out in front of the school one hot July afternoon. We frequently ate dinner in the cafeteria: fruit cocktail, meat loaf, and peas; plastic trays; milk from a machine; and all around us the murmur and motions of our elders, the Lexington community.

Everyone knew us. They knew us in our diapers and they knew us in our pajamas. They knew us running around the basketball court at halftime during the big deaf-school tournaments. They knew us making candles out of melted crayons with the dormitory students, or chewing Mary Janes and Bazookas while reading the comics in the lobby with the weekend watchman. Lexington held our extended family; it was a large, interconnected neighborhood full of surrogate uncles and aunts.

During the seven years our family lived at the school, it had an annual enrollment of about four hundred students, from the infant center straight through high school. One hundred and fifty resided in the dorm. In the building's northern wing, the centers for hearing and speech, mental health, and research served thousands more deaf people from the greater New York area every year. Deaf people from all five boroughs, New Jersey, Westchester, and Long Island converged on Lexington for special events — athletic tournaments, plays, homecomings, lectures, and talent shows, all held in the gym or the auditorium. My sister and brother and I were at home among them. From the time we could walk, we were navigating forests of grown-up legs, ducking in order not to obstruct signed conversation and pausing to endure having our cheeks pinched, our height exclaimed over.

In our world, people were either deaf or hearing. We registered both with equal lack of concern: the designation was relevant but unremarkable. We were already accustomed to cultural differences, even within our own family — our father was Jewish, our mother Protestant; our paternal grandparents were deaf, the rest of us hearing; Andy (who was adopted) was black, the rest of us white. We didn't actively learn so much as acquire the special behaviors and customs of communicating with deaf people.

We knew always to look at someone deaf when we spoke. We knew not to exaggerate the movements of our mouths but to make sure we did speak clearly. We knew that we should use our voices, because a lot of people picked up some sound with their hearing aids and that helped them read lips. Our father got annoyed if we only mouthed the words. If we wanted someone's attention, we knew that we should tap the person's arm or stamp our foot to send vibrations, never poke or snap. If we didn't understand someone's speech, we knew that we should listen for our father's voice, which would come from behind and above in easy translation, and without ever breaking eye contact we would respond, our lips automatically precise, our voices pitched at normal volume.

If our father wasn't there to translate, I would wrinkle the top of my nose in between my eyes, and then the person would automatically repeat what she was saying. If I still didn't understand, and I was feeling very tired and was waiting to be taken upstairs and put to bed, I might smile and nod, guiltily faking it. When I got older and knew enough sign language, I might use some of that, and then the person would beam, bestowing on me such a look of cherishing gladness that I would feel my cheeks and neck go hot.

Many nights I found myself, at the end of some late event, weaving groggily about the auditorium or gym, waiting for the crowd to disperse so that my father could lock the doors and take me upstairs to bed. Someone would flick the lights on and off, signaling, "Go home, please go home." No one ever paid much attention. Finally the lights would go off altogether, making signed communication impossible, and people would genially drift out as far as the still-lighted lobby — only to resume conversation there. When at last everyone had been shooed from the building, there were always some who remained out in front, halfway down the steps, under the dim globe of a streetlight, anywhere that enough light remained to converse.

I imagined friends lingering out there long after I had been tucked under the covers, vivid silhouettes communicating deep into the night. That the task of clearing the building after community events was so challenging never struck me as odd. Long goodbyes and deafness intertwine in my mind as far back as I can remember.

My connection to Lexington extends even further back than my memories. It begins long before my birth.

Around the turn of the century, my father's father, Sam Cohen, arrived in this country from Russia. Because he was still a child, his parents were able to hide his deafness from authorities at Ellis Island, who could have sent him back across the ocean with a single chalk mark on his coat if they had detected any impairment. Sam went on to become a student at Lexington, then located in Manhattan, on the avenue for which it is named.

My grandmother, Fannie, attended P.S. 47, the city school for the deaf downtown, on Twenty-third Street. She and Sam met after graduation, on a boardwalk near Ocean Parkway where groups of young deaf people gathered during the summers. Fannie, too, was part of a wave of Eastern European immigrants, but when she and Sam married, the culture that infused their home was not so much Russian or Romanian as it was deaf.

After a social evening — a dinner party or a few hands of

cassino with another couple — they would stand at the door of their basement apartment in the Bronx for over an hour, saying goodbye. The other couple might live only blocks away. They might be going to see each other the very next day. It didn't matter. Always they would linger.

This reluctance to part, to sever the connection and enter the vacant night — this is an integral part of deaf culture. After a day spent surrounded by the hearing, at work, on the subway, at the market, those evening hours with other deaf people were never enough. The last prolonged moments by the door grew out of a hunger for connection. Sam and Fannie, in their lifetime, had few alternatives to satisfy that hunger.

The teletypewriter (TTY), which enables deaf people to communicate through phone lines, did not become widely used until the late 1960s. A large clattery machine indigenous to newsrooms, it transmits typed messages instantaneously to someone who is also operating a TTY. Originally, the number of households that owned TTYs was quite modest, and virtually no public agencies — schools, hospitals, libraries, police stations — owned one. Certain localities offered a service called Deaf Contact for use in emergencies. A deaf person would call on a TTY; a Deaf Contact operator, acting as intermediary, would then telephone the hearing party and deliver the message by voice. Both its hours of operation and the purposes for which Deaf Contact could be used were limited. Very often, deaf people resorted to beseeching their hearing neighbors to place calls for them, or they simply ventured out on foot.

Today the old machine has been streamlined into the compact, portable telecommunication device for the deaf, which, in addition to being cheaper and more convenient, increases deaf people's autonomy. Today Deaf Contact has evolved into twenty-four-hour, toll-free relay services across the nation that facilitate simultaneous voice-TTY conversations. Today we have closed-captioned television, on-line computer information programs, and legislation mandating increased interpreter services. But even all of these modern developments have done little to quench deaf people's thirst for time spent physically together. When so much of the world is indecipherable, so much information inaccessible, the act of congregating with other deaf people and exchanging information in a shared language takes on a kind of vital warmth.

My first home was steeped in this warmth. I took it for granted, responded to it unconsciously, just as I took for granted that Lexington was in some way special, set apart from what lay beyond. Something survived intact within these walls, something perfectly removed yet vibrant in itself.

It seems to me that during my childhood, the fact that I was hearing was kindly overlooked. This may have been due to my lineage; people's feelings for my grandparents may have prompted a special graciousness toward me. It may have been simply my age; children are usually granted surrogate membership in the larger community in which they are raised. But I staked a further claim, one purely my own: after I was born, I was taken straight from the hospital to Lexington School for the Deaf. As far as I was concerned, in that motion alone my birthright was sealed.

What interests me now is not whether this fantasy was legitimate but why it mattered at all — why I longed so deeply for a place among deaf people. For if by blood I am bound to Lexington, by involuntary desire I am bound to the deaf community.

For the first century of its existence, Lexington was housed in a great gabled building across the East River, on Lexington Avenue and Sixty-eighth Street in Manhattan. It moved into its new lodgings in Jackson Heights in 1968, three months after I was born. I remember learning this fact when I was very small, and it struck me as further evidence of a special tie. With this information, I fully anthropomorphized the school; we were nearly twins. She was larger than I, but we were the same age. We turned five together, and six; I remember patting her walls in recognition of these shared anniversaries.

Just before Astoria Boulevard and the Grand Central Parkway mark the end of Jackson Heights, Lexington claims one full block in the midst of the neighborhood's varied ethnic landscape. Up by the Roosevelt Avenue subway, where the elevated Number Seven rattles overhead, women in jeans and sneakers shop for Asian herbs, videos from Bombay, tropical fruit in terraced displays. Within a block, business gives way to residences — grand old Tudor houses and garden apartments whose Anglophilic names seem incongruous with their current occupants, who have settled here from Korea, Colombia, Russia, Argentina, Venezuela, and Uruguay. The immigrants' voices rise from stoops and drift through open windows, punctuated by bursts of flat American slang from their children, playing stickball in the streets.

On the other side of Northern Boulevard, the ethnic mixture changes sharply. Old Italian, Irish, and German families live here, in brick rowhouses that squat for blocks like fat red hens, each indistinguishable from the others except for an occasional pink metal awning hung over a front door, a cement lawn cherub tucked in a nave of sculpted hedges in a yard, or worn AstroTurf lining an exposed porch floor. Always a woman in a housedress is pruning a rosebush, a man in an undershirt is hosing down his drive. From every tidy plot of land radiates a dual sense of patriotism and homogeneity.

At the northernmost edge of this neighborhood stands Lexington, a cultural community in its own right and a visible presence in the area. Storekeepers recognize Lexington students by the hearing aids behind their ears; residents can pick them out a block away as they sign to each other while they walk. In spite of their quarter-century in Jackson Heights, the deaf remain as culturally distinct as any newly arrived immigrant population.

During the late 1960s, Lexington was in the early stages of changing its stance on sign language. American Sign Language (ASL) dates back to 1817, when Thomas Gallaudet, a hearing preacher from the United States, asked Laurent Clerc, a deaf teacher from France, to help him start the first public school for the deaf in this country, the American School for the Deaf in Hartford, Connecticut. Clerc introduced manual education to this country, teaching the students his native French Sign Language, which became the ancestor of contemporary ASL.

Despite the achievements of Clerc and Gallaudet, most hearing people considered sign language to be primitive, an indication of deficient intelligence. This attitude prevailed for more than a hundred years. Not until the 1950s did research begin to show that ASL is a legitimate language rather than a sloppy English-substitute for deaf people who functioned too poorly to learn to talk. But even though Lexington no longer regarded sign language as an abomination, it still prohibited its use in the classroom and treated the whole subject with moody ambivalence.

So my sister and brother and I did not grow up bilingual. Our lack of fluency in the language did not prevent us from using it among ourselves, however. Just as we scribble-scrabbled with crayons on newsprint when we were preliterate, we played at signing to one another in elaborate gibberish. The signs themselves were nonsense, of course, but other features of the language we reproduced with native perfection: pacing, eye contact, various placements of the hands on the body, facial movements, even the incidental click of lips and teeth. I liked those sounds that deaf people made — unchecked, intimate, like tiny, natural lullabies.

For the longest time I never fully believed that I wouldn't eventually become deaf. All around me, children were deaf. I observed the older ones: the wonderful way they chewed their gum and wore their hair and cavorted in the snack bar, and most especially the way they talked, with such enviable panache, such thick rapport. At that time Lexington still adhered to oralism, the educational philosophy and practice that focuses on teaching deaf children to speak and read lips, but outside the classroom the older children signed to each other and no one much bothered them about it. I loved the rapid rhythms of their conversation, the effortless weave of eyebrows and fingers and shoulders and lips, so full of careless grace and yet freighted with meaning.

Reba and Andy and I could fingerspell the alphabet, sign the numbers up to ten, say *I love you* and *More milk, please*. I knew the signs for colors and members of the family, knew *apple* and *ice cream* and *good* and *home*. But that was about the extent of my signing abilities.

I played at signing the way other children play dress-up; part of trying on possibilities, practicing for the future, it was laden with excitement and anticipation, even aspiration. I wanted to grow up and be deaf, be a Lexington student, with all the accouterments: hearing aids, speech lessons, fast and clever hands.

When I was four and five years old, I was one of a few hearing children who attended Lexington's preschool as part of an experiment with integration. In many ways I seemed no different from any of my classmates, making doll cakes in the sandbox, playing chase outside on the patio, eating just the middles of my bread-and-butter snack, as was our fashion. But I was not the same.

One afternoon, while playing with my classmates outside, I sought to remedy my most blatant difference. I selected two pebbles — urban pebbles, rough bits of dark gravel — from the ground and set them in the shallow cups of cartilage above my earlobes. When the teacher spied my improvised hearing aids, I was thoroughly scolded. "Never put *anything* smaller than your elbow in your ear!" was her mystifying admonishment. Puzzling over this helped deflect some of my embarrassment and hurt, but it did nothing to help me fit in with the others.

I sorely envied my classmates their speech lessons. Whenever I had occasion to peek into one of the closet-size speech rooms along the hall, I drank in the scenery, the exotic paraphernalia — mirrors and flash cards, balloons and balls, feathers and tongue depressors — with a lustful, wondering eye. I didn't know then that many deaf children loathe speech lessons, experience them as something designed for humiliation and failure. (Once, when I was six and attending public school, I faked a lisp for the speech therapist who visited our class so that I could finally discover what really went on during speech lessons. They turned out to be crushingly dull; the therapist — a beige, squarish woman — presented me with an entire box of plastic drinking straws and directed me to practice saying my s's around them at home.)

But the time I remember being most alienated as a student at Lexington was during story hour. The other children and I would pull our little wooden chairs up to the table, and each of them would plug a special hearing aid into the metal box that sat on top, an FM unit that amplified the teacher's voice as she read the story into a wireless microphone. With their regular hearing aid receivers strapped around their chests on white harnesses and their heads crowned with large blue earphones, the other children leaned together, tightly connected, all joined to the same circuit.

I never felt so apart. The privilege of being able to hear paled in comparison to the privilege of being close, of sharing that common experience with the other children. The ability to hear, this extra sense through which I received so many signals and that allowed me to process information and make connections on another level, seemed to me at age five a mean gift.

It was not actually my ability to hear that set me most apart, though. At any rate, it was not my hearing per se, although it could be considered a symptom of my ability to hear: it was the fact that I spoke the teacher's language. This was my most important feature as a student. This, before anything else about me — personality, cognitive ability, learning style — was what shaped my experience in the classroom: I knew the same language as the teacher and the world at large.

One of my Lexington classmates had also started school knowing a language system. Like me, he had not been taught his first language; he had acquired it the way we all do naturally, through exposure, by seeing it used by parents, an older sibling, adult friends. However, his parents were deaf; his language was ASL. Unlike me, he knew a language that was not used, nor even condoned, by the teacher, who could not therefore know him or communicate with him in the same way that she could with me. The primary focus of this boy's education was learning English; everything else came second to that.

As for me, I was a language-smitten child, thrilled by the patterns and shapes of words. In my mind each letter of the alphabet had a particular color and personality. Every inanimate object — the wooden door wedge, the saltshaker, the windowsill — hummed with stories on its own special frequency. I related these stories all the time, told them to my brother and my sister, to my socks and my shoes. I dictated the stories to my parents and teachers, who transcribed them in English. Engaging with adults in this way, I could feel that I was the recipient of their delighted attention. I didn't know how lucky I was to have a vehicle for telling these stories, how lucky I was that my parents and teachers understood and encouraged me.

The messages my classmates received from hearing adults were altogether different. They did not qualify for most adult praise until they could use English. Most of them were not fluent in any language. They knew bits of English and were just learning to recognize words visually, although those words appeared slightly different in the mouths of their teachers, their mothers, their fathers. They were learning to connect the lip shapes with the concepts. They were being taught to locate their own vocal cords and position their throats and tongues and teeth and manipulate all the muscles just so, and when the teacher told them they had reproduced the sounds correctly, they were praised.

The process was arduous, and there was so much they continued to miss. They could not *overhear*. While lining up at the low sink to wash my hands for lunch or gathering my mat for naptime, I was constantly absorbing the banter between teacher and assistant, picking up new vocabulary, cadences, and constructions; the others were not. They were forced to devote a significant portion of their school hours to speech and auditory training, learning to use their residual hearing and read lips. Every bit of time they spent at speech lessons, I spent learning content.

Because most of my classmates had no contact with older deaf people, they had no opportunity to learn sign language. In the sixties, ASL was still considered anathema. Many hearing parents, typically besieged by grief and guilt over having a deaf child, perceived in oralism an alluring promise. Deaf children who could use their voices and understand English speech seemed less alien, more intelligent. In other words, more hearing. Normal.

For more than a century, doctors and educators had typically advised parents not to allow their deaf children to learn sign language and not to learn it themselves — it would impede progress toward mastering English. As long as parents didn't fall prey, the experts warned, to the manualists — those who believed that sign language was a more appropriate method for instructing deaf students — their children would become fluent in English and be eligible to reap the rewards of the hearing world. The parents, generally new to deafness and eager to salvage whatever relationship with their deaf child was possible, clung to this advice, which offered the hope of communicating on their terms.

In spite of their good intentions, they ended up withholding from their children the one language that could be acquired visually. And because deaf children do not acquire an aural, spoken language naturally — they must be taught every minute element that hearing children absorb effortlessly — they were sent to school with no language system at all. A bit of English and a few crude homemade signs were the only tools that most of my classmates possessed for making sense of the world.

Oralists are not willful oppressors. When Lexington, the oldest oral school for the deaf in the United States, began in 1864, it heralded a new option for deaf people. Until then, all schools for the deaf in this country used a manual system of communication. Lexington's founders were offering a hitherto unavailable choice, one that they believed was better, would grant deaf people more opportunities. But after more than a century (during which oralists had only qualified success in proving the merits of their method), research began to show that ASL is not an inferior language and that restricting its use constitutes a disservice and an injustice to deaf people — educationally, psychologically, and culturally.

During my lifetime, a civil rights movement has developed among deaf people. Spearheaded mostly by highly educated deaf professionals, its ranks are filled with people from the grassroots deaf community. With the issue of language at its core, the movement has grown influential at all levels, from local school boards to Congress. Political ramifications now apply to everything from personal style of communication to the portrayal of deaf people on television.

At Lexington, the movement has manifested itself in disputes over the use of sign language in the classroom and over the hiring of more deaf employees. During the past several years Lexington has gone through great changes, and it continues to change, in response to several forces: activism in the deaf community, a steady increase in the number of students of color and immigrant students, a national trend toward mainstreaming disabled children in public schools, and controversial medical technology that is almost certain to reduce the number of culturally deaf people (members of the signing deaf community).

My father, Oscar, has led Lexington through many of these changes, as its superintendent for the past eight years and its principal for eight years before that. Hearing people, especially those affiliated with oral education and the medical profession, are seen by some deaf militants as members of the establishment that has long oppressed deaf culture and tried to make deaf people assimilate into the hearing world. As a hearing person, then, and as the director of a famous old oral school, Oscar is one of the enemies. But as the son of deaf parents and as a person who grew up signing and has spent his life living and working with deaf people, he is trusted and respected. He is framed by these dual images, regarded suspiciously by some, welcomed warmly by others.

As I grew up, l was slow to realize that the deaf community I had idealized was fraught with political tensions. I was even slower to understand that my status as a hearing person would forever restrict my membership in that community. For most of my childhood, I continued to nurture a secret belief that I belonged to this special world, and it to me.

I was seven years old, halfway through the second grade, when we moved to Nyack, a village on the Hudson River about thirty miles north of the city. Our mother no longer worked at Lexington, but our father had become the principal and commuted to Jackson Heights each day. After the compact railroad apartment we had inhabited at the school, our new house seemed vast, echoey. Beyond its cool stucco exterior stood a row of dark, towering fir trees, a perpetually shady back lawn, dense hydrangea bushes — nothing familiar, no one we knew. It was here that I began to use sign language to remove myself, to retreat into a comforting, secluded place.

Our parents had chosen Nyack partly because of its reputation as a well-integrated community, but we soon discovered that almost all of the other children on our bus route were white. There was always a group of big boys, fourth-graders, who would menace us. "Oreo. Zebra," they would say, seeing Reba and Andy and me together. They would lurch down the aisle of the moving bus and stand over our seat. "You fuck your sisters, don't you?" they would say to Andy. Andy was six.

Furious, frightened, I would channel my response into my hands, discreetly spelling passionate words into my lap. Our parents told us that if we ignored the boys, they would stop. They advised Reba and me to sit on either side of Andy, hemming him in for his protection; if he lost his temper and entered into combat, he would surely be beaten. So I sat on the aisle, pressed tightly against my brother, willing us all to remain mute, composed, while in my lap I unleashed silent furies. Fingerspelling, I imagined I was working spells, weaving cryptic incantations around my brother and sister and me. This private language was a kind of power I retained over the awful boys, an invisible shield beyond which they could not go.

When the taunting eventually subsided, as our parents had predicted it would, I did not stop signing. The habit became ingrained; whenever I was bored or angry or hurt or threatened, my fingers would start to spell. I found in this language a way to absent myself, to grow remote and slip into private, imagined conversation. It was like a tangible cord that stretched from my fingers all the way back to the world I had left behind at Lexington. It was my flying carpet, my trap door. If being able to hear had set me apart when I was a student at Lexington, I used sign language to maintain this sense of separation when I was among hearing people.

I was not fluent then, but pestered my father endlessly for new vocabulary: "What's the sign for tuna fish? How would you say umbrella?" Every June, when he brought home a fresh copy of the Lexington yearbook, I would pore over the pages, longing to become deaf and go to Lexington. What I missed most was the closeness of the school, the physical intimacy wrought by sign language.

Deafness is classified as a low-incidence disability. About two million Americans are classified as hearing-impaired; only around two hundred thousand of those are culturally deaf. For seven years I had lived among members of this minority group, witnessing bonds that transcended language. I longed for the warmth of words left unspoken and nevertheless understood.

But as I got older I had to reconcile this desire with the fact that I was not deaf. I had become a full-grown hearing person. Although I could (and did) choose to socialize and work with deaf people, I could never be a member of the deaf community. Cultural identity is fixed. No amount of tricycling up and down Lexington's halls could ever change that.

And yet, certain details persist. Those were the halls of my childhood. I am Sam's granddaughter and Oscar's daughter. I once put pebbles in my ears, once wished I were deaf. These are bits of evidence, facts I can tick off on my fingers, count and possess like objects. Even today, when people ask me where I am from, the answer that comes first to mind is always Lexington.

2

Transition Lessons

S ofiya, Sofie, Sofa, Sophia. They took her name and twisted it every which way, until she decided for herself and it became Sofia. She is eighteen years old and no longer the new girl.

Two years ago, when Sofia Normatov first came from Russia, she was the new girl, and she was new again last year, when she first entered the high school. In between she attended Lexington's foreign language transition class, and on official school documents from that year, written in various sets of authoritative ink, her name, transliterated from the Cyrillic alphabet, appears in a full array of spellings, as if evidence of her transitional state.

At home her parents persist in calling her Sofa, which she is loath to have any of her school friends discover because then, surely, her name-sign will become *couch*. So she chooses *S-O-F-I-A*, which is so deliciously fingerspelled — rapidly, it's a blur of fingers unfurling from fist to flare to fist again — that she needs no name-sign.

"*Get Sofia*," her friends call across the lunch table, their fists springing open and shut. Someone tugs her sleeve and she looks up from a forkful of lettuce. *"You want to go to Pat and Joe's and get an ice cream after school?"* Sofia grimaces apologetically at her salad (she keeps thinking she has started a diet), then nods.

"Sure. If I can get Sheema to cover the store," she amends. This year Sofia is the comanager of the school store, as well as being on the volleyball team, the mock trial team, and the staff of the yearbook. But after school today she goes tramping off to Pat and Joe's with a bunch of schoolmates and fishes deep in the freezer case for an ice cream sandwich. The deli is full of Lex kids, buying soda and chips and gum, the ones with better speech acting as interpreters for the countermen and the cashier, kids signing to each other across the store, lending nickels and swapping candy bars. It feels so good finally to be in.

This is what Sofia yearned for during her year in the foreign language transition class. Everything seemed awkward and impossible then: learning English, learning how to pronounce things the American way, learning American Sign Language. The latter occurred mostly in the lunchroom, in the halls, on the school bus, in gym, and it was these encounters that decided her so firmly: she must move into the regular high school as soon as possible. The locker room exchanges, the study hall brushes with other students, both fueled and frustrated her. Her world was spinning, and she required ASL for traction; she needed to share the other students' language and enter their culture. So with a pure, sweet mulishness that would become her trademark, Sofia began to push for a transfer.

The foreign language transition class was formed in 1984 in response to the increasing number of immigrants who were applying for admission to the school. As New York City's population swelled with Caribbeans, Central and South Americans, Asians, Africans, and Eastern Europeans, so did Lexington's. And while the public schools could funnel these students into bilingual classes or English-as-a-second-language programs, Lexington faced a more complex task. Many of the students' home countries had no schools for the deaf. Some students had been schooled with mentally retarded children; some had never been schooled, never seen another deaf person, never worn a hearing aid. Some came knowing a few home-signs or invented gestures; others had no language system at all, signed, spoken, or written.

When Sofia entered Lexington in November 1989, the school had one foreign language transition class; two years later it had four. Lexington currently has first-generation students from thirty-four different countries. The languages of their families include Portuguese and Cantonese, Urdu and Arabic, Farsi and Tagalog. The languages of the school are English and sign. The languages of the students are mixtures, or fragments thereof, or absent altogether.

Sofia enrolled at Lexington after spending eight years in a residential school for the deaf in Leningrad, where she became fluent in Russian and developed excellent oral skills. With a strong base in a first language, she learned English far more quickly than those of her classmates who had never been to school. And while sign languages are no more universal than spoken languages (in fact, British Sign Language is distinct from ASL), Sofia's fluency in Russian Sign Language helped her to acquire a second sign language more easily as well. With these advantages, she was able to get herself switched into the regular high school by the following September. Her transition was successful in every way except one: she had to leave her little sister behind.

Sofia has two grown-up sisters, Adalina and Nadezhda (or Ada and Nellie, as they are called in the States), who are nearer her own age than Irina, seven years her junior. But it is Irina with whom she is closest, for Irina is also deaf. With disorderly hair forever liberating itself from the constraints of band and barrette and huge glasses magnifying and distorting clever brown eyes, Irina is the quintessential little sister — wheedling and obstinate, admiring and jealous, irrepressible and lovable.

The job of rearing Irina has been largely foisted onto Sofia, who, as a deaf person, is expected to discipline, tutor, and care for her little sister. With her good Russian oral skills, she is also expected to act as the interpreter between her Russian-speaking family and Irina, who has come to rely more on English and ASL. When both sisters entered the single foreign language transition class two years ago, Sofia felt stifled by the rather too close quarters. But from her vantage point in the high school, a different sort of burden now nags at Sofia: Irina has yet to transfer into regular classes.

"Hey, bubs, what are the hearing aids doing on your desk?" Margie Weissman circles in front of eleven-year-old Irina and leans on her desk. This teacher believes in audition. She has a solid, belting voice and almost never signs.

Irina launches into an energetic excuse, her lopsided ponytail galloping crookedly behind her. Her voice, all deep breathy rushes and warbly Russian trills, sounds like wind and water.

"What?" Margie squints, her glasses slipping until they straddle the round tip of her nose. "I can't understand you. Put 'em on," she directs, and Irina twists the molds into her ears and hooks the beige receivers behind them.

Beside her, Irina's classmate Walkiria has brought the voltage tester to her desk to check her hearing aids. She slips the round batteries, no bigger than grapefruit seeds, from her aids and holds them one at a time to a metal plate on the face of the small black box. Behind a little window, a needle springs to the right — good — and a second time — good also. Walkiria replaces the batteries, puts on her aids, and shoves the voltage tester onto Gianina's desk. They are both from the Dominican Republic.

Next to Gianina, Tericha waves for Margie's attention, then begins a question in a timid pastiche of gesture and sound. She is from Jamaica and the newest member of the class. Margie shakes back her blunt reddish hair and frowns in concentration. "You need a new battery?" she guesses. She knows that Tericha, who has no aids of her own, has been using a pair of Lexington loaners that work only sporadically. "Where's the tester? Wait for Gianina, she has the tester." But that's not what Tericha meant, and she tries again, pointing to her ear and then to her lap. "Oh, you want the group aid!" cries Margie. "Yes, me too, we're waiting for that."

The four girls in this foreign language transition class have all recently had ear mold impressions taken. From these, new aids are being made to fit a group system. When it comes, Margie will wear a wireless microphone; the children will have FM receivers, two each, worn in little harnesses around their waists and wired to their hearing aids. The receivers, tuned to Margie's microphone, will ensure that the signal of her voice remains constant no matter where she walks in the room; they will also diminish background noise.

A month ago such wizardry was beyond Tericha's ken. She was living with her grandmother in Jamaica and had never attended school in all her ten years of life. Tericha is not technically a foreign language transition student, since her parents' native language is English. She might more aptly be called a no language transition student, except that already, after only a few weeks of school, language, or the seeds of it, is visibly straining within her willowy body, tested surreptitiously on shy lips, strung together gingerly on long fingers, soaking into her brilliant dark eyes.

Irina and Walkiria, the class veterans, each having been here for two years, are far less taken with the notion of wearing group aids — having those bulky, chunky boxes hitched to their hips with institutional-looking nylon straps. At eleven and twelve years old, they fancy themselves boy-catchers and value certain standards of appearance. Margie has struck a bargain with them: if they wear the group aids in class, they may switch to the less obtrusive, behind-the-ear model on excursions to the library, cafeteria, art room, and gym.

This morning, still without the group system, Margie tests the girls individually. Covering her mouth with a sheet of loose-leaf paper, she addresses each one in a loud voice: "Good morning! Hello! How are you today?" "Are you down?" she bellows when one doesn't respond. "Are you on? Hello! Hello!" When they do answer her back, she offers modifications. "Do me a favor," she says, touching her throat. "Down a little, lower . . . lower the pitch . . . yes! How pretty! What a pretty voice!"

Nearly everything in the classroom is fodder for instruction. Room 2-217 is sometimes known as the zoo, since tanks of fish and turtles and hamsters and snakes claim every available countertop. When the smell gets dreadful, Margie pours lemon juice on paper towels and disperses these impromptu sachets around the room. The students don't complain; they are fascinated with the animals, especially the snakes. Margie has told them that snakes are deaf.

"What happened yesterday with the larger snake?" she is asking. "What's snake?" she calls to the Spanish-speaking aide who is sorting arts-and-crafts projects in the back of the room.

"La serpiente."

"La serpiente. What happened with la serpiente?" Margie adds for the benefit of Walkiria and Gianina.

"*The snake was sick —*" Irina begins to sign, eyes grave behind her glasses with their childish red plastic frames.

"You don't need to sign to me. Stop. I don't understand that." Margie screws her eyes shut and averts her face. Sometimes when hearing teachers say, "I don't understand you," they mean just that; other times they mean "I'm ignoring you until you use your voice." This one obviously means the latter. Irina shrugs philosophically and commences chewing on the collar of her turtleneck.

Walkiria stands and imitates the snake, thrashing and flailing in a little break dance. Rhinestone studs on her jeans catch the light and sparkle.

"What is that?" demands Margie. "Give me some language."

And gradually they do come up with English for their thoughts: "strange behavior," "sick," "spilled the water dish." Margie, standing by an easel, wields a felt-tipped pen, ready to catch all the vocabulary they can muster and transfer it to paper. All day she will do this, whether as part of a lesson or not; she will write their words for them to see.

Even their snack, delivered mid-morning on a cafeteria tray, becomes a lesson in similes. "This muffin is like a rock," Margie proclaims, and transcribes her sentence on the board. "Like a rock," she repeats. She holds the wooden pointer to her chin while her pink lips open and shut, then uses it to tap the extremely solid baked good. The students study her, then bang their dry sesame seed muffins observantly against the desks.

Throughout the day, scores of words appear in colored marker across the walls, labeling, linking, connecting life to language. Pens dry up and are traded. Every few minutes more words are inscribed, some flanked by their Spanish and Russian equivalents, for a key element of the program is maintaining and improving the child's home language while teaching her English. The first language becomes a scaffold from which to build the second; the two develop in tandem, weaving a bridge between family and school. In the classroom, words overlap and tangle as the faded confetti of yesterday's vocabulary, half erased, lingers across the board.

In the Soviet Union, the Normatovs lived in Samarkand, a city in south-central Asia near the Black Sea. Bukharan Jews, they spoke a dialect of Farsi as well as Russian, and many of their customs had a Middle Eastern flavor. They were well-off. Mr. Normatov did bookkeeping for a department store.

Mrs. Normatov obtained clothes and jewelry from non-Soviet countries and sold them in private transactions from their home.

They lived in a huge one-story house behind a white clay wall, with a vegetable garden and trees that produced apples, pears, cherries, and apricots. The walls and high ceiling of their living room were hand-painted with elaborate designs and Stars of David. They held parties with musicians and belly dancers and many dozens of guests spilling from the living room into the stone courtyard. During the summers the family slept on cots in this courtyard, and above them the stars shone through the grape arbor.

When Sofia was three, her parents sent her to School Number Twenty, an oral school for the deaf in Leningrad, so that she would learn to speak. Eight hours away by plane, Leningrad was so far north that on clear days Sofia could stand at the edge of the Baltic Sea and make out the vast gray shape of the Finnish coast. Sofia, and later Irina, lived most of their lives there, apart from the family, returning home only during the summers. School was their world, deafness their culture.

Early in the spring of 1989, Iluysha and Ister Normatov and their four daughters left behind their family and friends and their large house with the living room frescoes. They left behind their chickens and dog and vegetable garden and much of their china and many of their clothes. With the government-allotted sixty rubles per person, no English, and two diamonds (one smuggled in a suitcase lining, the other in Mrs. Normatov's back molar), they flew first to Austria, then to Italy, and after three months were permitted to pass on to their final destination, the United States, a country where they could practice Judaism publicly, with a rabbi in a synagogue, rather than covertly, behind their white clay wall.

One of the biggest differences they found in their new home, a modest apartment in Rego Park, Queens, was that it was only three subway stops away from the Lexington School for the Deaf. In addition to adjusting to a new country, the Normatovs had to adjust to having the deaf family members stay with them not for a summer holiday but permanently.

Even the flat white cardboard box containing the few photographs they brought with them from Samarkand bore testimony to the separateness of the two youngest children's lives. Picture after picture chronicled birth and death, wedding and holiday, years of family gatherings from which the deaf girls were absent. Except for an occasional school photo, showing them in uniform, with their red Pioneer neckerchiefs and tin Lenin badges, they were virtually unaccounted for.

Now, just as the Normatovs moved their religion from behind the wall, so Sofia and Irina emerged. In Rego Park they were no longer in someone else's hands, with their lives taking place eight hours away, on the edge of the Baltic Sea. They were directly within view, slightly alien blood relatives.

Across the hall from Irina's classroom, the older foreign language transition students are counting lollipops. Synthetic cobwebs sag across the doorway. Glitter, spilled and trodden into the carpet, winks from the floor like mica. Neatly printed on oaktag and taped on the wall of cabinets are the words WITCH, APPLE, JACK-O'-LANTERN, OCTOBER, BROOM, GHOST, CANDIES, PUMPKIN, MOON. This afternoon the students will host a Halloween party for the younger children.

This is Sofia's former class. The students range from eighteen to twenty-one years old. They have not much longer to remain in school; after age twenty-one, the state will not pay for them to attend. Some of them know they will never make the transition into the regular high school. They must gather what they can here, in this class: it will be all they take with them when they leave.

Right now the candy-sorting has halted because Jerry, a

quiet young man from Haiti, has become intent on ascertaining the French word for lollipop. He thinks he remembers a word, a loose assemblage of syllables, and he tries these out in a low, reedy voice, but the teacher, Marcy Rosenbaum, shakes her head helplessly. So he attempts to fingerspell it, but at this Marcy squints with effort and pleads, "Slower."

Jerry sighs. Sweet-natured, he is shaped like a string bean with a neat round head.

"*Put your glasses on*," advises Angel impatiently, thumping his desk to get Marcy's attention. He is less sweet-natured, and frequently indulges in rude ASL diatribes he knows his teacher can't understand. Since emigrating from the Dominican Republic, he has picked up ASL far quicker than English, which is meted out in wrenchingly tedious doses and confounded by misunderstandings that often result in Angel's lowering his head to his desk and refusing to look up.

Obligingly, Marcy slides down the glasses wedged on top of her cropped brown hair, but she still can't make out the word, so now Jerry rises, goes to the board, and writes out the letters he remembers, SUCEC, before giving up and diving for the battered French-English dictionary in his knapsack. By now the Dominican and Mexican students want to know their word for lollipop, too. Maria Joya, the Spanish-speaking aide, writes PALETA on the board. A visiting Russian-speaking aide adds LEDENETS to the list. At last Jerry fills in SUCETTE and the class resumes counting out lollipops and mini Nestlé crunch bars.

The students make these forays to the board all day long, whenever they are struck by the need to know something. If their teacher can understand neither their speech nor their signs, they resort to the board as an alternative mode of communication. Now Angel, studying a painted witch replete with glitter-encrusted warts who is hanging on the wall, goes to the chalkboard and writes WATCH, WATCHATION. He summons Marcy for her opinion.

She studies the board with her hands on her hips. "Maybe

you mean vacation?" she suggests. Angel, with great irritation, jabs a finger toward the witch decoration. "Oh. No, that's a different word," Marcy tells him. "Look: watch, witch." She emphasizes the movement of her mouth so that he can apprehend the distinction between the two vowels.

This prompts Angel hurriedly to write WOTCH on the board. He whips his head around to the teacher.

"Yes, you're thinking of the different vowels. You have a good idea, but that's not a word," Marcy tells him.

Angel underlines WOTCH and nods, adamant.

"No, that's not a word," the teacher repeats.

"*I think yes in Spanish,*" he persists.

"No, no, that's not Spanish."

"*Russian, I think,*" Angel amends.

Marcy chuckles and shakes her head.

"*Or French?*" Angel stares at the word, his mouth slightly open. Marcy is already on her way to help another student.

While Jerry is loading film in the Polaroid camera and Miguel and Jose are propping up the beanbag toss with a broomstick and masking tape, Francisco suddenly wants to know if Halloween is a religious holiday. The oldest member of the class, at twenty-one, he came from Mexico less than two years ago and must graduate this June. Strong and squarely built, he keeps his mouth in a constant firm line, tight dimples pressed in at either end.

"*Religious?*" he asks the teacher, using the correct ASL sign.

"I don't know what you are saying," she tells him.

"*Religious?*" he repeats, this time tentatively, less certain that he has remembered the sign accurately.

"I'm sorry, I don't know that sign."

He tries to fingerspell it. "*R-E-G-I-L-A-R-Y.*"

Marcy chews the inside of her cheek, then flashes Francisco a tiny, defeated smile.

"I think he's saying 'regular.' No?" Maria, the aide, has wandered up behind Marcy. Both Marcy and Maria are taking sign language courses at Lexington during the school day. Last spring, after 127 years of being a famous oral school for the deaf, Lexington began requiring all teaching staff who are not proficient in sign language to start taking classes. But for now, neither of them can comprehend Francisco. He shakes his head, dimples set in resignation. Marcy crinkles her eyes in an apologetic smile. The question goes unanswered.

Marcy Rosenbaum became a teacher of the deaf in the days of oral supremacy. Like Margie Weissman, she believes in speech and auditory training in the classroom. She is convinced that oral communication is the route to success, and it bothers her that so much attention has lately been directed to sign language and deaf pride. She agrees that these things should be given a place at Lexington, but not to the detriment of teaching English literacy, or, as she puts it, advancing the goal of "approaching the hearing population."

A half-hour before lunch, Marcy gives her students free time. They gravitate to the board, vying for a piece of chalk. The beanbags have given rise to a discussion about beans, only no one can think of a word for bean and they all have different signs for it. Francisco and Angel each manipulate chalk over a patch of board, drawing pinto beans and lima beans, snap beans and kidney beans, and this triggers in Jerry the memory of a French word, HARICOT, and Miguel comes up with FRIJOLES. Then Angel acts out peeling and crying, and Francisco triumphantly scrawls OINON on the board, and Jose knows the sign for it: a knuckle twisted at the eye. Chalk clicks furiously as the clock ticks on toward lunch. This is their vehicle; with a piece of chalk they can make themselves heard, and they continue practicing the art of conversation among themselves until the bell rings.

Sofia and her friends come out of Pat and Joe's, biting gingerly into their ice cream, and cross Thirty-first Avenue to join the milling crowds of Lexington kids waiting for the public bus. With their student passes, the mile to the Roosevelt Avenue subway is a free ride. The sky hangs low and white, like cotton batting. Leaves in sodden heaps clog the gutters. The afternoon has turned damp and cold; the ice cream thrills dizzily through their teeth. Three stooped women wearing raincoats and clutching shopping bags wait for the bus as well. They eye the signing students with wary curiosity.

Across Seventy-fifth Street, a crotchety homeowner steps out on his veranda to glare at a cluster of Lexington students chatting on the street corner. "Move along!" he tells them, padding halfway down his steps in worn leather slippers. "Don't stand there!" The students regard him blandly, watch his lips flap unintelligibly and his face grow livid. After a moment they lose interest and resume their conversation.

Sofia feels rain on her face. She glances at the sky, which seems to have sunk even lower, and peers along the avenue for the bus. Then she is caught up again in the activity and talk, all the movements boiling up around her as students relate opinions and gossip while their audiences press close and jockey for clear sight lines. The signing is fast and spicy and physical, with no apologies to the three women in raincoats or the man across the street. One of the students wears a T-shirt he bought at the school store; across the chest it reads "Deaf Pride."

When Sofia first came to Lexington, she didn't know her transition would be two-tiered. She managed to speed out of the foreign language transition class in only eight months, substantially less than the average duration of three years. By September 1990 she was an ebullient fledgling American, eager to merge with the rest of the high school sophomore class. And it was here that she encountered the second tier, the part that now allows her to stand boldly on the corner, blinking her lashes against the spattering rain, signing with friends in plain view of the world.

Here she encountered the deaf studies class. The course

comprised a variety of subjects, from the history and grammar of ASL to the physiology of the inner ear, from technological developments in devices for the deaf to the students' personal identities as members of the deaf community. In Russia there had been nothing like it — no talk of deaf studies, deaf culture, deaf pride.

The teacher, Donald Galloway, had created the course at Lexington only four years earlier. He had a wide-open pink face and a ready, gurgling laugh. He was the first deaf teacher Sofia had ever had. He asked the students to keep journals.

Sofia bought a wide-ruled, spiral-bound notebook. In this journal, with the involuntary poetry of one who is not fluent in the language, she recorded her explorations of deafness. Here, in this slim turquoise book, remnants of her journey into herself are preserved. "Who am I?" reads her final entry.

> I found out that who I am.
> I am Deaf and Jewish girl.
> I learned a lot about deaf culture and deaf's language. Before Deaf Studies I was negative that I am Deaf because I grew up in Russia. In Russia for deaf people didn't have ability to successful of their goal. Also no technology for Deaf people. That why I thought always I was negative.
> After Deaf Studies I learned a lot. In U.S.A. had tty, closed captioned and technology for deaf. Many deaf people has ability to be successful their goal or dream. Now, I am proud of me and everybody who are deaf. Also has club, college, universitet and good school, community for Deaf. I can do anything what I want.
> My favorite issue or sentense:
> "Deaf can do it except hear."

On the corner of Thirty-first Avenue and Seventy-fifth Street, the autumn rain is falling in earnest, and the students lift the backs of their jackets up over their heads like so many turtles. The rain is cold. It strikes an old bed frame and box spring that have been dragged to the curb for removal, drenches mashed cigarette boxes, and twists, oily, into the gutter. Sofia remembers the warm, pungent rains of Samarkand, her first home.

She is keeping them straight, her separate lives, as she moves between countries, as she moves between her hearing family and her deaf community. She is piecing them together from what has been available, from what she can gather: a family photograph in which she does not appear, the five American spellings of her name, the stories she has written in her turquoise notebook.

As cool water mats her hair and trickles down her socks, she huddles with the others, glad to be in America amid the strong deaf. "*I miss my Samarkand rain,*" she signs to a friend, but her smile is not wistful. Just now, down the avenue, the bus is coming into view.

3

Prince Charming

He wears his name in gold block letters pierced through his left ear, just beneath the hearing aid. His name-sign, thumb and index finger pinching earlobe, derives from this inch-long stud: JAMES. Around his neck he wears a gold chain, a heavy cord that dips several inches below his clavicles and suspends a large religious medallion. On three fingers of his left hand he wears broad gold rings, each stamped with a different image: a lion, the Virgin Mary, the Cadillac insignia. Just now he eases this hand into his jeans pocket, fumbles a moment, and withdraws it again, the fingers bare.

The guest speaker addressing the career education class is talking about how to cope with emergency. James knows this is the topic because it's written on the board, along with a drawing of a tightrope. He himself came to class late, missing the beginning of the lecture. He takes a seat in the horseshoe of chairs facing the chalkboard, peels the wrapper off a KitKat bar, and breaks off a couple of sticks for the girls on either side of him. When he looks up, the speaker is drawing a safety net under the tightrope.

Career education meets for one hour three times a week, and is required for all seniors. The speaker today is a counselor from Lexington's living skills center. Although he is hearing, he signs in ASL and does not use any voice. The little bits of sound that do spatter oddly from his throat are roughly hewn creaks and rasps, as though he were imitating a deaf person. James, who relies partly on audition and lip reading, has some trouble understanding him. He understands the words on the board, though: HOUSING PROGRAMS, FOOD STAMPS, WELFARE. James clasps his hands and leans forward, elbows on knees, a position of supreme attentiveness. Shortly, his lids begin to droop.

James Taylor is a success story. Everyone says so — teachers, counselors, administrators — commenting at length on his marked change in behavior since he first arrived at Lex. He came from St. Joseph's School for the Deaf in the Bronx, started here as a fourteen-year-old prefreshman, and his teachers all shake their heads at memories of what he was like then.

James missed 148 days of school in his first year at Lexington. When he did show up, it was in one of the two or three shirts and pairs of pants he always wore. The clothes were always clean. James was always hungry. He could never concentrate in class. So each morning, instead of going to first period, he reported to a little room within the high school office. Paul Escobar, his school friend from the Bronx, reported there as well, and an instructional aide helped them get ready for school, dispensing juice and toast, cereal, a pencil, a notebook — whatever seemed to be missing, whatever the school could supply. But James came so rarely — once a week, less — and generally wound up falling asleep in his hooded sweatshirt, cheek pressed against the white plastic table.

Now, in career ed, autumn light tilts through the window across his chin and James jerks himself awake. It has taken him nineteen years to become a senior in high school and arrive at today's lesson, "How to Cope with Emergency," and what they call emergency turns out to be a fair description of most of James's life. The speaker is discussing food stamps now, saying that it is illegal to sell them for cash. *"Drug addicts may do that,"* he is explaining. James jiggles his foot and sighs. A tremendously thick braid hangs down the back of the girl next to him. Absently, he hooks a finger through the broad plait. The girl glances to see whether he is calling her, then looks placidly back at the speaker, letting James bounce the braid softly against her spine.

In the five years since he entered Lexington, James has pared his absences down to about one a week, usually on Monday, when he must ride two buses and two subway trains from his mother's apartment on Webster Avenue in the Bronx. The other days his commute is simpler: down one flight of stairs. During the week he stays in Lexington's five-day residence, reserved for students whose home life "inhibits their progress in learning." The referral for James came easily — he was truant, he was failing, he was hungry. Now, beginning his second full year in the dorm, James is an honor roll student and president of the Black Culture Club. Too old to be on the wrestling team (he was a cocaptain last year), he has taken a job monitoring the bus room after school. Lexington pays him five dollars an hour, enough to keep him in sneakers and jelly doughnuts.

The guest speaker talks about the New York City Housing Authority. *"Sometimes you must wait forever for public housing. Single mothers with babies are the first priority. But if a single man fills out the application, he can wait forever."* The speaker is short and neat. He has a shiny head and a navy sport coat with four gold buttons at each cuff. He arcs a piece of chalk as he signs. *"Some of the housing projects are nice,"* he says. *"Some are really awful."*

None of this is news to James. He glances distractedly around the room. Crayon drawings of autumn leaves have been stuck up next to the door. In the mornings, this is the bus room for the little children. His classmates give the speaker their careful attention, even those who are certainly bound for college and good jobs. They know deaf people can be almost anything today: lawyers, psychologists, dancers, architects. But they also know that they will be facing the bleakest job market in decades, that even their hearing counterparts will be scrambling for positions, and that most employers are, after all, hearing. So they sit up straight and watch the speaker with respect.

"If an emergency happens," he is saying, *"if you lose your job or something, these safety nets can really save you. The city right now has lousy services for the deaf, not enough interpreters. Don't fall through the cracks. If you need to go for welfare, ask for an interpreter. They're required to provide one. Please, don't go without an interpreter. There may be something you don't understand and you'll get turned down."* Now he begins to mime, treading along an imaginary tightrope and holding out his arms, maneuvering an invisible pole for balance and taking another step, and the class watches, half laughing, half wincing as he bends and totters.

James does not see. He has dozed off again, his head hanging down, the religious medallion rocking gently. But then, James has already been through the cracks and back. The speaker's pantomime is no more gripping than the image of his own mother and the high-wire act she has performed all his life. She has raised an entire family on this wire, swaying and steadying through fire, eviction, single motherhood, disease, crime, and jail. Today's lesson doesn't teach James anything he hasn't already lived.

The English department chooses *Into the Woods*, an adaptation of fairy tales, as the senior class play. The seventeen teachers and instructional aides split up the various duties: directing, constructing the sets, making costumes. Two teachers adapt the script, spending more than twenty hours over a two-week period cutting, reordering sentences, and making the dialogue easier to translate into sign language. They all begin reviewing the fairy tales with their senior classes.

Although many of the students are already familiar with the stories, this sort of cultural literacy cannot be taken for granted in a school for the deaf. In grade school, while their hearing counterparts were listening to the story of Jack and the Beanstalk, Lexington students might have been learning what beans were. While hearing siblings were learning how to pronounce the names Rapunzel and Rumplestiltskin, Lexington students were sitting in speech rooms learning how to pronounce their own names, with plastic sticks pressing their tongues into shape. And while hearing children were learning to read stories, deaf children were just beginning to learn how to read their own parents' lips.

On the day of auditions, in mid-November, a great sheet of newsprint taped to the wall of what is called the mini-theater reads "Seniors: Sign your name by the characters you would like to act. Also tell your shoe size and clothes size." Some of the students are still a bit shaky on the plots and uncertain about which characters they would like to try out for. One dark-haired boy writes his name by each part, just to be safe. A girl with thick glasses and her mouth in an anxious pucker tells her teacher she knows there was a part she wanted to audition for, but she can't remember the name. "*It was a girl,*" she offers helpfully. Three other teachers hover over a blushing boy and speculate on his pants size. "He's thin," muses one. "I bet about a twenty-eight." He rummages helpfully around his waistband for a label.

They audition without scripts, acting out prescribed bits of action: the glass-slipper-fitting scene, the wolf-in-Grandmother's-bed scene, the Jack-milking-his-cow scene. Scripts would slow the proceedings by provoking fuss over translations and unfamiliar English words. This way, even the students who have trouble reading are free to ham it up as much as they like, and they do.

A would-be Cinderella takes the stage to soliloquize in a baseball jacket and stone-washed jeans. Gazing moonily at the ceiling, she appeals to the spirit of her dead mother. *"O Mother, why must I clean all day? I want a beautiful dress so that I can go to the ball!"*

The girl auditioning for the ghost of Cinderella's mother cocks her head in a streetwise manner. *"Cinderella, what's your problem?"* she inquires, setting off gales of laughter among the teachers.

"O Mother, it is my stepsisters. They are mean to me, and unfairly say I cannot go to the ball."

"Just ignore them," the mother advises sensibly. *"Don't let it bother you."*

A girl trying out for Red Riding Hood cups a hand to her hearing aid, pretending to listen for a "Come in!" before entering Grandmother's house.

A girl trying out for the part of a stepsister signs *no* with such vigor that she accidentally scratches Cinderella's nose.

A boy trying out for Jack's cow begins lowing in the middle of a scene, loudly, in his best estimation of bovine woe.

The teachers shriek and snort with laughter.

James sits to the side, his arms spread across the backs of two folding chairs, one leg flung across the seat of another, and laughs roundly with his friends. He finds this year's choice of play disappointing, the fairy-tale theme too immature for seniors, but when his turn comes he ambles gamely onstage, his clunky Timberland boots fashionably unlaced. His classmates hoot and pound the floor, sending vibrations to summon him, and when he looks around they tell him to remove his baseball cap onstage. He flings it amiably into the audience.

It's the Rapunzel-finds-her-blinded-prince scene. The long-lost prince, whose eyes were put out by thorns when he fell from Rapunzel's tower, wanders aimlessly onstage. James's rendition of blindness reveals a deaf person's special horror of losing his sight. He staggers and falls to the ground, creeps about extending shakily splayed fingers, and rolls belly up. A few students laugh as James collapses heavily onto his back.

Now Rapunzel steps in from the wings, happening upon the scene with fretful joy. She kneels and takes the prince's head in her lap. As she cries, her tears are supposed to water his wounded eyes and heal them, magically restoring sight. Rapunzel dutifully sobs and shakes imaginary tears over his face. James continues to lie there, thrashing weakly.

"You're healed, James," one of the teachers coaches futilely.

Rapunzel attempts to drag him to his feet.

"You can see now, James," another teacher calls to the oblivious prince. "Get up."

He doesn't, though. He is a blind prince, and deaf, and deeply into the scene. He allows everyone to see him helpless, and he extends the moment, big strong James lying as passive and defenseless as a baby, allowing everyone to see him vulnerable, in need of care.

Three years ago in September they went looking for him. James had, of course, been absent a great deal during his prefreshman and freshman years, but now it was the end of the second week of school and he hadn't shown up once. In fact, no one had seen him since June. The students had no news. So Friday afternoon the social worker and the high school supervisor drove up to the Bronx. They didn't like to make home visits, especially unannounced, but the Taylors had no phone and they were worried.

They parked on Webster Avenue, which was studded with bodegas and fried chicken joints, shops shut tight behind corrugated metal doors, lots strewn with rubble, rusted car parts and slashed furniture. Set back from the street, James's building rose, as thick and solid as a heavyweight boxer. The lobby, dim and stinking of urine, offered little relief from the hot, cloying brightness outside. The two women from Lexington waited alone for the elevator, but when it arrived they were joined by others, silent women who had been waiting hidden in protected corners. All together they packed the dank metal box for its ascent.

The social worker and the supervisor got out on the fourteenth floor, turned left past the meager squares of caged glass that permitted a suggestion of filmy light into the corridor, and knocked on the last door. Delores Taylor, a small, wiry woman, opened it for them, a dripping wooden spoon in her hand. Her face shone with moisture; crescents of finely beaded sweat were gathered under each eye and across her brow and upper lip. Behind her, in an otherwise bare kitchen, a pot of soiled bedsheets stood bubbling on the stove. Around the corner was another room, perhaps built as a living room, devoid of any furnishings.

Mrs. Taylor welcomed the visitors in her rich, dry voice. She disappeared into a third room to rouse James. From where the women stood, it appeared to contain a mattress and nothing else. Through the thickly painted yellow walls, sounds from other apartments sifted: a chorus of tinny radios, television game shows, voices in Spanish and English. In a moment James emerged, wearing shorts and pulling on a T-shirt, his eyes still puffy with sleep and now widening in surprise.

They spoke gently. James did want to go to school. He had no sneakers. He had no notebooks. There was no money. No, they hadn't been collecting Social Supplemental Income (SSI) benefits from the government. Both James and his disabled brother were eligible for these benefits, but Mrs. Taylor had little time to assemble all the documents necessary for the application: medical histories, proof of income, birth certificates, gas and electric bills, and proof of who lived in the apartment and how much each person earned, these last items being frequently nebulous and in flux. By the time she finally obtained one document, another would have become invalid. And all the while there were the other children to care for: Joseph, at fourteen the youngest and in trouble with the law; Andre, one year older, who had spina bifida and was in a wheelchair; James's older sisters, Linda and Denise, both of whom would become pregnant and eventually leave high school.

The Lexington women advised Mrs. Taylor on how to complete the SSI application and discussed the option of James's moving into the five-day residence. James promised to start coming to school. Everybody thanked everybody else. In the kitchen, the sheets boiled. The adults shook hands damply.

On Monday, James showed up as agreed and began his second year as a freshman, after failing the first. In February he gained admission to the dormitory, then decided not to move in. He was recorded absent 64 out of 180 days. His year-end grades were three F's, two D−'s, two D's, and a C− in speech. This was determined to be enough of an improvement for James, at the end of the year, to be promoted to the tenth grade.

The cast list goes up and James is Prince Charming. Rehearsals start immediately. From now until the end of the term, all seniors report to the auditorium during English period. The auditorium is cold, cavernous, elegant. The teachers post an attendance chart in the vestibule. Students initial themselves present and drift down the incline to clump onstage and form pockets in the aisles, kneel over the backs of blue plush seats and straddle the neatly bolted rows, all in order to see one another so they can talk.

The teachers must labor to get everyone's attention in this room, so large and scantily lit, with high pools of cool, waxy light submitting to shadow halfway down the walls. At the start of each rehearsal, one of the teachers stands center stage, waving her arms and stamping her feet. *"Can you see? Tap your neighbor, get everyone's attention. All right? Get him, is he looking?"* And when everyone is, she splits them into groups, different scenes with different teachers, some on-stage, others scattered throughout the house.

The script, already abridged and edited into simpler English, nonetheless teems with linguistic challenges. First, the students create name-signs for their characters. Some borrow existing signs from ASL: the baker, the witch, the prince, the wolf. But there are no standard signs for proper names. Fingerspelling grows tedious, and it's too hard to decipher from the back of the auditorium. So Rapunzel mixes her initial with a physical characteristic, becoming *R-long-curly-hair*, and Jack combines his initial with his behavior to become *J-thief*. Officially, Cinderella's sign is a *C* brushed straight down the cheek, but among themselves, in the descriptive fashion of ASL, the students dub her *Poor-Poor Clean*.

The greatest task falls to the two narrators, Robert Connor and Lisa Santiago, who are responsible for signing long passages throughout the play. Robert is gentle and stately, an articulate signer who rarely uses any voice. Lisa is more kinetic, forever swinging her lanky arms and snapping her fingers; she is the most oral student in her class. Together this disparate couple work in the far corner of the back aisle, consulting each other and Mary Jo LoPiccolo Maguire, one of the directors.

"Cinderella planted a branch on her mother's grave," Robert mumble-signs with one hand, reading from the script and thinking through a translation. He looks up at Mary Jo, forehead deeply wrinkled. There is no specific sign for branch, so he tests two possibilities. *"B-R-A-N-C-H?"* he fingerspells as he mouths the word exaggeratedly, his lips smacking dryly on the plosive. *"Or branch?"* This time he uses ASL classifiers to describe the shape visually.

"Yeah, I think it's better to show it," says Mary Jo. *"It'll be too hard to see fingerspelling from back here."*

Robert reads on. *"She wept so much her tears watered the grave and made the branch grow."* He looks up again, dropping his jaw in mock horror. *"How . . . ?"*

"*I know.*" Mary Jo nods in sympathy. "*When we did the adaptation, we said that part'd be hard to sign.*"

Robert hands his script to Lisa. She holds it before him so he can sign with both hands. He thinks a moment, then begins experimenting. First he sets up the grave, then the branch on the grave, then Cinderella crying. He shows the tears arching from her cheeks, dousing the branch, which now lifts and swells into a tree.

"*Good, very clear!*" Mary Jo tells him.

"*You don't mind that it's not in English word order?*"

"*No, whatever you feel most comfortable with. Lisa's going to speak and sign, so she'll be following the English, right?*"

Lisa shrugs and rocks on her ankles. "*Depends.*"

"*Depends on what?*"

"*I don't know.*" She's afraid that when she gets onstage she won't remember to use her voice.

"*Well, anyway, as long as it's clear, it can be signed English or ASL,*" Mary Jo assures them. At the actual performance, an overhead projector will provide the text on a screen above the stage, low-budget simultaneous captioning for anyone who doesn't understand sign language.

Props prove an additional obstacle in a play with signing actors. Cinderella, hindered by her feather duster during one speech, hands it to her stepmother. "No, no, that's not going to work," grumble the directors, sitting in darkness below the stage. "Tell her just to drop it on the floor." Jack, fresh from the giant's lair, bursts onstage with a golden goose and a harp in his hands, only to realize that he is rendered mute by his booty. "Can he stick them under his armpit or something?" the directors say, groaning. "Can we get him a knapsack?" Because they sit in shadows, invisible to the actors, each time they need to give direction one of them must hop onstage, into the light, before the actors even know that they should halt the scene.

Rehearsals progress; Thanksgiving comes and goes; painted rocks and trees and now a giant cardboard tower materialize onstage. Teachers wheel racks of costumes into the auditorium, pounce on idle students, and whisk them into capes and gowns. The directors all catch cold; they sit up front with boxes of tissues and bottles of juice; they lose their patience.

"James! You are the most unprincelike person this morning," snaps Adele Sands-Berking on the day of dress rehearsal, going into her bossy big sister act. Adele was James's English teacher his sophomore and junior years; he knows the routine and cuts his eyes, but not rudely, for he tempers all his irreverence with humor. A dimple flashes as his lips pull back, a chipped upper tooth setting off his saucy grin.

It is mid-December, one day before the performance. Chaos laps at the edges of the auditorium. Teachers baste gold braid onto costumes and nail extra supports behind drooping stage trees. Girls cross their arms and shiver in shimmery low-cut gowns. Boys, self-conscious in tights and tunics, grip one another in brutish headlocks. Adele has hustled James and Marina, who plays the baker's wife, into a quiet spot at the rear of the house to polish their tryst scene.

"What is this, James?" Adele, normally elegant and proper, assumes a stiff Bronx tilt to her neck and starts shifting and slouching like a homeboy. James can't help laughing at her mimicry. *"Come on, remember — formal!"* she tells him, snapping into a regal stance. He indulges her with a fair estimation and she appraises him sourly. *"Huh. Better."*

James and Marina run through the scene gingerly, balking at any romantic touches Adele tries to insert. When the prince is supposed to dip the baker's wife in an embrace, they teeter and laugh. When he is supposed to circle her with his arms and make the sign for *fun* on the tip of her nose, he fakes it, skimming air and leaning on her shoulder in a most comradely fashion. When he is supposed to lift her and carry her off into the woods, he complains that he's not strong enough.

"*James,*" hisses Adele, fixing him with a mean eye, "*you're a wrestler. She's not heavy.*" Marina, dainty and compact, giggles. James picks her up, and his eyes bug out and his cheeks grow shiny and puffed with exertion.

Adele mutters to herself, "Oh, James."

The lights go out.

"What happened?" James's voice comes anxiously, urgently through the dark. A breath of fear and helplessness wafts through the auditorium. All over the room communication is severed, except among hearing people, and now the teachers begin to call to one another through the dark. "What are you doing?"

"Testing some gels."

"Could we have the work lights back on, please?"

A moment later they chug on. James recovers his poise, then scowls at Adele as though she controlled the light switch.

"*Okay, pick her up again. I want to see your snakiest charm,*" Adele commands, not wasting a second. "*We all know you are sincere; now I want to see . . . snake.*"

James sticks his hands in his jeans pockets and uses his voice. "Later."

Adele glowers at him, shaking a blond curl back from her pale, pointed features. "Now."

James, his eyes insouciant, meets her gaze and tries to contain a smile. "Later," he challenges.

"Now."

"Later."

"Now now NOW." Suddenly she switches tacks. The bully vanishes and Adele appeals, "*Don't fight with me, James, the play is tomorrow. Tomorrow. It's just starting to get good and now you have to work it.*"

So he and Marina do the scene again. James begins to ooze a little snakiness and Adele perks up. Arrogant charm creeps across his face; his eyebrows lift in an expression of worldliness. With all the savoir-faire he can muster, he sweeps the baker's wife into his arms (this slip of a damsel? why, she's as light as air!) and conveys her grandly into the woods, tossing a last smug glance over his shoulder at Adele.

"*Yes!*" she cries. "*That's good, that's it!*"

James nods. He knows how to deliver. He has perfected the art of walking the line, the line drawn taut between tough and obliging, between cool and sweet. In his world, attitude is everything. Maintain strength; know when to bend. He knows exactly how to behave to get by.

This year, senior year, he increases his gold. A new ring, a chainlink bracelet, another religious medallion. It annoys him that everyone — the teachers, the dorm staff — makes such a fuss. "*Where did you get the money?*" they ask. "*Did you pay for that yourself?*" What they mean is, did he pay for it, period? And it bothers him, yes, but he keeps his anger in check. Always. His velvety eyes grow hard and remote, but everything else stays loose, disaffected.

But why shouldn't he have eight pairs of sneakers, Filas and Reeboks and Patrick Ewings and New Balances, trimmed orange and turquoise and purple and red and black? Why shouldn't he wear a beeper, one that vibrates rather than beeps, to keep in touch with his friends? Why shouldn't he wear gold now that he can afford it, now that he has a job and earns his own money? Why shouldn't he look like other young men in his neighborhood, hearing men, tough, sharp, in charge of their lives? A prince is entitled to his gold. To James they say, "*You look like a drug dealer.*" And his eyes go from velvet to ice, but everything else stays loose.

It was three weeks before the end of his sophomore year — almost two years after the home visit, almost four years after he entered Lexington — when James finally moved into the dorm. The referral for admission required a battery of tests, including a psychological evaluation, which found James to have "support and stability needs, and feelings of isolation and frustration," and suggested that "he may feel alone at times, especially at home."

He moved from the Bronx into his own room in the school, equipped with a small sink and a minifridge, a wooden bed and two desks, a dresser and a wardrobe and a closet, even his own bathroom. In the old days, this whole floor and the floor above it housed the dormitory. Now, with stricter state rules about who is eligible for residency, only five students live on a short leg of corridor, with more furniture and more space than they can possibly use. Living here, James gets help with his homework, does his laundry for free in the machines down the hall, and eats a hot supper, with seconds if he likes. When his siblings and hearing friends hear about his school and his room in the dorm, they whistle with envy. Somehow, being deaf, he is the lucky one, receiving special services and special care, getting a chance nobody offered them.

Baseball caps, orange and purple and aqua and black, dangle from thumbtacks on the wall behind his bed. More thumbtacks stretch a plastic Gap bag into a neat rectangle above his desk. A poster shows a trio of Latina women wearing evening gowns and holding long-necked brown bottles under the caption "La familia Budweiser"; another displays a white kitten with blue eyes and the motto "I'm perfect just the way I am." Tacked to a small corkboard are the business cards of James's vocational and guidance counselors, the phone number of the relay service on a pink memo slip, and a schedule for driver's education classes. A Lexington calendar displaying the entire year on one strip of paper is covered with marks, each one indicating another day lived. This is no mere inventory of dates; the marks are not the black X's of an adolescent's impatience with biding time — they are green slashes rising diagonally across the days, earnest and victorious.

James's prize possession is the secondhand radio and cassette player he inherited from some hearing friends. On this he listens to his music, his reggae and his rap, with the bass up high so that it vibrates in his chest and in the pit of his throat. Above 118 decibels he can detect sound with his right ear. He listens to his music and the rhythm of home, of his brothers and his sisters, of the sidewalk and the street. He listens until one or two or three A.M. some nights, behind a closed door, alone in his room in the school for the deaf.

4

The Least Restrictive Environment

The lobby this noon is thick with people. Teachers and secretaries are returning from lunch breaks with shiny cheeks, the smell of winter in their coats. The senior class has set up a bake sale just inside the glass doors, and staff members pause over the long folding tables to examine the goods. They shell out quarters and go back to their classrooms and offices bearing squares of chocolate cake with green icing on little paper salvers. Children pile in from recess, sweaty and sniffing, dragging their fat down jackets behind them like vivid cocoons.

Although they were supposed to meet at twelve-thirty, the committee of four who are to attend a public hearing of the State Education Department do not congregate in the main lobby until nearly one o'clock. Melissa Draganac, a high school senior, is the youngest of the group. She has dressed for the occasion in a smart black blazer and a short pleated skirt, and she clutches her printed speech in two hands. Donald Galloway, the director of Pupil Personnel Services, is there too, wearing a bright tie and chewing peppermint gum. Brenda Fraenkel, the assistant principal, joins them breathlessly with a fine clicking of heels across the tile, her earrings knocking against her jaw. Oscar arrives last, dispelling (as usual) the myth that hearing people are more punctual than deaf people. *"Ready?"* he asks, and they step outdoors.

It is December tenth. The air is as sharp as alcohol, shot through with clear gold light. The plane trees that line the strip of parking spaces have shed from the top down; their upper branches look lean and free, while leaves collect like gold coins at their roots. The quartet drives from the lot. They are on their way to give testimony before the education department, which is preparing to draft a new State Plan for Education of Students with Disabilities. If the plan endorses the increasingly popular trend of mainstreaming, schools for the deaf may be facing extinction. So their mission today is a grave one: they are going to try to save Lexington, and Lexington is so much more than their school. For deaf people (90 percent of whom are born into hearing families), schools are the locus of deaf culture.

As they pull away from the red-brick building, so broad and solid and teeming with activity, it seems implausible that Lexington's future might be threatened. But they have all heard the news about other schools for the deaf. The Maryland School might be closed down this summer; enrollment at the Governor Baxter School in Maine has dwindled to fourteen students; out on Long Island, the Mill Neck School has shut down many of its sports programs because there are not enough students to form teams. As the mainstreaming movement gathers momentum across the country, diverting more and more deaf students into hearing schools, schools for the deaf tally their budgets and watch their enrollments and wait.

Lexington's two-car convoy travels for just five minutes along Ditmars Boulevard to the Marriott Hotel, one of eleven locations in New York State where the Education Department is holding hearings today on the draft of the new plan.

The hotel stands directly across from La Guardia Airport; jets roar overhead, sending quivers through the air and the pavement as the foursome hurries across the lot. A six-foot evergreen wreath looms over the hotel entrance. Don pauses beneath it to spit his gum into a trash receptacle.

Oscar navigates through the Marriott's lobby, which is grandly appointed with lustrous chandeliers and thick mauve carpets. He has done this sort of thing twice before, presenting position papers in Washington before both the Congressional Commission on the Education of the Deaf and the House Appropriations Committee in 1987, and his manner is somewhat paternal as he guides the others down the mirrored staircase to the Jackson Heights Room, which is small and distinctly less grand.

The hearing has not yet begun. A woman and a man from the department sit at a small table up front. A handful of presenters are scattered among the five short rows of chairs facing them. The *Nutcracker Suite* is being piped into the hall, and strains of the music filter wanly into this room, which is chilly; several people remain in their coats.

The interpreter, a round-faced woman in a bulky black cardigan, spots the Lexington contingent and immediately goes to greet them, like their own private hostess. She is one of the better-known interpreters in New York; they have all met before and now stand chatting in the doorway, soaking up the warmth of familiarity. Don spots a little table by the door stocked with pitchers of icewater and a bowl of hard candies. He helps himself to several of the latter, then looks around with a stagy pout and explains in his defense, *"This is my lunch."*

"If you present well, I'll treat you all to lunch upstairs in the restaurant," Oscar proclaims.

"And if the presentation is lousy?" asks Don.

"You can have some more hard candy."

Brenda laughs. Don rolls his eyes at her. *"He's terrible. But what can we do? He's our superintendent."*

Don and Brenda are examples of a recently blossoming

tradition at Lexington: deaf teachers who rise through the ranks to become administrators. Until this year, Don taught math and deaf studies; Brenda chaired the English department. And while Oscar may be acquiring a reputation for cultivating and nurturing deaf administrators, the practice is proving a mixed blessing, since the new administrators keep leaving to accept higher positions at other schools. Within the past year, Lexington has lost two of its top deaf staff members: Susan Sien, who vacated the assistant principal's position to become one of three deaf female superintendents in the country, at the Austine School for the Deaf, in Vermont, and Reginald Redding, who left his job as director of educational support services to become the nation's only black deaf assistant superintendent, at the Minnesota Academy for the Deaf. By the end of this year, Brenda will move to Austine as well, as its new principal, and although Oscar will be pleased for her (and for Austine), he knows the departure of deaf staff members makes Lexington more susceptible to criticism from the deaf community.

Now, for the first time in history, the deaf community wields enough political clout to hold sway on search committees, and schools are pressured to actively seek deaf candidates to fill high-level positions. Mounting tensions have brought every hiring process under intense scrutiny; even the most modest job openings have become battlegrounds fraught with political ramifications. Just last month at Lexington, a deaf teacher undertook a short-lived effort to rally students to protest the hiring of a hearing man as a school bus assistant. The month before that, members of the deaf community threatened to boycott Mill Neck's annual Apple Festival if no deaf people were considered for the new superintendency there. (The Mill Neck search committee scrambled to attract a viable deaf candidate and managed to appease the militants just in time.)

In programs for the deaf, it has become increasingly awkward to hire a hearing applicant instead of a deaf applicant, even if the deaf applicant appears to be unqualified for the job. The matter is especially volatile in schools for the deaf, which many see as the rightful domain of the deaf community. *We have been patient for too long*, comes the warning. *After years of personal and job discrimination, the time has come for reparations. We are entitled to jobs in schools for the deaf as compensation for our losses, and for the losses of all the deaf children who have been denied deaf teachers, deaf role models.*

Hearing administrators who consider themselves to be in service, and in a sense accountable, to the deaf community, as Oscar does, must consider this point of view seriously. A dilemma arises when the interests of these deaf adults seem at odds with those of the schoolchildren — for instance, when satisfying the wishes of the former means providing inadequate services to the latter. Some would argue that because hearing people have always controlled the definition of adequacy, that concept is invalid. Others hold that any deaf candidate is preferable to a hearing candidate for a position working with deaf children. The debate spins around with the fervor of the 1960s civil rights movement. Oscar, at the eye of the storm, watches the gap between the hearing and the deaf widen, and while he continues to seek out the Susans and Reggies, the Brendas and Dons, he knows that much more needs to be done.

Today's hearing, however, is not about hiring policies. It is part of a more elemental struggle: to keep schools for the deaf alive.

In 1975, Congress passed Public Law 94-142, the Education for All Handicapped Children Act. This law was intended to establish public education policy for American children with physical, emotional, and learning disabilities. It said that all of these children must have available "a free appropriate public education which emphasizes special education and related services designed to meet their unique needs."

During the 1980s, while policymakers were deciding how to implement the law, they focused on one rather obscure and ambiguous section, the provision "to assure, to the maximum extent appropriate, [that] handicapped children . . . are educated with children who are not handicapped." With these words, the idea of the "least restrictive environment" took hold. The reification of this phrase spawned the most prevalent outcome of the law: mainstreaming. Mainstreaming's proponents (many of whom are unfamiliar with the special circumstances of deafness but see special programs as a way of isolating and stigmatizing learning-disabled and emotionally disturbed children) believe that the least restrictive environment for all children is the same: regular public school. The goal of social integration must now be achieved at any cost. As desirable as this outcome may be for many children, for some it amounts to bad pedagogy. For the deaf, it means the dissolution of their culture.

So when Oscar, as superintendent, received notice of today's public hearing, he took the liberty of inviting two deaf staff members and two students (one of whom could not attend) to give testimony as well. The other presenters are chiefly administrators of private school programs for physically and mentally disabled children. They are service providers whose jobs would be threatened by the decline of these special institutions; their careers are at stake. Certainly Oscar, Brenda, and Don share some of the same interests. But today their primary concern is not so much to preserve careers as to preserve a community and a culture.

The hearing begins. Oscar is the first of the Lexington group to testify. Presenters sit directly in front of the State Ed. people and speak into a microphone, through which their testimony is recorded and delivered to Albany. Oscar reads from the position paper he is delivering as the chairperson of the 4201 Schools, an association of New York's eleven state-supported schools for the physically handicapped. From where they sit, Brenda and Don and Melissa can see only the back of his broad, gray-suited shoulders; they receive his speech through the interpreter on his right.

"Mainstreaming is commendable," he allows sincerely. He knows that too often educators use special education to label and segregate children whom they have difficulty educating, and that too often the designations fall along lines of class and race. But he is here today to speak about deaf children. "However," he continues, "if equitable communication access cannot be achieved for children in the regular education setting, then it is our ethical and professional responsibility to assure children with deafness access to specialized educational opportunities that may only be available in regional day schools and residential schools."

In the context of American democratic ideals, segregated schooling is an abomination. The passage of P.L. 94-142 constituted a victory not only for the disabled community but for those champions of civil rights who, with a kind of tenacious enthusiasm, seek to wield the law like a scythe across the field of specialized education. Confusing equality with sameness, they believe in doing away with special schools and educating all children together. This is laudable, in theory. How, then, to explain that their interpretation of the law may sever deaf children from a culture that offers them strength?

Deaf people, unlike members of other disabled groups, have their own language. They have their own social clubs and athletic leagues, their own theater companies and television programs, their own university, their own periodicals, and their own international Olympics. Unlike members of ethnic minority groups, they do not receive their culture through their parents. Cultural transmission, formally and informally, has been carried out by schools for the deaf. In practice, few public schools can offer what most prelingually deaf children need: a visually oriented setting, communication access to all activities, interaction with deaf peers and deaf adults, and at least minimal sign language fluency on the part of teachers and peers. And no public school can offer the richness and nurturance of a deaf cultural environment.

Historically, deaf people have succeeded rather well at living and working independently in the larger community. Prior to the mid-1970s, 75 percent of deaf children attended residential schools, and deaf people enjoyed comparatively high levels of employment compared to other disabled groups. In fact, deaf white male workers in 1972 were employed at a higher rate than that reported for the general white male population. This era of "segregated schooling" was actually a time when deaf people were quite economically productive and independent.

Today, although more than 80 percent of deaf children attend regular public schools, unemployment rates among the deaf exceed 60 percent. This is not to imply a direct causal relationship; schools all over the country are contending with social problems that dilute the impact of their efforts. But it suggests the need for pedagogy specific to deafness. It would be damaging to dismantle schools for the deaf and funnel deaf children into public schools, where success is largely measured simply by how well students assimilate into the hearing world.

"The deaf communities in this country and state are largely unhappy with what they consider a national policy of 'wholesale mainstreaming' of children with deafness," explains Oscar at the end of his presentation, "a policy they had no hand in making, by virtue of having been excluded from policymaking and program planning for the past fifteen years (as well as the past two hundred years). Unfortunately, the majority of the deaf community in America is left feeling that public education officials and educators do not seem to care about the loneliness, pain, and suffering of deaf children who are being communicatively isolated in public school classrooms across the nation."

Now it is Melissa's turn. She goes to the front of the room

and, following protocol, sits with her back to the others. The interpreter sits in the adjacent chair, corkscrewing her body so she can see Melissa's signs, and takes up the microphone. "Hello," she voices as Melissa begins. "My name is Mel —"

Her amplified voice is directly interrupted by simultaneous outbursts from Oscar and Don, both of whom have risen from their seats at the back of the room. Don and Brenda cannot see Melissa and so have no access to the speech.

Don holds up a hand and emits a sound like a quick, strong sigh.

Oscar says, "Excuse me, can she stand?"

The man and the woman from Albany put their heads together for a moment. "Let's pause," decides the man. The woman switches off the official tape recorder. They wait somberly while the student goes to the podium and arranges the pages of her paper. The other presenters stir curiously. Melissa smiles, her cheeks flushed and taut, and tucks a handful of dark tresses behind one ear.

"*Can you see me okay?*" she signs discreetly to the interpreter. Melissa stands poised, her feet planted firmly and her rib cage lifted. She is an experienced public speaker, having litigated for Lexington's mock trial team as well as having served as the president of the student government, where meetings adhere to Robert's Rules of Order. Currently she is the president of the senior class and the student adviser to the student government.

"*I entered Lexington when I was in the third grade,*" she begins, her signs cutting the air with sinewy precision. "*My family is deaf and my parents are from Peru.*" As she delivers her personal testimony, she looks around the room, her wide brown gaze alighting earnestly on the various faces before her. The interpreter holds a copy of the speech in her lap, so that as she follows the signs, she does not make her own word choices but stays true to the English text that Melissa composed.

Melissa recounts her early experiences with mainstreaming, as a student at P.S. 149 in Queens. *"I came home crying because I was unhappy. The students made fun of my speech and punched me when I refused to speak. As a result, I withdrew and went into my shell."*

The State Ed. people do not look at Melissa while she presents. It is as if they are unable to connect the deaf student standing beside them with the spoken message they hear over the microphone. One watches the interpreter, the other the tape recorder.

Melissa tells about transferring to Lexington as a shy and passive child who cried when she made the slightest error. She describes the arduous process of gaining self-confidence, and the wonder of realizing that at this school she could communicate with her fellow students and teachers. She smiles modestly as she lists the various school activities she participates in now. It is difficult to imagine any deaf student at a hearing school doing what Melissa has done at Lexington: performing the lead in the school play, arguing on the debate team, leading student government meetings, being captain of the cheerleading squad, working as a peer counselor, choreographing for the dance troupe.

"I know," she states simply, turning to the representatives at their little table, *"that if I had stayed at a mainstreamed school, I would have fallen apart."*

A smattering of applause greets the end of her speech. In the stiff air the sound is like ice breaking up, and it surprises the people from Albany, who look up sharply from their legal pads just in time to see Melissa return to her seat. Brenda, Don, and Oscar hold their thumbs up and wink. Melissa ducks her head, going rosy as she slides back into her seat.

Don's and Brenda's presentations follow. They speak both as school administrators and as deaf people. Three hundred and fifty people will deliver testimony throughout the state today; Melissa's, Don's, and Brenda's will be among the very few delivered by members of the populations whose fates are being determined. The impact of deaf people's testifying for themselves is important. For hearing people unfamiliar with deaf mores, their testimony can also be seasoned with discomfort.

When it is Brenda's turn, she speaks on behalf of the current student body president, who has not been able to attend. *"I have a videotape of a student who could not be here today,"* she explains, the interpreter voicing as she signs. *"So what I'm presenting is a summary of the videotape."*

"Unusual, but okay," the man from Albany declares. "Wait, before you start, is she going to be reading his testimony?" he asks the interpreter, who performs her job by signing each word as he utters it. Then he recognizes his mistake, only to repeat it as he acknowledges to the interpreter, "I'm sorry, I should be addressing *her*."

Brenda smiles at this second gaffe and responds smoothly to the initial question. *"No, what I'm going to do is summarize his videotape. He signs on the tape and there's a voiceover."*

"Okay." Looking faintly nonplussed, the man accepts the tape.

When Don's turn comes, he introduces himself according to deaf custom, by telling first where he went to school. (Schools being the loci of deaf cultural roots, vast information is contained in such details as whether a person was mainstreamed or attended a school for the deaf and, in the case of the latter, whether it was residential or a day school.) As Don fingerspells the name of his graduate school, the interpreter flounders. She tries to signal to Don that she has missed something and wants him to stop and go back, but he is looking down at his paper and doesn't see her.

Oscar, who has the advantage of being extremely familiar with Don's style of signing and of knowing where he attended college, steps in. *"I attended Bethany College in Virginia, where I got my master's degree in math,"* he interprets from the back of the room. The change in gender and location of the voice is jarring. People crane their necks to see who spoke, looking puzzled and irritated. Some evidently do not make the connection between Oscar's voice and Don's speech; they look disapprovingly at Oscar for piping up so rudely with this seemingly bizarre comment. The interpreter quickly regains composure and continues voicing for the rest of the speech.

At last the State Ed. people declare a recess. The doors are propped open; warmer air and more Tchaikovsky come in from the hallway. People rise, arching their backs and cracking their knuckles.

One of the spectators, a woman with large red eyeglasses, approaches the deaf people as they move toward the exit. Describing exaggerated shapes with her florid lips, widening her eyes behind rhinestone rims, fairly patting their heads, she assures them that they have all done a marvelous job. Then she turns and confronts Oscar for more academic conversation (Does Lexington get many state-referred students? What kind of support services does it have? How many in a classroom?), leaving Don and Brenda and Melissa to wait against the wall like well-behaved children.

When Oscar is able to disengage himself, he joins the others by the modest refreshments table. *"Did you want to take some more hard candy?"* he innocently signs to Don.

"Oh, thanks. I did a lousy job?"

Oscar grins. *"I'm kidding."*

"I know." Don rakes up a small handful and waggishly offers one to Oscar. *"Here, you can have one, you were lousy too."*

But at the top of the stairs, as the others turn toward the main doors, Oscar waves to catch their attention. *"Throw out your candies. We'll have lunch."*

The hotel restaurant looks out on the western tip of La Guardia Airport, where a new U.S. Air building is being constructed. Already the sun is lowering. The building's exposed girders gleam red and gold as the day tapers to late afternoon. Airplanes float toward cold landing strips, and the picture windows tremble.

Oscar collapses heavily into a chair. He was up this morning at five-thirty, sitting at the kitchen table editing Don's presentation while he waited for tea water to boil. He continued the editing when he arrived at Lexington at seven-thirty, then at ten handed the paper over to Don, who worked on the changes until it was time to meet in the lobby. Don is a bright, subtle, and witty thinker; nonetheless, he peppers his writing with odd constructions. Like that of many deaf people, his English does not reflect his intelligence; it reads like a slightly foreign language. (Last year Oscar offered to have three deaf administrators tutored in the mechanics of writing at Lexington's expense. He felt that they were at a stage in their careers where their lack of English proficiency would hold them back and keep them at a disadvantage with hearing colleagues. Because the subject is emotionally charged, he made the offer quietly, casually, trying to be respectful of his colleagues' dignity. None of the three responded to the offer; he did not mention it again.)

Now, having gotten through the hearing, the group develops a giddy, irreverent mood. Don immediately seizes the centerpiece, a leafy poinsettia in a foil-wrapped pot, and sticks it beneath the table. (Deaf people need a full view of the torso as well as the face for comfortable communication; he is simply making the environment a little less restrictive.) They discuss the proceedings, which everyone feels went well. In retrospect, the hearing people's lack of ease with the deaf presenters has acquired a wickedly humorous cast, and they chew over certain details, making one another laugh. The humor is the sort born of ironic necessity; they use it to salve the wounds of insensitivity.

When Don whisked the plant from the center of the table, he employed a kind of radiant force that could suggest either playfulness or neatly diverted frustration. At the end of the meal he remembers to replace it. The others smile in deep camaraderie when he quips, *"Now it's a hearing table again."*

*

The following week, on the last day before the holiday break, the entire high school converges for Color Olympics. Once again the main lobby seethes with bodies and excitement. The students have festooned themselves with a sort of tribal devotion: the yellow team has dismembered Rapunzel's wig and braided strands of the yellow yarn into their hair; the greens wear verdant stickers on their noses and foreheads; the blues have drawn navy lightning bolts on their cheeks and arms; the reds have somehow managed to scrounge up felt Santa Claus hats. They swarm through the lobby to the gymnasium, where the ceiling lights bathe them in edgy orange as they squash into the bleachers and break into their team cheers, a visual-acoustic cacophony that reverberates with exultant frenzy.

This is what Oscar calls "licensed bedlam." The tradition began ten years ago as an attempt to alleviate the multitude of disciplinary problems that tended to arise on the day before the two-week holiday. Since then, there have been fewer problems on this day than on any other. Tensions are now channeled into games instead of fistfights, but they still run high. For many students, the coming fortnight heralds a vast silence, an abyss: fourteen days engulfed by hearing people and loneliness.

Today they come together with a kind of fierce intent. Color Olympics consists of four teams competing for six straight hours in a relentless series of events, including relay races, skits, trivia contests on deaf history, human pyramids, towers constructed of raw spaghetti and masking tape, teachers mummified in toilet paper. The tasks grow weirder and more feverish as the day progresses. The teams shuttle from gym to auditorium to cafeteria for different events, plowing down the halls preceded by the din of their cheers. They chant their team colors in rapid synchronism, both hands fingerspelling simultaneously. *"Voice! Voice! Voice!"* encourage the team leaders, on this one day taking up the plea usually reserved for speech teachers. The yell of preference is a kind of projectile hoot that arcs off the palate, loud enough for many of them to hear, kinesthetically satisfying even for those who can't.

The impulse for physical contact crackles with an almost biological imperative. As the participants travel from arena to arena, their body paint smudged and beaded, they pass one another and clasp hands glossy with sweat. They sprawl on the floor with limbs interlocking, lounge against each other's knees, breathe over each other's shoulders, softly tug at each other's sleeves and ponytails. All this touch might be considered awkward or brash among hearing adolescents; at Lexington it is implicit.

To amplify their instructions, teachers stand on chairs or stepladders, the visual equivalents of a megaphone. "Here's my rendition of shouting," a young hearing teacher on the blue team cries to her colleague, and she pumps the blue cheer straight over her head with both arms. No matter how urgently the teachers flick the lights, no matter how large the screen for the overhead projector is, they could not address the group without the students' compliance, for deaf people must be willing to look in order for communication to take place. And they are willing. In the stillness of all these riveted eyes, the warmth of all these attentive bodies, there resides the awareness that tomorrow there will be no school, nor the next day, nor the day after that.

At two-thirty, dismissal feels turbulent, jumbled. The temperature has dropped below freezing; the sky hovers, as dense and white as a hard-boiled egg, and every time the door opens the air smacks bitterly into the vestibule. Jointed blue foil letters spell out holiday wishes on the bus room wall, and beneath these signs the littlest children, freighted with wrapped parcels and candy canes, wait for attendants to lead them outside. Hearing aids come loose and whistle; a teacher's jingle-bell earrings tinkle as she crouches to zip jackets and tie hoods. (*"There should be jingle-light earrings for deaf people,"* suggests one student.) Long after the last bus quits the lot, older students remain talking in chilly gray huddles, reluctant to leave even though their breath spurts in hoary plumes. Across the street, the holiday lights that crisscross the privet hedges have come on.

The lucky ones are those on the girls' basketball team, for they have license to stay a few hours more. Janie Moran, the social studies teacher who coaches the team, graduated from Lexington eight years ago. When two boys wander in and beg permission to do lay-ups at the opposite end of the court, she doesn't have the heart to turn them away. And when Oscar pokes his head in at four o'clock, she shoots him an amused look.

"Want to play?" Her signs, as always, are terse and robust.

"Yeah."

"You're not dressed for it."

"I have shoes in the car."

He returns from the parking lot minutes later, his feet shod in dirty white sneakers. Oscar and the two boys scrimmage with the girls' team for half an hour. They play hard, with more concentration than merriment. The gym, devoid now of all the bodies that packed it during Color Olympics, echoes harshly. The lights over the bleachers are off; shadows from that side of the room seem to lunge onto the court. The girls and boys pound back and forth. Oscar lopes along with them, his necktie streaming out in back.

At four-thirty Janie reminds the team of their holiday schedule; they will practice a few times over the break. She also gets directions to the house of one of the students, who needs a ride. (Although her five younger, hearing siblings are afforded the privilege of using the subway, this girl's parents don't let their deaf daughter do so; basketball practice will be the only time during the next two weeks when she will see her friends.) Then practice is over and there are no more excuses to stay in the building.

It is a shame that the State Ed. people couldn't have visited the school today. When the new State Plan for Education of

Students with Disabilities comes out in seven months, it will not reflect any of the testimony that the Lexington representatives delivered. It will mandate the "education of the pupil to the maximum extent appropriate with other pupils who do not have a disability." It will stress that "the child should be educated in the school which he or she would attend if not disabled." Creamily bound in red, white, and blue, it will state its terms in the neat, unemotional jargon of bureaucracy. It will make no attempt to recognize that to many people, deafness is not a pathology but a cultural identity.

At quarter to five, Janie and Oscar turn off the lights, lock up the gym, and gently herd the remaining students outside. An aspirin-moon has risen, small and round, over the roofs across the street. Somewhere nearby, "Silent Night" is playing on a car radio, and now the last students drift out into it.

5

Words Left Unspoken

M y earliest memories of Sam Cohen are of his chin, which I remember as fiercely hard and pointy. Not pointy, my mother says, jutting; Grandpa had a strong, jutting chin. But against my very young face it felt like a chunk of honed granite swathed in stiff white bristles. Whenever we visited, he would lift us grandchildren up, most frequently by the elbows, and nuzzle our cheeks vigorously. This abrasive ritual greeting was our primary means of communication. In all my life, I never heard him speak a word I could understand.

Sometimes he used his voice to get our attention. It made a shapeless, gusty sound, like a pair of bellows sending up sparks and soot in a blacksmith shop. And he made sounds when he was eating, sounds that, originating from other quarters, would have drawn chiding or expulsion from the table. He smacked his lips and sucked his teeth; his chewing was moist and percussive; he released deep, hushed moans from the back of his throat, like a dreaming dog. And he burped out loud. Sometimes it was all Reba, Andy, and I could do not to catch one another's eyes and fall into giggles.

Our grandfather played games with us, the more physical the better. He loved that hand game: he would extend his, palms up, and we would hover ours, palms down, above his, and lower them, lower, lower, until they were just nesting, and *slap!* he'd have sandwiched one of our hands, trapping it between his. When we reversed, I could never even graze his, so fast would he snatch them away, like big white fish.

He played three-card monte with us, arranging the cards neatly between his long fingers, showing us once the jack of diamonds smirking, red and gold, underneath. And then, with motions as swift and implausible as a Saturday morning cartoon chase, his hands darted and faked and blurred and the cards lay still, face down and impassive. When we guessed the jack's position correctly, it was only luck. When we guessed wrong, he would laugh — a fond, gravelly sound — and pick up the cards and begin again.

He mimicked the way I ate. He compressed his mouth into dainty proportions as he nibbled air and carefully licked his lips and chewed tiny, precise bites, his teeth clicking, his eyelashes batting as he gazed shyly from under them. He could walk exactly like Charlie Chaplin and make nickels disappear, just vanish, from both his fists and up his sleeves; we never found them, no matter how we crawled over him, searching. All of this without any words.

He and my grandmother lived in the Bronx, in the same apartment my father and Uncle Max had grown up in. It was on Knox Place, near Mosholu Parkway, a three-room apartment below street level. The kitchen was a tight squeeze of a place, especially with my grandmother bending over the oven, blocking the passage as she checked baked apples or stuffed cabbage, my grandfather sitting with splayed knees at the dinette. It was easy to get each other's attention in there; a stamped foot sent vibrations clearly over the short distance, and an outstretched arm had a good chance of connecting with the other party.

The living room was ampler and dimmer, with abundant floor and table lamps to accommodate signed conversation. Little windows set up high revealed the legs of passersby. And down below, burrowed in black leather chairs in front of the television, we children learned to love physical comedy. Long before the days of closed captioning, we listened to our grandfather laugh out loud at the snowy black-and-white antics of Abbott and Costello, Laurel and Hardy, the Three Stooges.

During the time that I knew him, I saw his hairline shrink back and his eyes grow remote behind pairs of progressively thicker glasses. His athlete's bones shed some of their grace and nimbleness; they began curving in on themselves as he stood, arms folded across his sunken chest. Even his long, thin smile seemed to recede deeper between his nose and his prominent chin. But his hands remained lithe, vital. As he teased and argued and chatted and joked, they were the instruments of his mind, the conduits of his thoughts.

As far as anyone knows, Samuel Kolominsky was born deaf (according to the Lexington records, his parents "failed to take note until child was about one and a half years old"). His birthplace was Russia, somewhere near Kiev. Lexington records say he was born in 1908; my grandmother says it was 1907. He was a child when his family fled the czarist pogroms. Lexington records have him immigrating in 1913, at age five; my grandmother says he came to this country when he was three. Officials at Ellis Island altered the family name, writing down Cohen, but they did not detect his deafness, so Sam sailed on across the last ribbon of water to America.

His name-sign at home: *Daddy*. His name-sign with friends: the thumb and index finger, perched just above the temple, rub against each other like grasshopper legs. One old friend attributes this to Sam's hair, which was blond and thick and wavy. Another says it derived from his habit of twisting a lock between his fingers.

Lexington records have him living variously at Clara,

Moore, Siegel, Tehema, and Thirty-eighth streets in Brooklyn and on Avenue C in Manhattan. I knew him on Knox Place, and much later on Thieriot Avenue, in the Bronx. Wherever he lived, he loved to walk, the neighborhoods revolving silently like pictures in a Kinetoscope, unfurling themselves in full color around him.

Shortly before he died, when I was thirteen, we found ourselves walking home from a coffee shop together on a warm night. My family had spent the day visiting my grandparents at their apartment. My grandmother and the rest of the family were walking half a block ahead; I hung back and made myself take my grandfather's hand. We didn't look at each other. His hand was warm and dry. His gait was uneven then, a long slow beat on the right, catch-up on the left. I measured my steps to his. It was dark except for the hazy pink cones of light cast by streetlamps. I found his rhythm, and breathed in it. That was the longest conversation we ever had.

He died before I was really able to converse in sign. I have never seen his handwriting. I once saw his teeth, in a glass, on the bathroom windowsill. Now everything seems like a clue.

One afternoon, after the last yellow buses had lumbered away from school, I went with my father down to the basement. He sorted among his plethora of keys while we descended the stairs, finally jangling out the master as we approached the heavy brown doors to Lexington's storage room, an impressive if forbidding catacomb of huge proportions. Great sections of the windowless room were fenced into compartments very much resembling penal holding tanks; these enclaves contained spare equipment and ancient records belonging to the different departments. My father unlocked the gate of the largest one. Thin light shone murkily from dangling fixtures, and the pale, wet odor of mildew encouraged us to work quickly.

Picking my way through cardboard boxes, film projectors, and sheets of particleboard, I nearly tumbled into a familiar figure: our old TTY, donated to the school when our family acquired a newer, portable model. The original stood at waist level, a stout gray metal beast with a keyboard that had clacked and collected oily clumps of dust. My grandmother, when visiting us, would demand an old toothbrush and, with the rapt solicitude of a paleontologist, clean between the keys. She still possessed one of these old models; she called hers the Monster.

Up ahead, my father stood before the high banks of file cabinets. We suspected them of being wildly out of order; I was prepared to spend the afternoon down here, inhaling particles of mold and sifting through drawers of brittle documents. My father had asked one of the maintenance workers whether we could borrow a work light to prop above the files; he had intended to wait with me only until the light was delivered, but the spirit of the search had cast a spell, and now, in spite of himself, he scanned the rows of cabinets. Hands on hips, shoulders rounded over scooped chest, his posture mirrored his father's. After a moment he embarked on the middle aisle. I trailed after him doubtfully. There were perhaps forty cabinets, not all of them labeled.

I can't say why I sank to my knees just where I did. I suppose my father had paused, thereby blocking me from going further. I suppose that because he was tall, I assumed the task of inspecting the lower drawers. I suppose it was as simple and meaningless as that.

I knelt and pulled out the drawer directly in front of me, stuck my fingers a third of the way in, and parted a couple of thick brown folders. I had landed in a batch of Cohens. "Dad . . ." I picked through them gingerly; even so, flakes of discolored paper fluttered to the bottom of the drawer. "Dad, I think . . ." I passed Charlotte and Joseph, Lester and Millie, Rachel and Ray and Rebecca, and there, quite complaisantly, followed Samuel. "Dad."

I held the folder out to him. Somewhat to my chagrin, he did not say, "Go ahead, look," but accepted it from me. I stood on tiptoes behind his shoulder.

The first thing inside was a note, typed on a relatively fresh white index card. "This is it," my father murmured, reading the card. "This is Grandpa's." The note read:

1/12/79

This new file was made up since
Mr. Samuel Cohen's original file was
destroyed in a fire that occurred in
the old school at Lexington Ave. &
68th St., Manhattan.

Paperclipped to the note was a long brown envelope. My father shook out its contents: one wallet-size photograph of a boy in late adolescence. "This is it," my father repeated. The boy wore a heavy dark sweater over a white shirt, the left shoulder of which bulged messily against his collar. His hands were clasped just below the chest, and his chin and neck were thrust forward so that his Adam's apple protruded above the knot of his tie. His hair was slicked back in a glossy wave. His lips were just parting. The pockets of skin below his eyes were gathered in mirth; he looked slightly up, as though he were gazing at the photographer rather than the lens.

I knew about the fire that destroyed the original file; my father had warned me not to expect much of this reconstructed one, if we even located it. But the folder was gratifyingly thick. We took it upstairs to examine in better light.

On the way to my father's office, we met a maintenance worker wheeling a garbage can down the hall.

"Do you still need that light, Dr. Cohen?" he asked.

"No. No thanks, Fernando. We got it." My father held up the brown folder, showing what the "it" was, then, almost shyly, extended it. "This is the file of someone who was a student at Lexington in 1916," he explained as Fernando gently, quizzically opened the cover. "The student's name was Sam Cohen," he went on, pausing to let the connection take hold. "My father."

"Your father was a student at this school?"

"Yes."

"Then he don't hear?"

"No, he was deaf."

Fernando and my father beheld each other for a moment and smiled. Then Fernando handed back the folder. "Okay, see you later," he said, and went on dragging the big garbage can on wheels down the hall.

On the wall behind my father's desk hangs an old photograph, creased and cracked and now pressed under glass. In the photograph, eleven men kneel or stand in the dark athletic uniforms of the Hebrew Association of the Deaf, their hands clasped behind their backs, chins tucked in, chests out. On the floor in the center rests a basketball on which is inscribed "1937–1938 Champions." The young man standing second from the right, trying to look serious, is Sam Cohen.

When visitors come to my father's office for the first time, he will invariably point out the photograph. Often he will invite people to step behind his desk for a close look at the faces. Sometimes he will ask them to guess which man is his father. I have seen him display the picture to a deaf leader visiting from Moscow, a couple of black women pilots giving a presentation for Black History Month, the ambassador from Grenada, the deaf president of Gallaudet University, and a frightened high school student who was sent to his office for in-school suspension. He uses this photograph like a passport. With hearing people, it becomes a point of reference. With deaf people, it is a port of entry, proof of affiliate membership.

It was back to this office that we brought Sam Cohen's file, and it was here, thanks to the fact that my father's calendar was crammed with prior commitments, that I had the opportunity to peruse its contents alone. I read slowly, handling each spotty, crumbling document with care. They rustled and whispered as I turned them over, laid them softly down: the crackling onionskin, the mossy carbon copies, the yellowed memos scrawled with a fountain pen, their old-fashioned flourishes and curlicues gone a parched brown.

In 1916, Lexington was known as the Institution for the Improved Instruction of Deaf-Mutes, or, more familiarly, as the Deaf-and-Dumb Institution. Those words appear on nearly every page in the folder, weighing heavily, like lead sinkers lashed again and again to his name: Deaf-Mute Sam, Deaf-and-Dumb Sam, making him the responsibility of the authorities, turning him over to the institution. One set of papers makes him a state pupil, "to be educated and supported . . . at the expense of the county of Kings." Several other papers, signed by Sam's father (also named Oscar), authorize the institution doctors to examine the child, remove his adenoids and his tonsils, inoculate him, give him glasses. Most of these permissions consist simply of a signature, but the one that includes a brief note may well reveal the core of my great-grandparents' attitudes toward the role of the authorities regarding their deaf son. In hasty, looping script, my great-grandfather wrote, "I am satisfied that you are going to do the right thing for him. and oblige yours truly Oscar Cohen." The grim lead weights, son and all, dropped neatly out of sight.

In 1928, after twelve years of school, Sam graduated and moved back home to Brooklyn. Within months his father was appealing to Lexington for help, writing, "Sam tried very hard to find work, but it was impossible. He had no trade as your school did not teach him a trade. We do not know what to do. We are all upset. He is a boy of twenty-one years old and is nearly a man and has to earn a living."

Mr. Harris Taylor, the principal of the Institution for the Improved Instruction of Deaf-Mutes, responded defensively that although everyone at the school was extremely fond of

Sam, "he was one of those boys who wasted an enormous amount of time," and "we have never been able to make a worker of him, and unless he learns to work harder he will have trouble." He cited specifically Sam's poor speech and language skills, as well as his slovenly work in the sign-painting and printing departments. Then, with mighty benevolence, Mr. Taylor wrote that the twenty-one-year-old Sam was "a good boy," and assured my great-grandparents that "in any failure or in any trouble that may arise, you may count upon our sympathy, because everyone is a friend to Sam."

Indeed, the same day he wrote that letter, the principal advised Sam, via Western Union, "May have job for you. Come here tomorrow morning at eleven." Further correspondence in the file testifies to the school's continued attempts to help Sam find a job, as well as to the apparent lack of success of these efforts. The following February, my great-grandfather again wrote to the principal on his son's behalf: "During the time he has been out of school (he has been out a year now) he has only worked for two months at sign-painting for $12.00 a week. Then he was layed [sic] off. Since then he has gone out to look for work every day and can't seem to find any because of his being handicapped, it seems. Perhaps it is in the power of your Institution to help Sam find work? If so will you please let me know?"

I picture my great-grandfather as a sturdy man bundled in a thick overcoat and fur hat, plodding through snow to post the letter, his great bushy eyebrows bunched with worry. And I picture the principal as a clean-shaven man in a brown suit, a goodhearted man who had abandoned other, more comfortable careers to help deaf-mutes improve their unfortunate lot; I picture him reading the letter at his desk, perhaps rubbing a hand across his smooth jaw, sighing.

But in all the letters, the telegrams, the documents, the medical records, I couldn't locate Sam himself. I didn't know how to picture my grandfather in any of this, until one day when my Uncle Max was visiting. I had taken the bulky brown folder home to study more carefully, and Max sat at the kitchen table, jiggling his knee and leafing through it. He came to his grandfather's letter, read it, and snorted.

"Pop went out to look for work every day, my ass," barked Max, tugging at the corner of his blond mustache. The skin under his eyes creased faintly in a private grin. "He was out playing ball."

The final picture slid into place. Now I could complete the image: my great-grandfather dropping his letter anxiously into the box; Mr. Harris Taylor shaking his head behind a big polished desk; and my grandfather, Sam, on the court, away from language lessons and hearing employers and jobs where he couldn't talk with anyone, just Sam on the court, flying up and down the asphalt, his heart and lungs and limbs all engaged in what they did best.

The spring Sam turned seventy, we sent out dozens and dozens of birthday party invitations, hand-lettered by my mother and watercolored by me. We cleaned our whole house — the dust mice under the armchair, the peanut shells in the hearth, the dog-nose smudges on the windowpanes over the couch. We bought two six-foot submarine sandwiches, at which Reba, Andy, and I marveled; still in their amber cellophane wrappers, they spread importantly down the entire length of the dining room table. And all along the one-mile route from the Tappan Zee Bridge to our house, we thumbtacked markers to telephone posts, colored balloons with signs reading SAM.

It was not our family's custom to throw large birthday parties, even for septuagenarians, but something greater was being celebrated this year. My grandfather had finally been elected into the Hall of Fame of the New York State Athletic Association for the Deaf. This was his life's dream, the one he had given up hoping for nearly two decades earlier.

Shortly after his marriage, Sam had landed a job cutting

terry cloth for women's bathrobes. This remained his occu-
pation throughout his life. A member of the International
Ladies' Garment Workers Union, he provided the sole income for his family — his wife, Fannie, and their two hearing sons. Each morning he rode the elevated train along Jerome Avenue to work; he punched a clock and cut cloth all
day with heavy shears; at night he returned home so tired
that he was notorious for sleeping past his stop on the train.
It was a fine job for a deaf man in the middle of the twentieth
century, and with these hours of his life he provided suste-
nance for his family.

But Sam lived for his moments on the court. He had always loved basketball. In grammar school, he played it alone
in the rain and snow during lunch recess and after school in
the Lexington courtyard. At home during the summers,
when his parents imposed limits on his playing, he would
toss his sneakers and shorts from the window of their sixth-
floor apartment and tell his mother he was going out to buy
a newspaper, then return hours later, most often without the
paper.

As an adult his life continued to revolve around basketball, and around the Union League, one of the oldest deaf
clubs in the country. Every Thursday night my grandfather
would go to the Ansonia Hotel in Manhattan, where the club
members met to play cards and talk. He attended so de-
voutly that on Knox Place, Thursday was fingerspelled *U-L*;
my father likes to say that he grew up believing the days of
the week were Sunday, Monday, Tuesday, Wednesday, UL,
Friday, and Saturday.

Sam played basketball for the Union League, the Lexington Boys, the Hebrew Association of the Deaf, the Peli-
cans, and other deaf teams. He was the only deaf player on
two semiprofessional teams, the Philadelphia Spas and the
Castle Hill Beach Club. He coached and played basketball
until 1959. When he stopped, my father, just out of high
school, wrote a letter to the American Athletic Association of

the Deaf (AAAD), the first of many letters he would write on his father's behalf. It explained that Sam, then fifty-two years old, had developed cataracts and was awaiting an operation; moreover, the factory where he had been employed for twenty-five years had shut down, so he was out of work as well. "For the eighteen years of my life," my father wrote,

> I have regarded my father as a happy, jovial person who seems to enjoy life more than any person possibly could. During these past five weeks I have seen him turn into a depressed, despondent individual. On the outside he still acts the same but on the inside there has been a change that only one as close to him as myself could notice.
>
> Just yesterday while looking through some papers I found the letter that you sent to him in 1956 concerning his nomination to the AAAD Hall of Fame. Knowing my Father as I do I realized that he most likely forgot all about answering your letter, as his main interest is participating in sports events and not the publicity or notoriety involved.
>
> So now I can tell you the purpose of this letter. I thought of any possibility that might have a chance of cheering him up a little and I thought that if there was a chance of him making the Hall of Fame this would be a terrific lift. I am not asking for any charity nor do I want you to feel sorry for my Father for he is not a man to feel sorry for but a man to envy because of his great talents. I know how good an athlete he was and still is because he taught me everything I know about basketball and I have a few trophies to show for the learning he has given me. I would like to say again that my Father does not know anything about this letter, if he did he would probably beat the daylights out of me because of the tremendous amount of pride instilled in him.

My father signed his name in neat black script, sealed and stamped the envelope, and then I imagine him tramping through the snow to the mailbox, following the ghost-prints of his dead grandfather. The letter went unanswered, yielding no results, and Sam never knew what his son had done. It was eighteen years before Sam's nomination resurfaced and he was finally inducted into the Hall of Fame. He received news of the honor just four months shy of his seventieth birthday.

The day of the party, my grandfather appeared mildly bewildered when he first emerged from one of the rear doors of the car that friends had driven up from the Bronx. All of his friends and relatives clustered expectantly in our yard, holding hunks of submarine sandwich and beer and cake, grinning at him while he blinked uncertainly back. (Later we learned that my grandmother, in a cunning effort to prevent him from seeing the posters along the roadside, had snatched his glasses from his face as soon as the car left the exit ramp, on the pretext that they were shamefully filthy, and proceeded to scrub them vigorously with her skirt for the next mile, effectively keeping the party a surprise.) When my grandfather was finally apprised of the occasion for this gathering, his thin, wide mouth opened in unabashed appreciation, and he went around most of the afternoon beaming, his eyes glittering behind clean, clean lenses.

Late in the afternoon someone bounced a basketball out of the toy box in our garage. We didn't have a hoop, but one was mounted on the Rotellis' garage, next door, so we all gathered at the edge of their driveway and my grandfather took the ball out to what seemed like half-court. I had no faith at all that he would make it — him at seventy years old, with hair as white as birchbark and teeth that came out at night — and it made me queasy to think of him missing, today of all days. We watched in silence as he gently coiled his frame, his hands a smooth socket for the ball, then sprang his body open and let the sphere arc above us. It sank through the net, steady and definite. In this arena he never missed.

Three years later, in July, we held his funeral gathering at Max's house in Brewster. People drove up from Mount Hebron Cemetery in Queens and walked through the house depositing armloads of food, pot roast and kugels and soups and challah and pickles and olives and pastries and fruit baskets and nuts and chocolates, and then they continued out to the back lawn, where the acre of neatly trimmed grass rolled to the edge of the woods. The grownups reclined in plastic chairs and metal chaises, the women plucking damply at the necks of their dark blouses. We children kicked off our good, uncomfortable shoes and stepped barefoot over bees in the clover. We got sick on too much fruit and chocolate and sat in the grass, eavesdropping on the hearing people and watching the deaf people sign to one another; all of it seemed equally incomprehensible.

After a while I retreated into the cool, wood-smelling shade of the living room and stood looking through the square panes of the sliding doors. Uncle Max had wept at the service, but my father had not cried at all. I saw him now through the polished glass, moving about on the lawn, his shoulders rounded beneath his white shirt, a forgotten drink suspended perilously from his fingers. He nodded while someone signed to him. I had not been able to speak to him all day; I felt a little bit afraid of him, his iron sadness, his awful grace.

Some hearing children of deaf parents say that they had to assume parental roles when they were young, that they had to function as interpreters, caregivers, providers, instructors. They talk about growing up under the crushing weight of these responsibilities.

My father has never had much use for essays and articles expounding on this subject. He is quick to point out that *he* never supported the family, *he* didn't buy the groceries, *he* didn't feed the family or take care of the apartment — that it was his parents who tended him, who nurtured him emotionally, who were the rock.

Watching him on the lawn that day, his broad shoulders so bent, his muscles gripping in a kind of mineral stillness, I both craved and dreaded to witness some slippage, some chipping or crumbling. It would be ten years before this happened, before I heard my father's voice thicken and break, before I heard the full story of my grandfather's death.

On Saturday afternoon, July 25, 1981, Sam and Fannie had been heading to the Union League when Sam, walking a few steps behind Fannie, collapsed. Someone touched Fannie's arm; she turned and saw a crowd gathered around her husband. He lay crumpled on the bright sidewalk; blood came from his head. Police came, then an ambulance. He was taken to the Cabrini Medical Center on East Nineteenth Street and admitted to the Cardiac Care Unit.

When my father arrived at the hospital that afternoon, he explained to the CCU staff, nurses, and physicians that Sam was profoundly deaf and could not speak intelligibly. He emphasized the importance of having someone who was able to communicate in American Sign Language so that Sam could know what was happening to him and so the hospital staff could obtain information about symptoms and medical history and responses to their questions. My father said that he would serve as an interpreter. He gave the hospital his telephone numbers at home and at work. He said he would come to the hospital immediately whenever he was called.

On Sunday at three P.M. he tried to visit his father, but he was barred by the worker at the front desk, who informed him that because of doctors' rounds he could not visit at that time. My father explained that he wished to be present during doctors' rounds to serve as an interpreter during the examination. The worker replied that the hospital had an interpreter program for the deaf and that my father's services were not needed. She refused to let him in. Later my father learned that no interpreter had been available; the Cabrini interpreter did not work on weekends.

That night my father called the CCU to inquire about Sam's condition. The nurse on duty said the doctor was not there. My father asked for the doctor please to return his call on Sunday night at home. No one returned the call.

On Monday morning at nine, my father called the CCU again and was told that Sam had improved, that a heart attack had been ruled out, and that he had been moved from the CCU to the fifteenth floor. My father called Fannie on the TTY to give her the good news.

Fannie arrived at Cabrini at 11:15 A.M. to visit her husband. Requesting a visitor's pass, she was told that Mr. Cohen was not a patient. After she insisted that he was, the person at the desk made some phone calls and then directed her to the fifteenth floor. No one tried to call for an interpreter. On the fifteenth floor she was directed to a waiting room. Because the nurse could not communicate with her, Fannie did not understand what she was waiting for. Finally a resident who spoke with an Indian accent, which was extremely difficult to lip-read, came and described in technical terms that Mr. Cohen had not survived the second of two cardiac arrests that had occurred at about eight that morning. Fannie did not know what "cardiac arrest" meant, nor could she understand the resident's speech very well. But when he shook his head, she understood.

In a state of shock and confusion, she was sent to the hospital lobby. The doctor called my father at work. Dazed, frozen, behind a tightly stretched skin of silence, Fannie waited for him. But it was Max who arrived first. When she saw him striding jauntily up the passage toward her, unaware of his father's death, the blond ends of his mustache curved in greeting, Fannie dissolved, her sobs breaking against the lobby walls.

In the days afterward, there were many questions. Why had no interpreter been present to help Sam understand why he was being moved from the CCU on Sunday night? Why had no interpreter been present during the crises on Monday morning, to give Sam the doctors' instructions or tell the doctors what he might have been trying to communicate? Why had no interpreter been present at any of the examinations, after my father had offered this necessary service and been told that Cabrini would provide it? What possible explanation could the hospital have for preventing my father from serving as an interpreter during the doctors' rounds on Sunday afternoon? And why had no interpreter been present to deliver the news to Fannie of her husband's death?

My father wrote to the medical center administrators requesting answers to these questions. Months passed; it was November before he got a response. It acknowledged no fault but concluded placatingly, "You can be assured that we have reinforced our staff training programs in our continuing effort to communicate with our hearing impaired patients. . . . I want you to know that your persistence in pursuing this matter will impact favorably on other hearing impaired patients treated at the Cabrini Medical Center."

As a child, I was only partially conscious that something had gone awry, that something wrong and bad had happened beyond the fact of death itself. Years later, I asked my father to tell me the story. He obliged, reliving its chronology, and I finally witnessed the crack for which I had searched in vain a decade earlier. The craggy planes of his face darkened and shifted; something staggered painfully in his throat. For a moment I saw him fold softly into grief. I saw him miss my grandfather.

And I wondered at his vision of Sam, so clearly one of indomitable strength. When I go looking for Sam, it seems I come up only with papers, sheaves of dry correspondence about him and for him but never by him. If he was a rock, he has long since gone to dust, and any fossils left behind were left by others, just as the ink on the pages has been left by others, by Oscar his father and Oscar his son. Sam's own motions — the words of his hands, the path of his body as it worked the court — are traceless; once realized and finished, they left no mark.

6

A Recovery

First there is the snow, a thin white film of it blotting out the city, and for a moment Sofia imagines she is back in Leningrad, waking up in her old school dormitory. But in the bed next to hers, beneath that forbidding lump of pink blanket, lies not a schoolmate but her sister Irina. And in the icy dark outside her curtainless window, the yellow eyes of early morning traffic are sliding warily along Woodhaven Boulevard. Perhaps more than anything else it is the poster of the New Kids on the Block watching over Irina like ersatz guardian angels while she sleeps that roots Sofia firmly in Rego Park. She rises and stands for a moment in the narrow space between the two beds, watching flakes cling to the bars of the fire escape, fall past the branches of sycamore trees, and coat the frozen courtyard.

Then she goes to the bathroom and sees the blood, and that is when the trouble begins.

"Mama." She creeps into her parents' room, feels her way around the bed, and in an agitated stream of Russian tells her mother. She has gotten her period. Today. The day before she is to enter the temple formally by having a bat mitz-

vah. Orthodox Judaism says that while a woman is menstru-
ing she is impure, and today, the day before she is to stand
on the bema and read from the Torah, the day before she is
to become a bat mitzvah, a Daughter of the Commandment,
she has become impure. In the dark of the bedroom Ister
Normatov listens to the news delivered in the voice of her
third daughter, a voice with oddly taut and flattened vowels,
and she thinks, "Then there won't be a bat mitzvah after all."

Iluysha and Ister Normatov had not wanted their daughter
to have a bat mitzvah in the first place. A year ago, when the
rabbi who gave religious training at Lexington School first
broached the subject, their answer was no. Why should a
deaf child have a bat mitzvah? Their two hearing daughters,
after all, have done without the honor; they grew up in the
Soviet Union, where Judaism was forbidden. But gradually
Mr. Normatov accepted the idea, even grew to like it. As the
date for the ceremony approached, he helped Sofia study
Hebrew, reading aloud with her in the evenings. But Mrs.
Normatov remains opposed. Not this child — she doesn't
want this child speaking aloud before a hearing congregation. Perhaps this is God's way of saying he doesn't want
Sofia to have a bat mitzvah either.

Mrs. Normatov, awake in the dark, thinks about this
daughter, about how strong-willed, even defiant, she has become in this country, and so she steals out of bed and follows
Sofia into the kitchen. "What are you planning to do?" she
inquires suspiciously, and sure enough, Sofia replies, "I will
call the rabbi. Maybe it will be all right." They argue then.
Snow continues its clean descent past the little window at
Sofia's back while she reads the words on her mother's lips:
you are creating a sin, your bat mitzvah will mean nothing,
bad things will happen to you.

Her mother's words follow her out the door that morning,
a visual echo reverberating across her mind: the lips, the
teeth, the dark, knowing eyes. The school bus is already
waiting at the curb and she has to run for it, her hair half

combed, her stomach empty. She scrambles across the skid marks and turbid slush that already mark the snow. Irina, lagging behind breathlessly on plump legs, protests, but Sofia takes no notice. She will talk with the rabbi. They must hurry and get to school so that she can call the rabbi.

Only a week ago Wednesday Sofia had been sitting in the school library having her last Hebrew lesson before the bat mitzvah, and everything had finally seemed all right. She had arrived just a few minutes late and Rabbi Donna Berman had already been there, at a round table tucked against the back wall by the fish tank and the heaters. The rabbi stood up, tall and slender in green jeans and sneakers, smiled her warm, impish smile, and kissed Sofia hello.

The first time Sofia met her, slightly over a year ago, she was shocked and delighted to encounter a *woman* rabbi. Of course, by that time, shock and delight had become almost routine sensations for Sofia. School in America had proved full of surprises: deaf teachers, hearing teachers who signed, Jewish holidays on the school calendar. Every time she turned around, it seemed, another old certainty came crashing splendidly down.

Last fall, when Rabbi Berman started her religion class at Lexington, Sofia stood out instantly from the other four pupils. The group met only one hour a week and offered no academic credit, but Sofia treated it like a core course, taking the Hebrew alphabet home to study and diving eagerly into this language — her fifth, after Russian, Russian Sign Language, English, and ASL — with innate ability. She began to wear a gold *chai*, a letter of the Hebrew alphabet and a symbol of luck, on a chain around her neck. She cried upon seeing her first real menorah; until then she had only known the makeshift candle-gouged potato used at secret Chanukah celebrations in Russia.

What had once been denied was now being offered. Like a load of fresh chickens suddenly stocking yesterday's barren shelves in a Russian grocery, the promise of Sofia's religious heritage now appeared before her. She had known too much denial, too many restrictions, not to reach for it. It didn't matter that this was the fifth alphabet she had to learn, or that she was struggling to learn English at the same time, or that she couldn't hear the new language, couldn't sound out the strange words, couldn't ever — it was hopeless, she was sure — pronounce the Hebrew *ch* sound. None of that mattered. She would practice for it all day and all night, patience and desire pressed together in her heart like two gold coins in her fist.

After three months of classes, Rabbi Berman, or Rabbi Donna, as Sofia called her, pulled Sofia aside and asked whether she would like to have a bat mitzvah. Sofia had never actually attended a bat mitzvah. She didn't know exactly what having one entailed, nor was she entirely sure that her parents, who had practiced Orthodox Judaism since coming to New York, would approve. She did know that at eighteen, she exceeded the traditional bat mitzvah age by five years. But when the rabbi assured her that this was not a problem, Sofia decided to swallow her other qualms, and without initial parental consent, she spent the next nine months preparing for the ceremony.

It wasn't until this final lesson, sitting cozily back by the fish tank with Rabbi Donna, that Sofia finally let herself believe it would happen. Bent over the rabbi's fat leather book, her right thumb looped through the chain from which her *chai* dangled, her left index finger gliding horizontally along the page, she read aloud. The fingers on her right hand dipped and curled as she unconsciously fingerspelled portions of each Hebrew word.

The rabbi pulled her chair close and read over Sofia's shoulder. She stopped Sofia intermittently to correct her pronunciation, attempting to fingerspell the proper sound. The rabbi's fingerspelling was earnest and imperfect; frequently, Sofia had to smile gently and correct her signing as the rabbi corrected *her* Hebrew.

Behind them, a class of five middle-school girls had entered the library. The children wore hearing aid receivers strapped around their waists on wide elastic straps. They danced and jostled around the card catalogue in search of books on lizards. Unable to locate the proper subject heading, a few of them buzzed up to Sofia's table instead and peered interestedly over her shoulder until their teacher shooed them away toward the reptiles.

"They wait for you to hand it to them," commented a librarian, leaning across the shelf by the fish tank.

"Always," agreed the teacher, switching off the microphone on her lapel. She watched her students sashay at last in the general direction of nonfiction. "On a platter."

Sofia, oblivious, read on. Her hair curled like black flames down her rounded back. Rabbi Donna sat close, half curved around her, and Sofia could see her approving nods from the corner of her eye. She worked her thumb in and out of the loop of her necklace, following Hebrew across the page, spelling sounds on her fingers, molding them in her throat. Finally she came to the end of the passage, sighed, smiled, and raised her eyes for approval.

The rabbi laughed. "You need a sweatband."

Sofia frowned.

"A sweatband? Sweatband." The rabbi sketched one across her own forehead.

Sofia nodded. "Oh yah, yah. I know that." She used only her voice with the rabbi.

For the past few months, Rabbi Donna had sensed an ambivalence on Sofia's part; she seemed to be dragging her feet. At one point she had even wondered whether Sofia had changed her mind about the bat mitzvah, and had asked, "Am I forcing you?"

Sofia had shaken her head. "No, no . . . I just have to check with my mother."

Now the rabbi gently brought up logistics. "Sofia, are you making an invitation?"

"Not yet. I want to." There would be no engraved cards

with sprays of roses for this bat mitzvah, no thick creamy envelopes, no neatly stamped and addressed printed reply cards. After school one day Sofia would print something out on the laser printer in the second-floor computer room — if she ever got a moment in which to do it.

"Maybe after your bat mitzvah, when you have more time?" suggested Rabbi Donna. She laughed again and laid a warm hand across Sofia's shoulder blade.

"How many people?" asked Sofia.

"The temple has a lot of seats."

"Not too many. Better limited," she suggested anxiously.

"Can I come?" teased the rabbi.

Sofia smiled tiredly.

She hadn't dreamed that a week and a half later she would be grimly riding on the bus through the snow, preparing to ask the rabbi that very question in earnest.

As soon as she arrives at Lexington, Sofia places a call, via telephone and TTY and relay service, to the rabbi's office number. She gets an answering machine and leaves a message to please contact her through her guidance counselor, Louann Katz. She makes the call from Louann's cubicle in the guidance office. Louann, one of the handful of Lexington staff members invited to the bat mitzvah, is all compact efficiency, warm and brisk and solid. With her strong, rapid signs, she promises to contact Sofia as soon as the rabbi calls back. Then there is nothing to do but get a pass and go to class.

Sofia tries not to dwell on what the rabbi will say, but the day seems mined with subtle references that propel her back to the subject. In American history, the lesson focuses on religious freedom.

"Why did dissenters leave the Massachusetts Bay Colony in 1644 and establish their own colony in Rhode Island?" quizzes Janie Moran, smudging the date as she hits the board for emphasis.

Sofia responds instantly, as though she just happens to have been thinking about that very topic. *"They wanted to believe in God on their own, in their own way. Because it's personal."*

"Right. Remember, the Massachusetts Bay Colony was incredibly strict." Janie signs *strict* sharply, two crooked fingers snapping over the bridge of her nose. It looks like a bridle, with the rider yanking back on the reins.

Sofia rubs the side of her face and looks over her shoulder at the clock. Not yet ten.

The morning drags on, miserably chill and damp. In English class, when Sofia asks whether she may go down to her locker and fetch her book, Liz Wolter starts to harass her a bit. *"What is it doing in your locker?"* she asks sternly, hands on hips. Liz is another Lexington teacher who has been invited to the bat mitzvah — she is to interpret — but Sofia neither details that morning's events for her nor plays up to the scolding. She only responds wearily, *"Yes or no?"*

Liz lets her go and she runs the three flights down the dim, empty stairwell to the basement, wondering again what the rabbi will say. Sofia has to pass near the guidance office on her way back to English. Might the rabbi have called by now? She returns to class without checking.

Liz Wolter reads out loud from a paperback copy of Rosa Guy's novel *The Friends,* which she props open on the table, a stapler weighing the pages down and leaving her hands free to sign. She simultaneously reads aloud and signs, using English-like signs to match the text with generous snippets of ASL tossed in for clarity. Her fine-boned face lifts and contorts with feeling; her narrow shoulders shift as she takes on different characters. Her fingerspelling has the clean precision of an elementary school teacher's penmanship.

Sofia rests her chin on her stacked fists and prepares to soak her harried brain in fiction for an hour. But too many details in the novel remind her almost uncannily of her present situation. In today's chapter, the protagonist, a teenage girl who has immigrated to New York, is sitting in a class-room unable to stop thinking about her mother. Then Liz gets to the part where the fictional class begins to taunt the teacher. *"'She ain't nothing but a Jew!'"* reads Liz. Her chin puckers in disgust as she takes on the part of the students, signing their cruel chant, *"'Miss Lass is a Jew-ew.'"*

The scene is disturbingly familiar. Sofia knows what it is like to be called "dirty Jew." At her old school, in Leningrad, her dark, Middle Eastern looks made her an easy target for anti-Semitism. When she first came to Lexington, two years ago, she wrote an essay about her experiences which was translated from Russian to English by a school interpreter.

> I want to tell you something about how Jewish people live in Russia and America. In Russia, there is discrimination against Jewish people. In Russia, the government tells people that they can't believe in God and the government closes some churches and synagogues. Also, in Russia, some Jewish people do not know their religion. They are not free to learn about the holidays or eat kosher food.

Sofia's own family had practiced Judaism secretly at home in Samarkand. But she spent most of her childhood away at the school for the deaf in Leningrad, cut off from both her family and her religion.

She touches the *chai* on the chain around her neck. She has traveled halfway around the world to a country where Judaism can be openly practiced; she has met a rabbi willing to work with a deaf student; she has labored over Hebrew and religious studies; she has wrestled with her family's reticence. Now it looks as though she may have surmounted all of these obstacles only to be thwarted by the time of the month, a phase of the moon.

After English there is biology, and after biology, math. When it is finally one o'clock, Sofia makes her way anxiously to the guidance office instead of the lunchroom. Louann Katz is at her desk, and yes — before Sofia has even quite sat down — yes, the rabbi has called, she says, they talked for thirty minutes and everything is fine, *fine,* and here is the rabbi's home phone number for Sofia if she wants to call.

A sweet tiredness washes through Sofia's muscles as Louann tries to convey everything the rabbi has said: that having her period is a wonderful thing, a God-given gift, that there is no more appropriate time to have her bat mitzvah than during this time of potential creativity, this time of celebration. But knowing that this perspective might clash with the Normatovs', the rabbi has emphasized that she will respect Sofia's wishes and support her either way. She has left the ultimate decision in Sofia's own hands.

Sofia thinks of her mother, who she knows is still embarrassed by the idea of her deaf daughter's speaking in public. She thinks of her father, who only a month ago began to show his support by helping her practice the Hebrew readings. She thinks of Rabbi Donna and the Lexington staff members who have helped her prepare, who are rooting for her, who are planning on attending the ceremony tomorrow. She thinks of herself. And she tells Louann her decision.

"My family believed in God and they always celebrated holidays," Sofia had written in that school essay two years ago, "but I couldn't celebrate with my family because I was in a residential school. I was in a dorm school for the deaf." For too many years she has been apart. Too much has been left out, too many connections have been missed. It is time to start recovering the pieces, filling in the holes.

"Sofia, I watched the sun rise this morning."

They are standing on the bema, facing each other. Behind them colored light glows dully from two panels of stained glass. The room is long and low-ceilinged. A fake candle atop the ark flicks pointy orange light at odd intervals.

"I watched the sun rise because I had a great deal of trouble writing this piece. I had tried several times during the week to jot down some thoughts. Last night I stayed up late ripping up page after page, dissatisfied with anything I had written."

Sofia glances at Rabbi Donna, tall and gentle in her dark robe and many-colored tallis. Then she looks back at Liz Wolter, who stands beside the rabbi, interpreting her words.

"And so I got up early, watched the sun rise, and realized why I was having trouble writing about you — because how do you do justice to something or someone so beautiful?"

It is December seventh, the sixth day of Chanukah. Sofia has chosen this day to have her bat mitzvah because Chanukah is her favorite holiday; it celebrates religious freedom. She chose the date almost a year ago, and now that it has arrived it is perfect: blue and gold and spare.

Driving out to Long Island with her family this morning, Sofia watched the trees that lined the roads. They looked kind and elderly, like great-aunts. Snow lay in patches deep in the woods. It seemed to come up between piles of leaves like milk through cereal. In Port Washington, they drove down streets where large plywood snowmen decorated the lampposts.

They reached the Port Jewish Center, a modern square cement building with a rutted parking lot. Sofia's mother and grown sisters, Ada and Nelly, picked gingerly across muddy potholes in their high-heeled shoes. Sofia asked only a handful of guests outside her nuclear family: an uncle, a few teachers, a Lexington student named Ruben. She has closer friends at school, but these she did not invite. Ruben is another deaf Russian Jewish immigrant; his mother has become friends with her mother.

Inside, more and more strangers kept arriving. The rabbi sent a letter to the congregation shortly before Thanksgiving, inviting them to participate, both by attending the service and by preparing food for the reception afterward. "Sofia's family is struggling here in the United States," she explained in the letter, "and yet I feel strongly that there should be some kind of special *oneg* after the service." All morning, in answer to the call for a celebration, the tables in the back corner were quietly stocked with Tupperware bowls, pans wrapped in aluminum foil, paper shopping bags, plastic bottles of seltzer.

By ten-thirty, more than fifty people had taken their seats in the congregation. A man in a blue velvet yarmulke set up a video camera in the back. A woman with white hair and glasses on a chain around her neck sat at the organ. The Normatovs assembled themselves on the right half of the front row, the Lexington teachers and Ruben on the left. Irina, who had been racing about all morning, looking importantly flustered in a birthday-cake dress of pink ruffles and striking up conversations with anyone who spoke English or Russian or ASL, now aligned herself with the Lexington contingent.

Upstairs, Rabbi Donna broke one of her own rules; she gave the bat mitzvah girl a gift, a tallis of her own, embroidered with glossy white threads. She helped Sofia arrange the prayer shawl over the shoulders of her suit, which is really Ada's suit, a grown-up suit of ivory lace with rhinestone buttons on the jacket.

"How do you feel?" the rabbi asked, giving her a squeeze.

"I feel Jewish."

Then they started together down the stairs.

Now Sofia, standing at the bema after the cantor's first song, looks out at all the familiar and strange faces and says in as clear a voice as she can, "Please rise."

The congregation hesitates, unsure of what she has said, until a man toward the back repeats her request and they hastily get to their feet. Sofia reads the prayer with her eyes cast down, dark hair spilling over her tallis, its fringe dripping like candle wax. Her right hand, perched on the podium under a small gold lamp, unconsciously fingerspells the words she speaks in her Russian-deaf accent. Mrs. Normatov rises, carrying Ada's one-year-old son, David, on her hip. She walks the baby, who is not crying, out of the room.

After the opening prayers, the cantor sings again. Sofia

seeks out Louann Katz, seated down in front, and smiles. Irina sidles up to stand just in front of the bema, squirming a little to get her sister's attention. In one hand she clutches a bag of Chanukah chocolates, coin shapes wrapped up in gold foil. With her free hand she signs, *"This is boring. All this standing up and sitting down and standing up and sit—"*

Sofia replies with tiny, discreet movements: a thumbnail touched to her lips, fingertips lightly slapping the back of one wrist. *"Just be patient — I'm warning you."* An indulgent smile twitches at her mouth and she looks away. Some of the congregants are smiling back at her in amusement.

The service continues smoothly after that, except for one slight gaffe, when Sofia announces in the middle of the cantor's song, "We continue silently," which elicits suppressed giggles from the congregation and a sideways glance from the cantor. Ada and Nelly take turns ducking into the aisle in their stocking feet to take photographs. Irina almost sits still. Mrs. Normatov, still holding little David like a shield, remains hovering around the doorway, but once she catches Sofia's eye and waves the baby's hand at her.

When the rabbi summons them, the entire Normatov family steps up to the bema. They participate in opening the ark and bringing out the Torah; they read from it — a privilege that they would have to pay for in their own synagogue — and all together they march around the temple with the Torah carried before them. Even Sofia's mother walks with them now, hiding her smile in the baby's neck while he waves a soggy piece of pumpernickel bagel in the air.

Then Sofia takes the pulpit. She thanks everyone who has helped her, apologizing first to her parents for choosing to sign her speech and have it interpreted. Then Ada makes a speech and presents Sofia with a gold bracelet from the family. "We have a very strange feeling, my family. It's hard to explain, but we are related to everyone here and would like to thank you." She pauses, breathing through a sob.

The skin under her eyes shines wetly. "That strange feeling? It's a happy feeling," she explains. Then someone hands a bunch of red and white carnations to Sofia. Around the congregation purses snap open and shut, releasing tissues. The man working the video camera blows his nose spiritedly.

Now the rabbi takes her place at the microphone. Sofia looks into Donna Berman's eyes, and at Liz, and back again.

"How do you do justice to someone so beautiful?" the rabbi says, and Sofia feels something rise and quake in her chest. "Where do you find the words to describe her adequately? Sofia, a flood of adjectives comes to my mind when I think of you. You are strong, even stubborn." Here Sofia grins. "You are determined, highly intelligent. There is a nobility about you, a grace, a dignity that is unique. Say 'Sofia' to anyone at the Lexington School for the Deaf and they will smile. People are warmed by you.

"Sofia, to look into your eyes is to see worlds. There isn't anything you can't do — God has blessed you with so many gifts. It is up to you to decide which world or worlds you will explore. Your mind and your heart have wings; let them carry you to a place of fulfillment and peace."

Behind Sofia, her family watches and listens. They are all squarely built, with jet hair and firm mouths, strong and ordinarily stolid. But now they sit in damp-cheeked wonder. What are these worlds that Sofia can decide to explore? As a deaf woman in Russia, she could have worked either in a factory or as a seamstress. The entire fall term before the family emigrated, she was kept out of school in order to take sewing lessons with a dressmaker in Samarkand.

"Sofia, you have been our teacher today. You have taught us about courage, about diligence, about the value of freedom and the preciousness of our faith. You wanted your bat mitzvah to take place during Chanukah because Chanukah celebrates religious freedom. Having come to this country in search of freedom, this was a most appropriate choice. But there is another reason why Chanukah is such a perfect time for your bat mitzvah, and that's because you, Sofia, have a special light within you, and like the shammes on the menorah, you go through your life inspiring others to let their own light shine forth. It is a special gift you bring to the world."

Sofia brings a hand to her face and artlessly sweeps it under each eye. The rabbi waits until she is again looking at the interpreter.

"And so as I watched the sun rise this morning, it made me think of you. Like a sunrise, you are brilliant — brilliant in terms of your intelligence and ability, brilliant in terms of the sacred light which shines through you."

Sofia has had only coffee this morning. Wings seem to beat in her stomach. Her eyes swim.

"Welcome home," says the rabbi.

When they hug, Sofia's hearing aid gets jogged and it whistles, a high pipping sound. It sounds like a signal, like a message in code. Something has been recovered.

7

Falling Within
the Banana

James sits behind the sealed door of the soundproof chamber. His connection with the rest of the world consists of one large plate of Plexiglas that appears semi-opaque, as though it might have been smeared with shortening. He takes a Mr. Potato Head from the shelf beside him and idly begins removing its plastic features.

"Your new girlfriend," comments his friend Paul Escobar, who is waiting in the antechamber for a pass back to class. A glass passageway connects Lexington's Hearing and Speech Center, at the northern edge of the block, with the rest of the building. The center serves the outside community as well as Lexington's students, who come here when they need a hearing aid repaired or their hearing tested. The state recommends that students be tested once every three years, but Lexington conducts hearing exams annually for students under the age of eight, every two years for older students.

James catches Paul's remark through the bleary window and snaps his head back in derision. Paul grins slowly, his eyes half lidded, freckles curving across his light brown face.

A small girl in a navy blue coat wanders into the room. James waves Mr. Potato Head's spindly arm at her and she smiles, all huge pink gums and little baby teeth, until she spots an otoscope on the desk across the room and eyes its shiny metal cone with grim recognition. She taps Paul's knee and points to it, her eyebrows lifted.

"Goes in ear, shines light," he explains in sign and voice. Paul's speech is extremely intelligible, although he tends to pronounce just the English glosses for his signs rather than complete sentences. He speaks a hybrid tongue common among many deaf people — not quite English, not quite ASL.

The girl, her suspicions confirmed, makes a great show of recoiling from the object. She shakes her head vehemently at Paul, a fat pigtail wagging from her crown.

Now the audiologist comes into the room brandishing James's file. The holidays have just ended, and appointments are running slightly behind schedule. As she sits at the desk opposite James's window, she flips the file open, reaches for a pen, and checks the dials on the pure tone audiometer, the device that will transmit a series of tones, at different frequencies and decibels, into the chamber where James waits.

The little girl ventures further into the room and stands beneath James's window. She waves, hoping for further contact with Mr. Potato Head, but James is looking beyond her at Paul, laughing at something he has signed.

The audiologist's back stiffens. A harried edge glimmers through her thin glaze of amiability. She turns to the little girl and points to the hall as she speaks broadly. "Okay, I think you need to find your mother now. Mother. Go out and find your mother." She watches the child's retreat, then addresses James through the window, her hands stiff-fingered and halting. *"I didn't understand you, sign it again."*

He squints, puzzled, then shakes his head. *"No, no, I'm talking to him,"* he says, indicating Paul, who sits against the opposite wall, legs luxuriously splayed and ending in pristine white high-tops the size of cinder blocks. His eyes like deeply hooded slots, his face muscular and sealed off, Paul inclines his modest goatee in acknowledgment.

"Oh." The audiologist shuts her eyes briefly; it is almost possible to perceive her count to ten. She swivels in her chair, rises, and stands above Paul. "Okay. Will you move to that other chair, please? Because you'll make him laugh." She doesn't sign now. Paul receives her message through residual hearing (which he happens to have a fair amount of) and lip reading. He regards her coolly, appearing to consider her request.

"I've known him seventeen years," he tells her, his speech clear, if faintly hollow-sounding. "Grew up together."

"Wow," she says brightly. "Seventeen years is a long time."

"Yeah, he's a boring man."

"He is not boring," contradicts the audiologist, confused by the apparent non sequitur. But Paul has shifted slightly, unhooked an arm from the back of the chair next to him; she can tell he is going to acquiesce, so already she has lost interest in the conversation. "Okay, just move to this chair," she reminds him once before returning to her desk to administer James's hearing test.

"Boring" carries a greater variety of connotations in ASL than in English. In sign language, especially in the hands of young adults, it can mean "dull" or "intensely annoying" or "detestable" or "worthless." Paul applies it to James as a generic term of disparagement; of course, what he means is that James is his homeboy and he loves him more than he would ever be caught dead expressing.

James and Paul actually met thirteen years ago, when they were both in first grade at St. Joseph's School for the Deaf in the Bronx. Lexington has the only high school for the deaf in New York's five boroughs, but the Bronx, Brooklyn, and Manhattan all have primary schools for deaf children, who usually attend in their home borough. When he was three and four, James went to a prekindergarten program in public school with hearing children. Then he became deaf.

Lexington's social history of James lists his etiology simply as "illness at the age of five." On his audiological chart, this has been construed to mean bacterial meningitis, the most common cause of deafness in people who lose their hearing as children. But James's mother remembers it differently; Delores Taylor says her son became deaf from the kiss of a dog. She tells the story easily, as though describing the plot of a television show. It was a Saturday evening in late summer when somebody brought a stray dog into the hallway of their public housing project, where the five Taylor children were playing. She tells how this dog, sweet and sloppy and wriggling, full of beans, licked James on the face, right on the mouth. Her voice is as rich and grainy as crystallized syrup.

"And all of a sudden, Sunday morning when I got him up to feed him, I noticed he didn't get out the bed. Now James was five and he never wet the bed, but this morning we kept calling him and waking him up and he didn't answer us, he didn't move, and he peed the bed. When I told him, 'Come on, Jamie, get out the bed,' he just looked at me, and he didn't say anything, he just looked."

When Mrs. Taylor lifted her son and set him on the floor, he collapsed. His skin felt hot and papery and she could swear he was losing weight before her eyes, just vanishing. So she picked him up and ran with him down fourteen flights of stairs, across three blocks from Webster to Washington to Third Avenue, to the Dr. Martin Luther King, Jr., Health Center. From there they were rushed to Montefiore Hospital.

"The doctors took the clothes off, stripped him buck naked, and he was just . . . limber. The first thing the doctor came and told me was 'Miz Taylor, what animal bothered him?' He knew. 'What you got to do,' he said, 'when you get home, you call the cops and you have them find that dog. And hope the dog didn't lick nobody else, because whatever that dog had, he gave it to your son.' "

Three months later James was well enough to return home, but the illness had left him weak. He was like a newborn baby, according to Mrs. Taylor — couldn't walk, couldn't talk, had to learn everything over from scratch. And he had lost his hearing.

James remembers it differently still; he believes he became deaf from a fall. He has a vision of going fast down a flight of stairs, his body pitching forward, out of control. Or else, he thinks, it was the result of high fever; there is that, too — an image of being hot and dry, his mind weaving and branching like curls of smoke inside his own body. These two memories, slippery and incomplete, have somehow become entwined with the cause of his deafness.

But for James, the history of how he became deaf is not important, just as the story of how he lost his most recent hearing aid (four months ago, at a Labor Day party in Prospect Park, when he took it off because the bands were playing so loudly it hurt, stuck it in a pocket, and never saw it again) is not important. Marginally more important is the future, both in terms of planning how he will fend for himself as a deaf man in a hearing world and in terms of how he will obtain a new hearing aid. Today, however, he would simply like to get a Lexington loaner aid.

Hearing aids can cost between $400 and $800 apiece. Lexington buys aids wholesale or secondhand for about $100 each; these are lent to children who are waiting for their aids to be repaired or replaced. When a student loses a loaner, Lexington sends a letter home asking the parents to pay $50 toward the cost of replacing it. During the past five years, James has lost three. Lexington has not received any money for them. His chances of getting a loaner today do not look promising. James is neither hopeful nor hopeless; with his standard equanimity, he will wait and see. He leaves this decision, like almost everything else, to fate or higher powers.

The audiologist is sending a series of tones into the chamber where James sits. Whenever he hears a tone, he raises his hand. For each frequency, the audiologist records the lowest decibel level at which James can detect sound. She maps these responses on a graph. The responses for each of the three middle frequencies are averaged; this number is called the pure tone average. Although a complete audiological exam includes various other data — impedance testing to check middle-ear functioning; spondee threshold and speech detection threshold testing to measure the volume at which the subject can identify actual words — the pure tone average is the figure most commonly used to describe the degree of hearing loss. Volume is measured in decibels, or dBs. James's pure tone averages are recorded as 118 dB in the left ear and 120+ dB in the right ear. This means that without a hearing aid, he can detect only sounds that are 118 decibels or greater, such as the sound of a lawn mower or a jet plane.

A child must be profoundly deaf to be admitted to Lexington. Most students meet this criterion by having a hearing impairment that measures 80 decibels (about the volume of a garbage disposal) or greater. A few students are able to attend by meeting other criteria; although their pure tone average is under 80 decibels, they may have such difficulty in using residual hearing for spoken communication that they meet what is known as a functional definition of deafness. The common bonds — behavior, communication style, identity — are more cultural than medical.

James, listening closely for the pure tones, raises a hand to signal that he has heard something. The audiologist makes an adjustment and glances back at him — this time no response. Another adjustment — still nothing. She makes a motion as though turning yet another knob and checks James again, raising her eyebrows and holding thumb and index finger narrowly apart: *Do you hear it just a little?* James hesitates, then nods helpfully: *Yeah, faintly.* But this time the audiologist has sent no tone. She is not trying to trick James, nor is he wittingly offering false responses. An affirmative response to silence is not uncommon; in his effort, James may really believe he has detected a sound. The audiologist is merely trying to gauge how often James might volunteer these responses so that she can assess his overall results more accurately.

Paul, who has managed to comply with the audiologist's request to move to a different chair and still remain within James's view, now raises his own hand in parody. James shakes his head and laughs. The audiologist is instantly suspicious. Stories about students mischievously faking responses on their hearing tests abound; many deaf adults reminisce about such capers fondly. She narrows her eyes accusingly at James, who laughs helplessly and points to Paul. *"It's not me, it's him."*

She whips around. "What are you still doing here?"

"I need a pass to go back to class." He flips the signs with the bored finesse of a blackjack dealer.

"What? Use your voice."

"Pass. I need a pass."

"Oh." She writes it out on a yellow notepad; he palms it and saunters out the door. Paul will not graduate with James this spring; not yet twenty-one, he has decided to spend another year at Lexington.

Although they both live in the dorm this year, James and Paul are not as close as they used to be. Once they were wild together; they were trouble from their days at St. Joseph's straight through their first few years at Lexington, when they spent mornings drinking orange juice together in the high school office. Then, about two years ago, as James started doing better in school, he began spending more time with college-bound students. Casually, incrementally, he changed course, as if by instinct sluicing off old patterns that dragged him down, gravitating toward those that would buoy him. But it must never look deliberate; only inadvertently will James allow himself to be saved.

"Baseball," the audiologist is saying. They are on the home stretch: the spondee test. Spondees consist of two equally stressed syllables. James is supposed to repeat the words back to her. "Ice cream, cupcake." Speaking through a microphone, she holds a piece of paper over her mouth so he can't read her lips through the window. "Cowboy. Airplane." She increases the decibel level. "Snowman. Hot dog. Hot dog. Try and guess. Hot dog. Rainbow. Try, please? Just try. Rainbow. There's no right, no wrong. Just guess. Baseball. Cowboy. Cowboy."

At last they are through. James, rubbing his ears, opens the door of the soundproof chamber and steps down in his Georgetown sweatshirt and new bullet-shot jeans. *"Boring!"* he signs. *"Hurts my ears."*

The audiologist fishes in a desk drawer for a small cardboard box, from which she plucks a baggie labeled with James's name. "Okay, your new molds came in." She holds it up, displaying the chocolate-brown ear molds inside. A colorless plastic tube sprouts from each mold; this piece plugs into the aid itself, a plastic crescent that hooks behind the ear. "I'll fit the molds now," she tells him, using about one sign per sentence. "But I'm only going to give you the loaner when you have an appointment at the hospital."

Because Medicaid will pay for his new aids, James must have a referral from a Medicaid facility, which Lexington is not. He will need to repeat today's exam at Roosevelt Hospital before the new aids can be ordered. The audiologist, astutely predicting that once James has the loaner aid he will be less likely to pursue getting his own, will hold his molds and the loaner aid ransom, in effect, for proof that he has made strides toward that end.

She fits his brown molds to beige Lexington loaners. James twists them into his ears and the audiologist tests them, first the right, then the left. "Can you hear me?" He shakes his head. She adjusts tone and volume on the curved receivers. "Can you hear me now?" Nothing. She fiddles again with the switches. "Can you hear this?"

The sounds of regular speech can be plotted on an audiogram as a series of points that extend across the entire range of frequencies and form a curve between about forty and sixty decibels. If you colored the area with a yellow crayon, it would look like a banana placed horizontally on the middle of the sheet of graph paper. The audiograms of most Lexington students dip way below the banana. The idea of hearing aids is to give these results a boost, to make the sound a person could hear at, say, ninety decibels (as loud as a food blender), audible at sixty decibels (normal conversation). Amplification doesn't automatically yield clear speech, but it can produce clues to help a person decipher speech better. Ideally, hearing aids will give James at least partial access to spoken communication, will get him within the banana.

When the audiologist is satisfied at last that both of the aids are working properly, she seals them back in the baggie, which she dangles between finger and thumb. "Look. Look. In my drawer. When you've made the appointment, let me know and you'll get them." She drops them in and slides the drawer shut.

James flashes her a gloriously injured smile, then tosses his head back and laughs. *"Put me in jail! I keep losing Lexington loaners, they're going to put me in jail!"*

But as the audiologist bends to write him a pass back to class, the clownish good nature rapidly wilts and he shakes his head. *"Borrrrring."*

Under the clock, James waits alone. He has been sitting in this chair in the Developmental and Disabled Center at Roosevelt Hospital for fifty minutes, and the odd empty hum of lunch hour makes him drowsy. Red and white balloons, gone puckery in the three weeks since New Year's, droop from the ceiling. All he can glimpse of the receptionist, bent over papers behind a high counter, is the top of her head: rigid, gold-trussed cornrows. Now and then he feels as though someone might come through the swinging doors from the hall, but each time the vibrations subside with no evidence of life.

James is missing lunch, career ed, and woodshop to be

here. Louis Taxin, the dorm supervisor, offered to accompany him to the hospital, but James declined and took the subway out from Jackson Heights alone. As it was, he had to rely on the school social worker and then the nurse to make and confirm the appointment for him over the telephone. So many details of his life seem automatically to become common knowledge, parceled out and shared among teachers and guidance counselors and social workers and health workers and dorm staff. He figured that taking the subway to Columbus Circle and walking over to Ninth Avenue was something he could manage on his own.

A narrow woman dressed in black comes at last to tell him that the doctor in ENT can see him. She signs a little bit, this woman who turns out to be a nurse, crooking her narrow, big-knuckled fingers into semblances of meaning. She leads him through the swinging doors, down cool, pale corridors, into a cramped room, where James immediately takes up residence in the examination chair. He sticks his feet, impressively shod in brown leather boots, onto the metal footrest and anchors his elbows on the armrests, as though returning to his throne.

The doctor enters with his head low and his arms behind his back, one hand grasping the opposite wrist. He is a short man whose pallor nearly matches his lab coat. He straightens before James, rounds his lips. "I'm just going to look in your ears."

James removes his black-and-gold Michigan baseball cap. The doctor performs an impedance test, using a slender metal device to exert pressure on the tympanic membrane of each ear. It takes less than one minute. He jots something on James's chart.

"That's the easiest test you'll ever have!" the nurse congratulates James, who smiles politely and bobs his head.

The doctor and the nurse bend their heads together. James sees the doctor skim a finger down his chart. They appear to be making a discovery, or a decision. He cannot see their faces, and they do not look directly at each other, but hearing people often talk that way. James, waiting patiently, starts to remove his leather Polo jacket, which he bought on the street with the $150 his father gave him for Christmas.

"Tell him not to get too comfortable," the doctor tells the nurse, making one last notation on James's chart. "We're not going to be long."

It isn't until James gets back to Lexington, where the audiologist deciphers the doctor's scrawl, that he discovers he has been recommended for a cochlear implant evaluation.

The cochlear implant, a source of bitter contention between the deaf community and the medical community, is a device that changes sound waves into electrical impulses that are then transmitted to the brain and interpreted as sound. Implantation requires surgery to fit the device, with its magnet and decoder and tiny electrode-studded coil, into the snail-shaped cochlea of the inner ear. After surgery, another magnet fits on the skin behind the ear, with a transmitter and a microphone. A wire connects these to a speech processor, which can be clipped to clothing or worn like a pocket calculator.

The implants were researched and developed over three decades in centers around the world before the Food and Drug Administration (FDA) approved marketing them for children between the ages of two and seventeen in 1990. The National Association of the Deaf (NAD) reacted to the FDA's approval by establishing a task force of its own, which came out staunchly against implants in children. Calling the FDA's approval ethically and scientifically unsound, the NAD takes the position that implanting deaf children robs them of their freedom of choice.

During implantation, the tiny hairs of the inner ear that normally activate the auditory nerve get torn and crushed. Once this has happened, the effects are irreversible; even if the device is removed, any residual hearing that might have existed will have been obliterated. So if the implant is unsuccessful — the definition of success including not only healthy recovery from surgery but also learning how to interpret speech from the implant's electrical signals by working with rehabilitation specialists, who may include audiologists, speech-language pathologists, psychologists, and educators — the child won't ever be able to benefit from a regular hearing aid.

Advocates say that children are the ideal recipients of implants because they can become accustomed to deciphering the electronic signals early on and thereby benefit fully throughout their school years and as adults. The Cochlear Corporation targets children with a coloring book depicting an anthropomorphized cochlear implant. Drawn with a firm but friendly smile, clenched fists, outstretched muscled arms, and the letter *S* emblazoned on its chest like Superman, it is shown soaring through space to remedy the bad, damaged ear. The deaf community finds such propaganda grotesque, the message insulting and reeking of prejudice. They perceive the medical profession, in its patronizing zeal to "cure" deafness, to be attacking their worth as deaf people and absconding with the community's most valued and cherished resource, its very future: deaf children.

For centuries the deaf community has struggled to forge relationships with hearing parents of deaf children, both to ease their adjustment to deafness and to offer proof that deaf people do grow up to lead successful, happy lives. But many hearing parents resist these efforts, fearful that they will lose their children to this other, foreign family. Now the Cochlear Corporation is courting these parents with the opposite argument: we can make your children more like you, less like *them*. If parents can't be faulted for feeling relief at these words, neither can deaf people be faulted for feeling hurt and angry.

In the whole imbroglio, however, a few criteria on which both sides agree do exist. Because of the irreversibility of the damage to the inner ear that occurs during implantation, people who already benefit from regular hearing aids, who make any significant use of their residual hearing at all, are not considered candidates for the surgery. This is undisputed common knowledge. James's medical chart clearly shows him to fall into this category. Yet the doctor at Roosevelt Hospital recommends him for a cochlear implant evaluation.

Cochlear implants are still fairly new to most physicians, many of whom are more likely to have read in medical journals that they are the new panacea for deafness than to have any empirical knowledge of them. Roosevelt Hospital doesn't even perform the surgery; currently, only two facilities in New York are equipped to do that, the Manhattan Eye and Ear Hospital and, only recently, the New York Eye and Ear Infirmary. The doctor's assessment displays exactly the hasty enthusiasm that the NAD has rallied and cautioned against. It is a product of the well-intentioned but narrow-minded zeal of the medical profession in this matter.

The doctor may have based his conclusion on James's fairly good speech and the fact that he could hear until age five; the conclusion makes some sense if the doctor has read or heard that people who become deaf after learning English are better able to reconstruct the sounds of speech from the electrical impulses transmitted by cochlear implants. But his determination is short-sighted, or he is only partly informed, because James's medical chart shows that he benefits significantly from hearing aids and that his deafness was caused by bacterial meningitis. Within a year and a half of the occurrence of this disease, the inner ear ossifies, or develops a bony growth that virtually blocks the insertion of electrodes. Unless a child undergoes cochlear implant surgery immediately after the disease, before ossification, the device will be of little use. In James's case, thirteen years have passed, making him a highly unlikely candidate even if he were to meet the other criteria.

Suppose for a moment that James did meet all the criteria — that is, that his cochlea were not ossified, that he received no benefit from hearing aids or tactile aids (which vibrate rather than amplify sound), that he had strong parental support and commitment (even the Cochlear Corporation stresses the importance of this for successful rehabilitation), and that during psychological and cognitive evaluations he demonstrated the potential to learn how to adjust and make efficient use of the device. Supposing all of that, the doctor's recommendation still may not be sound.

What has yet to be considered is the social component of deafness, the cultural status of someone who has received an implant. Even with implants, a deaf person will not be able to function like a hearing person. It is incorrect to assume that implants will enable a deaf person to "pass" as hearing or to be "cured" of deafness; it is incorrect to assume that the recipient will miraculously travel from a world of loneliness and isolation into the heady warmth of vibrant communication.

Deaf people, as long as they are not deprived of contact with the deaf community, already have access to warm and vibrant communication. Within their community, identification of oneself as a deaf person and pride in being deaf are both highly valued. Cochlear implant surgery is often perceived as denigrating to the group, as a step toward trying to "be more hearing." For some, it conveys the same messages that straightening one's hair or medically lightening one's skin might convey within the American black community.

When doctors recommend cochlear implants for deaf people whose social identity is already rooted in the deaf community, they must have the awareness and sensitivity to ask themselves, at what cost? Does the potential of enhanced speech detection outweigh the potential loss of identity with the group? Will the overall quality of life in fact be bettered or worsened? Unfortunately, during their professional training, most doctors (as well as most audiologists and speech therapists and many educators) learn to treat deafness purely as a pathology, and they cannot begin to formulate questions that treat it as a culture.

Finally, in the examination room, the nurse turns to James, splays all ten fingers, and flips her wrists once. *"Finished!"* she announces. James relinquishes his seat and follows her out the door. He exudes the tranquillity of one who long ago ceased trying to guide his life. He allows the nurse to escort him to the elevator, allows the elevator to convey him to the street.

Outside it is quite white and wet, with monotonous rain sliding onto the streets like condensation dripping down the inside of a kettle. The clouds have sunk low, impaling themselves on the tops of buildings. Smoke from shish-kabab carts, moist and pungent, blows in shredded veils across the sidewalk. James draws the hood of his sweatshirt up over his baseball cap and heads for the subway.

On Sixtieth Street, a tall white man in a sopping windbreaker approaches him. "Want to buy a token for a dollar?" he asks, squinting as rivulets of rainwater course down the creases of his face. Drops splash against his mouth; his speech is impossible to lip-read. James hesitates for a fraction of a second, evaluating the man's appearance. Is he dangerous? panhandling? preaching? asking for directions? Then, jaw tight, eyes polite and cold, James shakes his head tersely and keeps walking.

On the subway steps, transferring from the D train to the Queens-bound E at Seventh Avenue, he is approached again, this time by a young black man in a business suit. "The uptown number one?" the man asks pleasantly, his body tensed as though in a rush. Once more James hesitates, his posture slightly guarded, his eyes working to understand what the man is asking. "The uptown number one?" the man repeats. James continues to stare at him, his own lips open in the effort to parse the words. The man thinks he's being mocked; the corners of his mouth tuck down sourly and he hurries away in disgust. James continues to the lower platform.

When he gets back to Lexington, the audiologist will look at his medical form, laugh at the doctor's misguided recommendation, and realize that the scheduled hearing aid exam, through some misunderstanding on the part of the hospital staff, never took place. James's trip today has been a waste. *"You'll have to go back,"* the audiologist informs him while he stands in the doorway, his face a mask. *"Did you tell them what you were there for?"*

"They never asked me any questions!" he exclaims in a rare burst of frustration, then drops his hands to his sides and looks away, his stony gaze skimming over a row of green ear mold impressions set out to dry on a paper towel before being cast in plastic.

For most of the spring James will remain outside the banana. It will be March before he gets another appointment at Roosevelt. On that day he will walk to the bus stop in Jackson Heights, remember the green Medicaid card he left in the dorm, double back two blocks to get it, and arrive late at the hospital, with time for only half of the hearing test. It will be April before he can schedule a return appointment to complete it, June before the new aids finally arrive. In the interim, James will borrow another loaner and promptly lose it, this time on a dorm field trip to see the Knicks at Madison Square Garden.

He doesn't ask for the new loaner today, though. He leans against the office door, his strong back accidentally crushing a few Christmas cards taped there. The audiologist gently scolds him for the mix-up at Roosevelt. His face draws shut like a pouch.

This is a kind of betrayal. In return for letting the professionals make decisions about his life, he is supposed to be absolved from responsibility for it. When the audiologist presses — *"But James, why didn't you tell them what you were there for?"* — he can only repeat, *"No one asked me anything!"* His role is to defer to authority, not to question it.

It is as though ever since the first spill, that remembered hurtling down a flight of stairs, he cannot reach out to catch himself. He will not grab for the banister. He will not scrape his knuckles against the plaster walls. His stomach will not even clutch in fear; fear has no use when he cannot hope to halt the descent. All he can do is let himself fall.

8

Tower of Babel

Before the meeting of the communications committee even begins, the deaf staff members get up and move their table. Curving one tip of the giant U inward, they create a marked separation between themselves and the hearing committee members. Their re-angling is motivated by only the most practical considerations. They must clump together because there is just a single interpreter; from their newly jointed leg of the U, they are afforded the fullest possible view of the committee's proceedings.

Oscar created the communications committee last spring. He circulated a memo throughout the school that posed a series of provocative questions on both sides of the oral-manual debate:

> Are we delaying deaf students' access to participation in the deaf community by not providing an exclusive sign environment?
>
> Are we embarrassing students or otherwise hurting their self-esteem by requiring speech?

Are we being paternalistic or showing lack of respect when we expect certain behaviors (e.g., the use of hearing aids) from students?

What is the message to deaf students, especially to below-average achievers, when the majority of deaf visitors invited to speak to them are persons of high oral skills who often maintain an anti-oral posture?

What will be gained or lost by yielding to certain factions within the deaf community?

Are we sufficiently promoting choice?

To what extent, if any, does being "pro-speech" mean being "anti-deaf"?

Then he recruited thirteen staff members from different departments to form a committee that would address the problem at the heart of these questions. The committee met once before the summer holiday, at which time its members set themselves a goal for the coming year: to formulate a school-wide communication policy.

Inherent in this goal is the admission that Lexington's current communication policy is nonexistent; within different departments, and even different classrooms within the same department, it is the teachers' own abilities and ideological preferences that tend to dictate the communication practices used in instruction. Political camps exist but are not discussed formally. No clear definition of "sign language" exists for staff or students; everything along a vast continuum from pure ASL to a sort of clunky creole of signs combined with English gets used indiscriminately. The students receive a mishmash of languages and contradictory messages about how they are expected to communicate. Students come to the school with different communication systems, so one classroom might contain oral and signing students who are unable to understand one another. In short, it's a mess, at least as far as policymakers are concerned.

Lexington bears no special shame for finding itself in this nebulous position. For nearly a hundred years it thrived, secure in its identity as a purely oral school. Only recently have two external factors arisen to challenge the appropriateness of this old system, and like schools for the deaf across the country, Lexington is changing to accommodate them.

The first factor relates to the politics of ASL, which was only "discovered" during the late 1960s, when hearing researchers determined that it was not a primitive system of coded gestures, as had hitherto been supposed, but a valid language with its own grammar and syntax, capable of expressing abstract thought as well as the most esoteric detail. These findings filtered out into an educational community that for a hundred years had viewed signing as unbecoming, imbecilic, virtually bestial. Schools had commonly forbidden the use of signs, and not only in the classroom — students were not allowed to sign among themselves on the playground; they weren't even supposed to sign with deaf houseparents in the dormitories at night. At some schools, children caught disobeying these rules sometimes had their hands struck with a ruler, or even bound together in an effort to force them to use their voices.

In the late 1960s, whenever Lexington's superintendent, Dr. Leo Connor, spotted groups of students signing on the sidewalk in front of the building after school, he used to dispatch Oscar, the brand-new director of child care, to send them on their way, as if they were engaging in an unseemly act. Oscar, who had grown up bilingual, who had ASL for a mother tongue, whose own parents communicated in ASL, never balked. Twenty-six years of living in a deaf household were no match for the voice of hearing authorities, the declamations of his professors at Teachers College, or the doctrines of Lexington School, that famous bastion of oralism. If they said signing reduced people to the level of animals, then it did. In his youthful disposition to please, Oscar accepted this credo so unflinchingly that when his parents came to visit our family at Lexington, he would ask them not to sign until they had crossed the threshold of our apartment and shut the door behind them. Sam and Fannie honored his request, traveling through the halls of the school with their hands at their sides, incommunicado.

If Oscar, with a college education, a family, a job, and a lifetime of exposure to deaf adults who signed, could internalize this negative view of sign language so deeply, then deaf children of hearing families were even more susceptible. Even as they learned sign language (for most did, of course — no number of rules, no system of enforcement could prevent that), they learned to devalue it. If they loved the language, if they found a kind of freedom in it, it was a shameful love, and the freedom was tainted with guilt. Many students from oral schools learned to look down on manualists in childhood, only to stumble upon the signing deaf community and find it exciting, appealing, in adulthood. It is not unusual for oralists who come late to ASL to experience frustration over not signing well enough to have immediate access to the community, as well as resentment over having been excluded from that community their whole lives. The passage from a strictly oral environment to a world of choices can be overwhelming.

Lexington has come to a crossroads no less overwhelming. When linguists validated ASL as an authentic language twenty-five years ago, many schools for the deaf made efforts to incorporate signing into their curricula. But instead of using pure ASL, they borrowed ASL signs and tried to fit them into English grammar and syntax, inventing clumsy hybrids, such as Manually Coded English (MCE), Signed Exact English (SEE), and Pidgin Signed English (PSE), that had little inner logic or integrity. (The latest studies suggest that there is not even any such thing as PSE. Pidgin is a simplified form of speech, usually a blend of two or more languages, with its own specific grammar and syntax. But there is no single PSE; the fact is that deaf people use a variety of "contact languages" that fall all along the continuum between ASL and English.) When Lexington began introducing variations of these sign systems in many classrooms two decades ago, it was more through happenstance than decree.

The second factor influencing Lexington to address its communication policy relates to a shift in its student population. As an oral school, Lexington once bore the reputation of possessing a sort of country club air. Oralism has long been linked with high socioeconomic status, since members of the privileged classes tend to have more resources to channel into their children's education and more choices about what form that education will take. Wanting their deaf children to have access to the same privileged circles they enjoy and perceiving the deaf community to be a step down, they have tended to favor oralism as the method that will best keep their children out of contact with the deaf community and on a par with hearing people.

Oralism's very inception was, in fact, a byproduct of socioeconomic motives. The systematic education of deaf people began in Spain in the mid-1500s, when word spread that Pedro Ponce de León, a Benedictine monk in San Salvador, had taught a young deaf man to talk. At that time the church barred deaf people from Holy Communion because they could not confess aloud; moreover, they were prohibited from inheriting their family's wealth. Spain had a small, wealthy nobility that was anxious to preserve its lines of succession; however, because of inbreeding, deafness was not uncommon among these families. When they heard of the work of Ponce de León, they sent their deaf heirs to him to learn to talk and thereby become eligible to inherit.

Lexington's existence does not stem from such blatantly economic motives; still, it is linked to social privilege. Recognizing this part of the early history of oralism is important now, as the old systems are being questioned or dismantled or rearranged, in understanding the deep-seated attitudes on both sides of the debate. In the basest stereotype, speaking has been equated with the higher classes and higher intellect, signing with the lower. Even though many people, deaf and hearing, understand intellectually that this stereotype is inaccurate, they still carry its emotional residue.

Lexington was founded by Hannah and Isaac Rosenfeld, an educated, affluent, well-traveled German Jewish couple whose daughter, Carrie, became deaf in infancy from a bout of scarlet fever. The Rosenfelds did not want their daughter to be educated manually — the only method that had ever been available in this country. They traveled to Germany, where they were put in contact with Bernard Englesmann, a teacher of the famous German method called articulation, which taught deaf children to speak and lip-read. The Rosenfelds hired Mr. Englesmann to begin a school in New York City where Carrie would be a student. In 1864 the first class, with six deaf children, began its studies in the Rosenfelds' home at 367 Broadway, below Canal Street. No one had any inkling that this gathering, which began the first oral school for the deaf in the United States, was planting the seed of an enormous controversy that would rage well into the next century.

Within three years, the Rosenfelds formally incorporated their little school as the Institution for the Improved Instruction of Deaf-Mutes and enlisted a group of community leaders to form a board of trustees. Word of the school's success spread and enrollment multiplied, necessitating moves to ever-larger spaces, until the Lexington Avenue building was constructed in 1880. In 1868, the New York City Board of Education donated two large chalkboards and three dozen desks and chairs to the school, marking the beginning of public aid. Two years later, the school applied for and was granted full state support for pupils' tuition and board. Private funds continued to fund teacher training, research, building additions, field trips, summer camps, and the like. A state–private school cooperative arrangement had evolved.

Meanwhile, Lexington was holding public exhibitions that

showcased its top students' ability to lip-read and respond orally to questions posed by members of an astounded audience. The popularity of oralism was catching on all over the world. In 1880, 164 delegates met at an international congress of teachers of the deaf in Milan, where, "considering the incontestable superiority of speech over signs in restoring the deaf-mute to society," they passed a declaration that "the oral method ought to be preferred to that of signs in the education of the deaf and dumb." By the end of the nineteenth century, virtually all schools for the deaf in the United States had switched to pure oralism. Sign language was occasionally permitted but never taught, and only among older students who were considered "oral failures."

The very concept of "oral failures" is a giveaway to the imperfection of the oral method, or at least to its inappropriateness for some deaf students. It would be equally naive to suggest that oralism is entirely without merit, or that its proponents are strictly motivated by chauvinist hearing ideals. The inherent value of ASL notwithstanding, English is the dominant language in this country; the ability to get along in English is helpful for anyone who lives here. Deaf people who are good lip readers, are literate in English, and have intelligible speech will almost certainly have an easier time with everything from getting a job to giving a cab driver directions to reading a newspaper to buying a carton of milk.

In fact, oral skills, originally taught to deaf children of the nobility and the upper class, are equally if not more crucial for children from less privileged backgrounds, who may not be able to rely on their family's financial support or social connections, who may not get prestigious jobs where an interpreter is provided, but who must fend for themselves in the hearing world. Despite Lexington's former country club reputation, it has educated children from all social strata ever since state funding began in 1870. Being in New York, it has always enrolled a large proportion of immigrants; today that proportion is growing. The city's urban problems have always found their way into the school also; as homelessness, drug use, violence, and unemployment worsen in the city, so they are reflected in the student body.

The popularity of mainstreaming has also contributed to the shift in Lexington's student population. Parents who have a strong desire to see their deaf children fit into the hearing world and who might once have sent their children to Lexington are now choosing to mainstream them in public schools. Traditionally, children who have strong parental involvement are the ones who succeed best at oralism. With this pool depleted, Lexington faces the more complex challenge of teaching children whose parents may not have jobs or green cards, let alone fluency in English. The social reality is that many of these children need a program of instruction that includes sign language.

Even if the political disputes about ASL were not hammering at the old system, Lexington could not remain a pure oral school — not if it wants to meet the needs of the city's deaf children. Not if it wants to continue to exist.

Once the conference tables have been dragged into position, the interpreter has taken his seat, and the committee members have uncapped their pens and turned to fresh sheets of their legal pads, Oscar welcomes the members, speaking and signing simultaneously. When he recruited them, he asked for both a commitment to the importance of audition and English for all students and an open mind concerning communication methodology. The two may seem mutually exclusive — they certainly don't leave room for those champions of ASL who reject any use of English or residual hearing. But given Lexington's history and reputation, the idea of having any discussion, of having any ambivalence about oralism, represents a significant divergence from course.

The discussion also represents a fair amount of courage, not just because change in itself can be threatening, but because in this particular case no clear path lies ahead. So many different voices must be heard: those of educators, parents, students, policymakers, and members of the deaf community. Some say it's criminal to force deaf children to use their voices and hearing aids, to instruct them in anything but ASL, their natural language, their birthright. Others say it's criminal to do anything but teach them English and speech from infancy, to help them compensate for their hearing loss, to allow them to communicate with their parents. Still others say the only solution is to provide a choice, but that becomes convoluted with the question of who chooses — parents, children, teachers? The din of voices promises to be confounding, and there are no guarantees; the committee's final report may recommend actions that Lexington will find itself unable to carry out.

The teachers on the committee have turned their classes over to substitutes today; the administrators have shelved their regular responsibilities. Coffee sits cooling in stiff white cups. A beehive stack of Danish sent up from the cafeteria glistens, untouched, on the back table. Under the quiet hum of fluorescent bulbs, the room brims with a certain heightened energy — excitement about attempting something new, trepidation about being able to meet the objective.

A trio of guest speakers has been invited to address the matter. Each is deaf. Each is a professional who holds a doctoral degree. And each approaches the subject from a startlingly different point of view.

Richard Stoker, the director of the Central Institute for the Deaf (CID), an oral school in St. Louis, speaks for himself, explaining that he never found the time to learn sign language. A product of mainstreaming, he says he aligns himself socially and culturally with the hearing world. Signing is absolutely proscribed at CID. When asked whether CID students ever rebel against the restrictions, Dr. Stoker retorts, "Sure, we have a handful of hotheads who have nothing but bad things to say about being educated at an oral school, and I assign the same value to them as I do to black supremacists."

At these words the committee members seem to flinch collectively. Still, it is impossible to ignore CID's record: as a private school, it has the right to admit only students who are able to succeed orally, and their test scores compare remarkably well with those of hearing students. If CID were state-funded, like Lexington, and required to accept students who need a manual program, Dr. Stoker declares he would sequester them so that the students who were succeeding orally wouldn't be tempted by any exposure to sign language. When he reveals that all of CID's graduating students read within one year of grade level, the Lexington staff looks momentarily sick with envy.

Then there is Sam Supalla, a linguist from the University of Arizona, whose view is 180 degrees from Dr. Stoker's. One of the 10 percent of deaf people who are born to deaf parents, he signs in his native ASL. Following the deaf cultural tradition, he begins his talk by outlining his school and family background, relating a few anecdotes that locate him within the culture. He explains that while he was growing up on an isolated Oregon farm amid a large deaf family, he naturally believed that deafness was the norm, and until he was three years old he thought that the word "hearing" referred to a person who couldn't sign.

After establishing his cultural identity, Dr. Supalla goes on to explain language acquisition theory. He says that because deaf children rely on vision rather than audition, they cannot acquire English naturally but must learn it as a second language. He cautions against using MCE, SEE, and PSE, the made-up sign systems that blend components of English and ASL. *"The languages are not compatible,"* he warns. *"When you try to mix them, something in the system goes haywire."* Auditory and speech training he does not advocate at all, saying that they injure a deaf child's self-esteem by emphasizing weaknesses rather than strengths. Children's first language ought to be ASL, Dr. Supalla asserts, with no compromises and no exceptions; to him, this is no less than an issue of human rights.

These two views alone are enough to send the committee members reeling. Practical considerations aside — How could they sequester the manual kids from the oral ones without imposing a damaging stigma? How could ASL be the students' first language when many of the teachers, let alone the parents, can barely sign? — the differences between the two seem impossible to reconcile. Yet both speakers point convincingly to the success of their respective views. Already the committee would seem to be at an impasse.

But it is Irene Leigh, the assistant director of the Lexington Center for Mental Health Services, who, with fine understanding, paints the most devastating picture. She doesn't use an interpreter but simultaneously speaks in a clear, throaty voice and signs in English word order. Like Dr. Supalla, she begins with personal information: her early training with hearing aids and speech therapy, her lack of deaf adult role models, and her experience of being mainstreamed with other deaf students in Chicago's public school system, where she maintained ties with two distinct groups of friends, one deaf and one hearing. More than either of the other two speakers, Dr. Leigh is personally familiar with both sides of the issue, being attuned to dichotomous cultures within herself.

She advocates neither oralism nor ASL, posing instead two rhetorical questions: *"Can you imagine all of your students succeeding orally? At the same time, can you imagine depriving students of the opportunity to learn speech?"*

Dr. Leigh offers no middle ground between Dr. Stoker and Dr. Supalla but a third perspective. As a psychologist who counsels hearing parents, she has heard fears that the deaf community makes "moonies" of deaf children, turning them into militants for deaf pride. As a member of the deaf community, she has heard charges that the hearing establishment makes zombies of deaf children, turning them into lonely, culturally bereft oralists. With the moonie-zombie paradigm, Dr. Leigh highlights the core of the issue, the truth beneath the cool, dry layers of pedagogy and linguistics and reading scores: "mode of communication" has become a shibboleth. No one will reach a solution to the communication debate without understanding and addressing the emotional stakes in the tug of war over deaf children.

"Let's not throw the hearing aids out with the bathwater." This is one of Oscar's fond sayings, which he delivers innocuously enough. Only it is not innocuous; in the present political climate these are incendiary words, depending on who utters them, and in what context, and to whom.

Oscar can afford to say them, partly because Lexington is an old oral school and nobody expects it to fall into quick concordance with the political trend toward ASL, and partly because he has been a sort of affiliate member of New York's deaf community since he was born. He is apportioned a little more trust and respect by deaf people than if he were a *know-nothing hearie* fresh on the scene. But mostly he can afford to say these words because he is relatively secure in his position as superintendent; at least so far, the deaf community has not tried to oust incumbents.

Ever since the Gallaudet University uprising in 1988, hearing professionals have been watching what they say. That week-long protest galvanized deaf people across the United States, enchanted the international news media, and ended victoriously with the instatement of Gallaudet's first deaf college president and first deaf president of the board. The Deaf President Now (DPN) movement was spontaneous, masterminded by no political strategists, planned in advance by no protest committee. Gallaudet was in the midst of hiring a new college president, and the announcement that the search committee had selected a hearing candidate should have been unremarkable, in light of the fact that Gallaudet had had hearing presidents since its inception in 1864. But it was as though the civil rights movement of the 1960s had finally seeped past the language barrier and achieved critical mass within the deaf community. The students erupted in rebellion. They marched to Capitol Hill. They took over their campus, pushing buses in front of the main entrance gates. At two or three or four each morning, student leaders set off the fire alarms, triggering strobe lights in each dorm room to rouse the residents; then they all trudged through the dark to the gymnasium to plan operations for the next day.

The story caught on rapidly with the news media; reporters, photographers, and television cameras descended on campus. Interpreters from all over gave up commitments and flocked to Gallaudet, donating their services to help the media conduct interviews. Deaf leaders flew in to lend their support. Politicians and celebrities joined in, endorsing the students' efforts and attracting more coverage. By the end of the week, the hearing president-elect stepped down, I. King Jordan became the university's first deaf president, and Gallaudet was internationally famous.

Schools for the deaf across the nation followed the situation avidly. Lexington had reason for particular interest. The president of Gallaudet's student government, who appeared on *Nightline* with Ted Koppel as a key leader of DPN, was Greg Hlibok, a Lexington alumnus. And the newly elected president of Gallaudet's board of trustees, Phil Bravin, was another Lexington alumnus, a member of the Lexington Center board, and a parent of two current Lexington students as well as a friend and colleague of Oscar's. In spite of the number of miles separating Jackson Heights from Washington, D.C., the unfolding events seemed not so very far away.

Many Lexington students and staff members openly cheered the Gallaudet victory. Others registered the outcome with veiled skepticism and concern. It was not difficult to imagine where DPN could lead. For years, the predominance of oralism had worked as an oppressive measure, effectively preventing deaf people from becoming teachers and entering the field of education, leaving the fate of deaf children exclusively in hearing hands, robbing deaf adults of jobs, denying them any input in decisions about how to educate deaf children. DPN taught deaf people that they didn't have to accept this anymore. It signaled an end to hearing people's unchallenged authority.

The deaf cause had become a media favorite, and hearing politicians wanted to capitalize on this popularity. With the backing of these two allies, deaf people were able to shift the centuries-long imbalance of power between the hearing and themselves. In the years since DPN, local members of the deaf community have followed the example of the Gallaudet students, putting pressure on school hiring committees and policymakers with rallies and boycotts. This has done much to raise consciousness among the public, the media, and politicians as well as among school officials who may previously have disregarded the rights, or even the existence, of the deaf community.

But it has also bred a certain amount of indiscriminate kowtowing to the wishes of the deaf militants. In some instances, an eagerness to demonstrate support for the civil rights of deaf people has overtaken the commitment to providing educational choices to deaf children and their parents. Some people say that in order to make up for all those years during which signing was prohibited and speech enforced, speech should not even be an option any more. Oralism, viewed as the tool of the oppressor, is regarded so negatively as to be discarded altogether, even if this means alienating hearing parents and driving a wedge between them and their deaf children, and even if it means denying children possible social and employment opportunities later in life.

Most hearing people within the field fall into one of two camps: those who believe that the changes herald a victory for deaf people and who support the militants with all their hearts, and those who do not. Among those who do not, most are savvy enough to tread lightly, speak vaguely, and take care not to alienate deaf leaders. The frontier between deaf and hearing worlds has become a political minefield laced with danger.

Tramping through this field with something like luck or grace comes Oscar. Rather than aligning himself with one camp or the other, he weaves down the middle in a stubborn cakewalk, questioning the certainties of both. Not that he stands pristinely aside while others clash ideological swords and jockey for power; he is in the struggle as much as anyone. But his agenda remains distinct.

An example of the kind of situation that Oscar fears will arise from too-hasty efforts to appease the deaf militants is the fiasco that occurred in 1991 at the elementary and high schools housed on Gallaudet's campus. The Kendall Demonstration School and the Model Secondary School for the Deaf (MSSD) adopted a new policy when school opened that fall: all communication would be conducted in ASL. This was enforced with such ludicrous rigor that a hearing teacher having a conference with hearing, nonsigning parents was required to use ASL and summon an interpreter to voice an English translation for the parents. By early winter, the school had received so many complaints that it suspended the rule.

Soon after that, word was out that Gallaudet had issued an expanded definition of ASL; now it was to include any variation of sign language, from nonvoiced pure ASL to signs in English word order combined with speech. Linguists groaned. Kendall and MSSD were conveniently able to reinstate the ASL-only rule without a lot of nonsensical maneuvering. The experts have continued to revise and hand down definitions, and deaf people have continued to get along in the same variety of contact languages they have always used.

While Gallaudet's ASL-only policy proved muddled and ultimately embarrassing, another, subtler scenario concerns Oscar even more. Last year, one of Lexington's high school seniors decided that he wanted to drop speech from his program. Three half-hour speech lessons a week are commonly scheduled for all high school students. The senior in question was Seth Bravin, the youngest son of Phil Bravin. An outstanding student and a class leader, bound for Gallaudet the following fall, Seth felt that he was old enough to make this decision for himself.

Oscar met with him and told Seth that he respected his wish and his right to drop speech, and that he agreed that this decision was unlikely to hamper Seth's future success or happiness. Then he asked him to consider his role as a class leader, someone whom other students admired and tried to emulate. He asked him to consider the role of speech for students who were not college-bound, who might be seeking blue-collar jobs with hearing employers and coworkers unaccustomed to deafness. He told Seth that he was worried that dropping speech could become faddish, cool, that students who might not have Seth's ability to choose in their best interests would want to drop it too.

There was a time when Lexington measured its students' success by their degree of assimilation into the hearing world. Carrie Rosenfeld, the first Lexington student, established the model for subsequent graduates when she wrote at age seventy, "Despite my handicap, I had the good fortune of being with normal hearing people. Most of my good friends were amongst them." Today, these words sound so sad. Who taught her to aspire to friendships with "normal hearing people"? Was she also taught to shun friendships with deaf people? She writes of being "blessed with a devoted hearing husband," of having children and grandchildren who were all hearing, or, as she puts it, "normal." How did she feel, as the one "abnormal" person in the family? If she was "blessed" with a hearing husband, was he "afflicted" with a deaf wife?

Today, Carrie is no longer the model. Lexington advocates oralism not for the sake of assimilation but for the sake of choice and increased opportunity. This was clear at the meeting between Oscar and Seth Bravin, and each respected the other's position. Nevertheless, Seth made Lexington history by going ahead and dropping speech. But he made it quietly, conceding to Oscar's wish for him to avoid setting a trend. No other students have since made the request. The whole event seems evidence, however, of a change in climate that could seep through Lexington's walls; the school would do well to prepare for that possibility.

Since mainstreaming has caught on as the oralists' method of choice, and since speech and audition are increasingly out of favor with the deaf community, Lexington has found itself edged out onto an increasingly narrow limb. The communications committee is now trying to define the exact terms of that limb. Its efforts are made much harder by the fact that Lexington is not seeking to ingratiate itself with those on either side of the debate, who, like Dr. Stoker and Dr. Supalla, propose rather straightforward communication policies.

Lexington will adopt neither of the extreme approaches. It seeks a third alternative, one that doesn't exist — one that will answer not to hearing chauvinists or deaf militants but to the needs of the students and their parents. Working within the complex portrait painted by Dr. Leigh, risking the stubborn cakewalk that Oscar has navigated between opposing camps, the committee will try to create one.

9

Salvaging

The first thing my grandmother lost was her name — Bessie. When she was five and became so ill, her family took the name away in order to fool the evil spirits. It worked; the spirits rode off in the empty shell of Bessie and left the real human girl to live. But they stole her hearing, and left in its place a fat white scar where the infection had been. The scar roped from behind one ear to the base of her throat. The spirits also snatched her hair; she had to wear a bonnet until it grew back. By that time she was called Fannie.

Fannie was born on the Lower East Side of Manhattan in 1914, the youngest of seven children. Five of her siblings — Hymie, Ida, Yetta, Izzy, and Loretta — were born in Bukovina, a region in Eastern Europe that spread across the north of Romania into the Ukraine, not far from Kiev, where my grandfather was born. In 1912 Benzion and Pearl Hager brought their family to the land of opportunity. Here in America their last two children, Arthur and Fannie, were born. All of them were hearing except Fannie, after her illness, and Izzy, six years her senior, who was born deaf.

Their father was a fur trader and a philanderer, both of which occupations took him on frequent voyages overseas. When he was home, Fannie remembers, he was stingy and chain-smoking. Even on the Sabbath, Benzion would go to the toilet and roll his own; presently smoke would curl from the crack beneath the door. He was a distant man, with one black boot firmly planted in Europe; his beard, as thick as the forest, smelling of sulfur and blue ash.

In photographs, Fannie's mother, Pearl Orringer Hager, is handsome and sad, with wide nostrils and wide dark eyes, long brows riding above them like wings. She spent much of the time in a sanatorium with a mysterious ailment. On rare visits home, she would kneel on the kitchen floor and rock herself, bashing her head against the wall. There were no words, no explanations for Fannie, just a sad mother coming through the door and going out again.

One day, when she was eleven, Fannie came home to find the family gathered around her mother. Pearl lay in a wooden box in the center of the living room. Fannie followed the others as they shuffled slowly around the box. She wasn't sure, but she felt her mother must be resting. Later she was told that her mother had died. The other children overheard whispers that Pearl had plunged out of an eighth-story window at the sanatorium, but the only story ever to reach Fannie was that her mother had expired of a nervous breakdown.

Benzion remarried a year after Pearl's death, and twice more after that. He divorced two wives and buried two before dying himself at the age of eighty-nine. Fannie did not grow up with her father, who moved to the Williamsburg section of Brooklyn. She attended P.S. 47, the school for the deaf in Manhattan, and at night slept on cots at her sisters' apartments in the Bronx, shuttling between Yetta's, where she stayed in the same room as her baby nephew, and Ida's, where she slept in the foyer.

In this way, by the time she was twelve years old, Fannie had lost her name, her hearing, her mother, and her father.

Shortly after her husband's death, my grandmother moved to Hallendale, Florida. For the past ten years she has lived alone in one of a row of biscuit-colored buildings that she calls, with her slightly skewed pronunciation, "condimims." Here, in air that is hot and dewy all year round, she practices the art of preservation. Nearly all of her groceries go immediately into the refrigerator, even a jar of individually wrapped hard candies, even a box of salt. The ironing board stays permanently erected; she is continually pressing the moisture from garments, hanging them crisply in closets like strips of cured meat. Photographs deck the walls and tabletops, lie under stiff blankets of glass — Sam and the boys, Max and Oscar, and the boys' wives and their children, and, recently, a great-granddaughter. Her family: the happy years.

The pictures of her own childhood are relatively few, her memories of that time correspondingly scant. For all the care she lavishes on storing items and details — the assortment of unused key rings hung in neat rows on the kitchen pegboard; the blood pressure and diet charts she picks up at the shopping center and posts on the freezer door; the drawer full of playing cards that come free with air travel, all still in their cellophane jackets — they are exclusively the items and details of her present life. Old jewelry, clothes, and photographs — these she has systematically discarded, foisting them on children and grandchildren, shucking their confusing weight. She is no caretaker of the past; it was never hers to cherish.

Not even her memory belongs to her. The facts of her childhood jog and shift, are worn down like bits of sea glass, the real memories supplanted by stories she has been told, for a deaf girl's reality is easily manipulated by the parcelers of information. Sitting at the wooden table in my parents' kitchen, she once gave me three different accounts of how she became deaf in the space of five minutes: she was born that way; she fell off an ironing board when she was one; she developed an infection at age five.

My father, bent over the cutting board mixing up tuna fish for lunch, broke in. "No, Ma!" he cried, setting the fork down so he could sign. *"That's not right, you weren't born deaf!"*

My grandmother looked at him, her mouth working the way it does when she's reading someone's lips. She is strong and blocky, with short light hair and a face cross-hatched by fine pale lines. She sat with her hands clasped. One thumb-nail began grinding against the fleshy pad of the opposite thumb.

"I fell," she said. "One year old. My mother had the iron-ing and she dropped me off the board." My grandmother's speech is easy to understand. The intonation is mostly flat, the end consonants are often missing, and her teeth and tongue and lips often clash unexpectedly, producing extra-neous sounds, so that her words may snap and sigh like a plastic bag caught in a breeze. But still, her speech is intelli-gible, and it is the mode of communication she uses most frequently with hearing people, even her sons.

My father signed back in rapid response. *"You think you became deaf from falling off an ironing board?"* As usual, he signed and spoke simultaneously. He sounded gruff because he was confused. His eyes appeared very gray, deep in their sockets under the dark ledge of his eyebrows.

"She dropped me. Off the board, the board for ironing. They told me I fell off. I don't know, I was a baby." Her teeth worried the inside of her lower lip; her nail ground ridges in her thumb. Suddenly she remembered something else: "My mother dropped me on the kitchen floor. When I was born. I didn't know that. Ida said. You understand what I mean, Ocky? She dropped me on the floor." My grandmother made the sign for *giving birth.*

"*You mean she had you at home, you weren't born in a hospital? No, I didn't know that. You never told me. And then when you were one, you fell off an ironing board and became deaf? . . . No, Ma! You can't have been deaf when you were one. You used the phone. You told me you remember using the telephone. You had to have been older before you became deaf. It was from infection, you told me.*"

She peered at him, again working the information with her knotty lips, the corners of her eyes twisted up in little winces. Then: the tiniest of shrugs, a nod. "You're right. That's right, Ocky. I don't know, you're right." She shook her head, dispersing the fragments of memory, and turned to look out the window.

After a moment, my father picked up the bread knife and began slicing rolls. I could feel him thinking in the quiet of the kitchen. "I don't know," he said to me after a minute. "That's strange, what she said." With his back to us, he could speak without my grandmother knowing.

I looked at her. She was watching a couple of sparrows dine in the birdfeeder mounted outside the windowsill. A bluejay swooped in, matter-of-factly bossing the little mottled birds off their perch.

"Mmm-hmm," I answered, eyeing my grandmother, be-ing careful to move neither my mouth nor my chest and risk gaining her attention. I was complicit and expert in this old habit of talking around her. How must that be — not know-ing the facts of your own life story, subsisting on only the morsels dished out directly to you, using your memories, relegated to dubious fictions, like thin gruel to fill in the gaps? My father went on fixing our lunch while I watched my grandmother watch the jay crack open his seeds.

She had been alive for nearly a quarter of a century before the happy part of her life began. This she defines as the time she stopped living with hearing relatives and moved into her own home. Earlier memories are sparse and sour.

From the ages of six to fifteen, Fannie was a student at P.S. 47. Like most schools for the deaf at that time, it was an oral environment; signing was forbidden. On her first day, Ida dragged her into the classroom, bald and sobbing, and deposited her there without any explanation of where she was or what was happening. Of the following nine years Fannie remembers almost nothing, except for one day, shortly after her mother's death, when she could not find her way to school. The big gray building on Twenty-third Street, the block, the subway stop, her very sense of place — all had abandoned her. In the most profound sense, she was lost. Shifting between the thin cots where she laid her head at Ida's and Yetta's, with Benzion so often at sea and Pearl vanished absolutely, Fannie was untethered, adrift.

On that day when she was eleven years old, this was manifested in a most literal fashion: her body lost the ability to navigate the same path it had taken every morning for five years. Instead, seemingly of their own volition, her feet led her to her father's furrier business in the garment district. She showed up dazed and murmured that she was lost. Someone fetched Benzion (he was not on one of his voyages); when he saw his truant daughter, he responded with pragmatic efficiency by delivering her straight to P.S. 47. A wordless question had been asked and answered; thereafter Fannie went to school on her own, never again wavering from her prescribed path.

Four years later, with a fat white gardenia pinned to her blouse, Fannie graduated with her class. She had done poorly in history and geography, well in composition and math. She had also distinguished herself in speech, a subject particularly prized in a school where, if a student was caught signing, a flag colored red for shame was flown outside the classroom door. Armed with these skills and a crisply scrolled diploma, Fannie landed her first job: cutting fabric swatches and pasting them in display books used in showrooms. The job had the earmarks of a position that a hearing person would think fitting for a deaf employee: it was solitary and dull. Fannie earned ten dollars a week, which she promptly handed over to Benzion.

The following summer she met her future husband while staying with her sisters in a rented seaside bungalow in Brooklyn. Her older brother Izzy knew Samuel Cohen from the Coney Island deaf club and had once shown him a snapshot of his youngest sister in a bathing suit. *"Just watch,"* Sam had told his friends when he saw this image of Fannie Hager. *"I'm going to get her!"* During the summer of 1930, amid the clusters of alumni from the various schools for the deaf who gathered at Ocean Parkway in their own animated social network, he had his chance. They met one afternoon on the beach; their courtship began when Fannie agreed to meet him again that very evening on the boardwalk. She was sixteen, Sam twenty-two. She didn't fall in love with him so much as succumb to the wonderful ballast of his love for her.

None of Fannie's relatives approved of the relationship. Sam could not talk. With Fannie's good speech, couldn't she at least get an oral deaf man, maybe even a hard-of-hearing man? Even Izzy, her deaf brother, tried to convince her to stop seeing Sam. With no speech skills, what were his chances of earning a living? Besides, Izzy had him pegged as a hapless charmer who cared more about basketball than steady employment. *"He's no diamond,"* Izzy warned, and slapped her across the face. But Fannie wouldn't be dissuaded.

Sam and Fannie dated steadily and married four years later. They moved in with Sam's mother and two sisters, who lived on Church Street in Brooklyn. Fannie hated it. She felt bossed and bullied by her hearing sisters-in-law. The young couple had to sleep out on the sunporch. And Sam did have trouble holding a job. He found sporadic work as a cloth-cutter but was always among the first to be let go during layoffs, an easy choice for employers, who figured the deaf guy couldn't complain.

It was a hearing woman, a social worker, who helped him

gain job stability. Mrs. Tanya Nash, a pioneer in advocacy for the deaf, could persuade potential employers to give deaf applicants a chance and pressure discriminating employers to use fair labor practices. Today, there are laws to protect the rights of deaf people, and a state agency — Vocational and Educational Services for Individuals with Disabilities — provides counselors and services to assist with continuing education and job placement. But at the time Mrs. Nash was unique, and her reputation circulated widely in the greater metropolitan deaf community: *Have a problem? Go see Mrs. Nash.*

Sam went to see her, and she helped him get into the International Ladies' Garment Workers Union. Once he had a union job, he and Fannie were at last able to move into their own apartment: one and a half rooms on University Avenue in the Bronx, with an alcove-kitchen, a bridge table in the foyer for meals, and a bedroom where they all slept — Fannie, Sam, and their hearing son, Max, born just a few months before they moved.

Fannie was twenty-four years old and, for the first time in her life, happy. When she describes the rooms of her first apartment, she grows excited and quite pretty, her cheeks leaping up, her eyes growing dark and rich with remembered images. In this apartment she got her bearings and her autonomy. No one gave her orders or made her feel inferior. It was a deaf home and she spoke the mother tongue.

Soon they were able to get a larger apartment, two rooms on Gun Hill Road, off Mosholu Parkway, and soon after that they moved around the corner to three rooms below street level on Knox Place, where they would remain for more than thirty years. By then they had two sons, Max and Oscar, both of them hearing. The boys grew up bilingual in ASL and English. The neighborhood was called the Parkway, and it teemed with street life; the boys knocked chestnuts and played curb ball and punch ball and stickball and never suffered for lack of exposure to hearing culture.

They never suffered for lack of good parenting, either. Fannie mothered with vigor, passion, and a sixth sense that was almost witchlike in its accuracy. Her devotion was such that she seemed to be compensating for the neglect that had characterized her own childhood. All three of her men lived under the powerful gaze of her love, which she leveled with a sometimes irritating, if not frightening, scrutiny. If one of them coughed and she was standing across the room with her back to him, she would spin around and demand, "What's the matter! You're sick?" Yelling her name from the same spot would trigger nothing, but a cough or a sneeze, as if transmitted along some rare, unknown frequency, yielded immediate action.

Every week she transformed Sam's modest salary into ample, delicious meals. Deaf or not, she prided herself on being choosy, and when it came to feeding her family she could be a battering ram, prepared to rush all communication barriers. Once, at dinner, she began to serve her family a steak she had cooked, only to find the meat rather tough. Fannie seized the serving dish off the table and marched it straight up to the butcher shop on Jerome Avenue, where she demanded that the butcher sample a bite. He never sold her another piece of tough meat.

If one of her boys was in trouble, she became the staunchest of defenders. When Oscar was a gym monitor in the eleventh grade at DeWitt Clinton High School, he once got caught playing poker in the locker room with several other boys. The dean, Abraham Feibush, summoned their parents to school for a talk. Oscar coached Fannie strenuously before the fateful meeting. *"Ma, just promise me, don't tell the dean it was the other boys' fault. Okay? Just listen and agree with him. And please, whatever you do, please don't tell the dean that I'm a good boy and blame the others. Okay? Promise me."*

At the appointed time, Oscar accompanied his mother to the school and sat with her outside Dean Feibush's office until she was called. Although Fannie's lip-reading skills are excellent, they are not sufficient for every situation. In the best circumstances, only about 30 percent of speech is visible on the lips; the rest is conjecture. To alleviate frustration and misunderstanding, Oscar went prepared to interpret, and when Fannie was called, he started to follow her into the office. He was halted at the door by the dean's bark: "Stay there, Cohen!" The door slammed shut. Twenty seconds passed. The door reopened. "Cohen, get in here!"

Dean Feibush sat behind his desk, trying to maintain a semblance of command. "Cohen, ask your mother if she knows what you've done."

Oscar flushed and signed to his mother, *"The dean says to ask you if you know what I've done."*

Fannie signed back, *"Tell the dean it wasn't you, it was the other boys."*

"Ma! I told you not to say that!"

"Go on, Ocky, tell the dean you're a good boy."

"What's she saying, Cohen?"

"Uh, she says to tell you I'm sorry and it'll never happen again, sir."

"Very well," pronounced Dean Feibush, brightening as he decided to make this an abbreviated conference. "Now Cohen, I want you to tell your mother to tell you not to play cards and to be a good boy."

Oscar's color deepened as he faced his mother once again to deliver the inevitable punchline.

As a deaf parent of hearing children, Fannie negotiated two worlds, sometimes working double-time to satisfy the demands of each. When Oscar had his bar mitzvah, she threw a party at Knox Place, preparing everything herself: thirty-three pounds of whitefish and carp chopped into gefilte fish, two roast turkeys, potato salad, coleslaw, and from the bakery challah and two sheet cakes. In the afternoon, the hearing relatives came. That night, the entire event was repeated for the family's deaf friends. The first party was obligatory, the second a pleasure. Two separate worlds, two separate events. And after they were over, Fannie took sick from exhaustion for several days.

She never asked for help. Sam and Fannie were able to support their family without ever receiving financial assistance from public agencies or hearing relatives. Of course, the hearing relatives still felt entitled to offer bountiful unsolicited advice, especially in regard to the boys. The extent of their interference was often patronizing and hurtful. Fannie's mothering, despite its keen force and great singleness of purpose, was never enough for them; they looked askance at the notion of a deaf woman rearing children. When Max contracted polio at age twelve, one of Sam's sisters decided that Fannie had caused it and flatly informed her, "You didn't care for him satisfactorily."

In fact, the relatives had passed judgment long before, appropriating Fannie's right to motherhood before Max was even born. Recently, I asked my grandmother how she had named her sons. She had come north for a visit; my father and I had just picked her up at La Guardia Airport, and we were heading up the Sprain Brook Parkway toward Nyack. I sat with her in the back seat, where she supplied me with endless tough caramels from her minty-smelling pocketbook, extending a palm for the wrapper each time I accepted another.

When I asked the question, she tilted her head at me, the soft folds of her face meeting in wary confusion. I signed the question to her again, rephrasing it, looking her full in the face so she could read my lips at the same time. *"How did you think of their names, Max and Oscar? How did you choose them?"*

I sensed my father listening from the driver's seat. He had never heard the story either.

Hundreds of skinny bare trees rushed by outside the car windows before she answered. "The relatives," she said at last, waving her hand in uneasy dismissal. "Grandpa's family, they took care of it."

It took a moment for the meaning of her broad, bluntly formed syllables to sink in. As a young deaf woman, she had been judged unfit, incapable even of naming her own children.

Living in Florida, Fannie has her routines, her daily markers and acquaintances. Walking to the Diplomat Mall down the street, she always passes somebody she knows: that young man with the big Adam's apple and the sunglasses, that sweet Russian lady with all the purple veins, that rich Canadian couple who come every winter. They mouth large, voiceless greetings at her, and if the sun is not in her eyes, making lip reading impossible, she stops for a brief chat. At the mall she visits the kosher meat market, where they know her, gets a free cholesterol check from a freckled nurse at a folding table, and buys a cup of coffee at the food court, where she slips a fistful of marmalade, cream, and sugar packets into her purse.

When I go to visit, my grandmother treats me to everything. We set out for the Aventura Mall, and she has all the change for the bus counted out (forty cents for senior citizens, eighty for me) and ready in her fist before we leave the apartment. The bus stops right outside her building and is crowded with retired people. We find seats near a man wearing a brown baseball cap on which is printed "OLD? My toupee is turning gray." We drive by a series of pleasant beachfront villas; my grandmother appraises them with a stern and eager eye, informing me that mafiosi live there. She rakes over such visual details — her own form of eavesdropping, like a magpie scavenging for glitter among trash.

Today she is consumed as well by the tremendous responsibility of looking after me. She frets over my bare shoulders on the air-conditioned bus, fishes around in her purse for some tissues, and tries to arrange these on my person like disposable shawls until I tell her to cut it out. She outlines the various bus routes for me with the solemnity of a general mapping maneuvers for his troops. She makes me travel to the front of the bus to get her a schedule, in case it has changed. Like a prudent tourist venturing out in a country where she does not speak the native language, she takes pains to equip herself with information beforehand.

At the mall, she leads us to the French Bakery Café, a bustling cafeteria-style restaurant. We get hard rolls and pour our own coffee. She points to the pot with the orange handle: decaffeinated. *"Deaf or regular?"* she asks, signing.

I frown and shake my head.

"You get it? D-E-C-A-F. Deaf."

Now I catch on and laugh at her sign-pun.

"That's what we call it. Deaf coffee. You want regular?"

The cashier, a young woman with black hair to her waist, recognizes my grandmother and greets her warmly. My grandmother likes to frequent the same places over and over; less effort is required in places where people already know her, know she is deaf. She knows the names of all her shops and refers to them affectionately, as if naming old friends: K-mart, Phar-Mor, Publix, Drug World. There, within the cool embrace of the automatic doors, among the orderly shelves of familiar products, she is never a stranger.

She has friends in Florida, the ones she meets on Tuesdays, when local deaf people gather in a nearby church basement to win or lose a couple of dollars playing cards, and the old friends who have also migrated from the Bronx. Those who have cars sometimes give her rides to the deaf club that meets every other Saturday in Broward County, or drive her out to Rascal's Delicatessen, a large kosher restaurant where 90 percent of the patrons seem to be fellow expatriates from the Bronx. Over fish and potatoes, they reminisce about their deceased friends and the days of the Union League, and share news about the new state telephone relay service and which television station has the best record for closed captioning and how to fill out Medicare and tax forms.

Without any embarrassment or shame, my grandmother

might ask for help in figuring out a bill or a notice from her building manager. Among deaf people, it is a cultural tradition to ask for and offer assistance with the ciphers of the hearing world. These evenings serve not only as social occasions but as vital exchanges of information. Afterward, my grandmother returns to her apartment alone, her pocketbook bulging with leftover dinner rolls wrapped in a paper napkin.

Most evenings she stays home. She likes to lie on top of the bedsheets, catching an evening breeze through the screen window and watching a television show called *That's My Dog*. The television in her bedroom is not hooked up to a decoder, but *That's My Dog* isn't closed-captioned anyway. It's a game show on which the contestants are dogs. The format never varies; each night two dogs vie for the championship by competing in a maze, an obstacle course, and a talent portion. Very little language is necessary to follow the program; in fact, my grandmother's viewing is probably enhanced by being deprived of the host's patter. The program's appeal is reminiscent of the physical slapstick I remember my grandfather enjoying on Knox Place. My grandmother tunes in faithfully; it makes her laugh out loud.

On Wednesday and Friday mornings at ten o'clock she walks three blocks down Hallendale Beach Boulevard to the Greater Hallendale Adult Day Care Center. Against her deepest principles — all her life she has struggled not to be taken advantage of; never would she have dreamed of working for strangers without compensation — she has taken a volunteer job. Sometimes she pretends to have accepted the position naively and puts on an act of haggling with the director for a salary, as though she has yet to reconcile this alien generosity with her more exacting nature. The director, a large, pale-haired woman whose brusqueness has won my grandmother's approval, just laughs. "Faye is wonderful, a great help," she tells me. My grandmother leans in to read her lips, then blushes and tries not to look very pleased.

My grandmother's job is preparing lunch for the people at the center, many of whom have Alzheimer's disease. She clips her nametag to the sleeve of her purple sweatshirt, pulls a hairnet over her bluntly cropped, straw-colored hair, and stretches on a pair of plastic gloves. The kitchen is small and bright and very clean. She consults a list to see how many people are eating lunch today and who gets a no-sodium or no-dairy meal, and then she distributes Styrofoam trays across the orange countertops and separates paper napkins and sets out fruit cups and spreads margarine on bread and starts brewing the coffee for herself and Hazra.

Hazra is the full-time salaried worker. On Wednesdays and Fridays she and my grandmother are partners. Hazra is from the West Indies, about half my grandmother's age but her equal in assiduousness. When my grandmother develops a more efficient method of dressing the individual salad cups — she snips open two little packets at once and squeezes them together to dress three salads in one shot — she shares this technique with Hazra, who is duly impressed. When they break for coffee, they commiserate heartily over the cheap trinkets they drew at the holiday grab bag — a plastic honey bear and a vial of ocean-scented toilet water called Ebb Tide — and agree that the gifts they contributed were of superior quality. They discuss their children, their health, their mutual passion for gambling and for the flea market held every weekend at the nearby greyhound track. My grandmother has taught Hazra the signs for *coffee*, *milk*, *good*, and *thank you*, but for conversational purposes she adapts to Hazra's language.

The two women look out from time to time at the activities going on in the main room. In the morning there is exercise. Twenty program participants sit slumped in their chairs; they look vacant, ethereal, barely there. The group leader calls out to them: Gussie, Bella, Jules, Doc! Revolve your ankles, lift your arms! Later she plays the piano while they sing "When Johnny Comes Marching Home" and "Listen to the Mockingbird," their bloodless voices ascending from strangely slack mouths. Here and there a narrow stalk ending in fingers jerks a rattle or a bell, and once a birdlike woman with harsh spots of rouge (the one my grandmother claims is the widow of a Mafia don) gets to her feet and begins to conduct, startlingly imperious in her kelly green suit.

In the afternoon a young man arrives to lead "adult education," which turns out to be current events. He sits with the participants, their chairs in a horseshoe around him, and with great animation paraphrases newspaper articles into a microphone. The participants either do or do not listen; it is impossible to tell. A sign on the wall offers the reminder that THIS CITY IS HALLENDALE. THE WEATHER IS CLOUDY. THE YEAR IS 1992.

My grandmother and Hazra peek out philosophically from the kitchen. They inspect the infirm with an almost brutal detachment. My grandmother projects the unsentimental curiosity of a child watching a beetle that has tipped onto its brittle back and lies flailing its useless legs.

The program participants at the Greater Hallendale Adult Day Care Center are all people who have lost crucial bits of information, the most basic details of their lives. The program here varies almost not at all from day to day, continuity being extremely important. The threads that bind these people to their own histories have worn thin, unraveled, snapped. The effects are evident in their gossamer bodies, their glassy eyes. Repetition and routine are their lifeblood now, the sap that keeps them going in the absence of memory.

My grandmother too is missing crucial pieces from her own life: details that she never had the opportunity to overhear, experiences that she, as a deaf person, was spared or denied. In their absence, she has created a web of daily markers. Her pilfered marmalade and sugar packets, her ironing, her television shows, her bus routes, her volunteer work, her Tuesday card games — she tends to these fastidiously.

But if she makes any association between herself and the adult day care participants, it is not a conscious one. She aligns herself with Hazra, this younger, hearing woman, her able and savvy kitchen partner. Sucking their teeth, they pass clinical gazes over the disabled ones in the main room. Then they shake their heads at each other and go back to work.

10

Stupid English

I t is too cold for grammar. January is not such a good month for parts of speech; this is the message clearly emanating from the students in Sofia's English class as they enter the room and spy the forecast on the board: GRAMMAR REVIEW. Punchy, frenetic, they waste as much time as possible before Liz Wolter can begin the morning lesson. Chris rattles his boxes of peanut M & M's, which he has been toting around in a cardboard satchel as part of a fundraiser for the Junior National Association of the Deaf. Juanita buys a box and pries it open with her short, narrow fingers, promptly setting loose an avalanche of candies across the table. Tamara rolls a bottle of white nail polish to Sofia, then asks to borrow lip gloss from Patti, who proceeds to search vigorously through her blue gym bag. Rushes of air pour with a hot congested sound from the heating unit under the windows, and sunlight prints brassy diamonds high on the wall.

This is the top-level junior English section; these are the best students in their class. In a hearing school, they would be the ones most likely to enjoy English, the ones for whom it ought to cause the least amount of grief. But at Lexington, even among the brightest students, English remains to some degree unnatural, like foreign territory. If literature inhabits the most accessible region of this territory, if the language barrier is transcended by the animation of stories and drama, then grammar, it could be said, lies frozen in the nether regions, arbitrary and inscrutable.

Sofia's first exposure to English occurred less than three years ago; that she qualifies for placement in the top-level class signifies her great knack for languages. But the fact that she is grouped with classmates who are all American-born is probably at least as much an indication that most deaf students approach English as a second language as it is of her particular talent. And successful though she has been, it has not come easily; it was English class that once drove Sofia, usually so even-tempered, to dash her pencil at the chalkboard during a lesson and wail, *"This is a stupid language!"*

Still, the students in this particular class can handle grammar lessons more readily than most; they have even requested them, asking Liz to administer periodic doses of grammar's crazy rules. Naturally, whenever she honors their wish they automatically disown it, mounting great displays, veritable pageants, of resistance. Even now, sailing M & M's and tubes of lip gloss across the table, they maintain a steady visual murmur against which the teacher must compete for their attention. Unruffled, Liz takes her seat at the doughnut-shaped table and zeroes in on Patti, directly to her right.

Patti is a model of preoccupation. Having reached one hand around the back of her head, she is expertly palpating her ponytail (which has been growing progressively lighter in shade over the past several weeks; today it is the color of burnt taffy). Finding it still damp at the core, she removes her shiny black scrunchie and shakes the hair free over her shoulders, that it might dry more quickly. Liz taps her fingers gently on the table before her.

"Patti, are you dreaming? Are you here?" she signs.

Liz is one of the better signers among the hearing teachers at Lexington. Both her speech and her signs are clear and precise; she fits them together like the teeth of a zipper. She knows that English is her students' most difficult subject and takes nothing for granted, answering every question in the same judicious tones. Taped to the board behind her hangs a list of vocabulary words from her freshman class: "Mustache — hair above the lips (men); Twang — sound from a bullet; Saliva — spit, the water in your mouth; Squeezing — hold very tightly (maybe a hug or maybe to make orange juice); Probably — maybe will; Tears — water from crying; Cinnamon — brown spice, sweet (eat with rice?)."

"Do you have any work for me?" Liz queries.

Patti, forever late with assignments, chews her lip and smiles sorrowfully.

"Do you have the book?" presses Liz.

Patti has still not returned *The Friends*, the novel they were working on before the holiday. Now she purses her lips and continues shaking her head.

"Not even one little lightweight paperback book? Boooo!" Liz fingerspells the exclamation on both hands for emphasis, her lips puckering into a comically long tube. Patti laughs and tries to look penitent at the same time. Dispassionately, Liz registers a mark in her grade book. Then she looks up, full of purpose, at the rest of the class. The students cease their antics.

"What do you remember about grammar?" Liz begins without preamble. She has a wonderful poker face, useful for eliciting sobriety; her eyes, pale and ingenuous, gaze from beneath hay-colored bangs that fall as evenly as the calibrations on a ruler. Under the combined influence of their teacher's manner and the subject at hand, the students become grave, focused.

"Pronouns," offers Sofia, unwittingly trilling the *r* in her Russian warble as she fingerspells the word.

Liz stands and writes it on the board.

"*Adverbs and adjectives,*" contributes Chris, managing to flip the letters off his long, knuckley fingers in such a way that they appear manly, virile.

Liz adds these.

"*Nouns, verbs.*" This from Sofia again.

Liz writes, then pauses. A teacherly wrinkle forms between her brows. "*What else? Nothing else?*"

"*That's enough,*" maintains Juanita sincerely.

Liz tucks in her lips to hide her amusement. "*Okay. What are some pronouns?*"

As the students dictate haphazardly, Liz distributes their examples in columns: first person, second person, third person. The columns grow long warped tails as she crams them full of words. Each time the students think they are finished, Liz coaxes a few more examples, and they trickle forth until the board is cluttered with a confusing, monotonous inventory: I, me, we, you, they, them, he, she, it, her, him, mine, hers, his, their, its, your, our, those, these, who, whom, whose, that, this. The students wait skeptically for meaning to emerge.

Now Liz switches to pure ASL. She makes the sign for a girl standing off to her right and for a boy off to her left, and then she shows the two figures coming together and kissing, rather sweetly. Her students smile. "*Okay, how would I say that in English?*"

"*They kissed,*" suggests Sofia, speaking and using signed English.

"*How about a little longer and more specific?*"

"*The boy and the girl met and kissed,*" offers Chris in similar fashion.

Liz writes that on the board. "*Now . . . what if I say,*" and this time she shows the boy approaching the stationary girl for a kiss.

"*He kissed her,*" responds Chris.

"*Right! And that's a little different. Or we could do it this way,*" says Liz. She reverses the motion so the girl becomes the initiator; the students translate that into English. They catch on and practice more sentences, bilingually manipulating subject and object pronouns, gliding from ASL to English, one after the other.

ASL conveys the differences between subject and object as specifically as English does. It simply employs a change of direction rather than a change of pronouns or of sign order. Liz uses the grammar of ASL, which is perfectly clear and reasonable to the students, to teach them English grammar, which they find so unwieldy. The former is nothing they were ever taught; they acquired it naturally through use, just as hearing students understand how to form proper English sentences before they ever receive any formal instruction. This method ultimately serves two purposes. As the students learn the rules of English grammar, they are also receiving a subtler message: that ASL has an equally complex and worthy grammar, a grammar they have already mastered.

Now Liz writes on the board, "Patti borrowed her friend's clothes." Patti has been gazing up at the colored origami cranes strung along the ceiling. Stirred by currents of hot air, they look as though they're flying in place. Tamara jostles her classmate's wrist and indicates the board with her chin. Patti reads the sentence and grins.

"Now," says Liz, *"can we change this sentence to use 'hers'?"*

Sofia drums her feet under the table in a flutter kick of inspiration. *"I think . . . Hers friend has a lot of beautiful clothes?"*

Liz arches her eyebrows. *"Tamara, you be the judge. Can we say that?"*

"No way."

"Sorry, the judge said no."

"A friend of hers . . ." begins Patti, but she abandons the effort, the tip of her tongue pinched gingerly between her teeth.

"A friend of hers lent her the clothes," declares Chris.

"Do you accept this, judge?" Liz turns to Tamara.

"No . . . I don't know." Tamara, wiry and alert, jiggles her knee and thumbs her lower lip in contemplation.

"Does it sound right?" Liz prods. The students understand that she means this idiomatically. Naturally, they cannot check the sentence phonetically the way hearing people can, cross-referencing it with vast stores of similar, overheard phrases.

"Yeah . . ." Uncertainly, Tamara reverses her decision.

"That's right?" clarifies Juanita, struggling to keep up.

"This is a correct sentence, yes," Liz allows. *"But how can we make it clearer?"*

Juanita, stumped, pushes her glasses up with two fingers and sucks in noisy desperation on her M & M.

"A friend of hers lent her clothes," tries Chris, kicking the rung of his chair rhythmically. Someone's hearing aid has started whistling, and Patti is striking her pen against the table with fierce, repetitive whacks. But this mounting cacophony, unlike the visual frenzy at the start of class, is a symptom of engagement rather than avoidance. Liz, the only one for whom it represents a potential distraction, chooses to ignore it.

"The grammar is right," she concedes now, *"but the meaning is a little confusing, with two 'her's."*

"Patti borrowed hers clothes," says Sofia.

Tamara's head clunks dramatically to the table.

"No way. We can't say 'hers clothes.'" Liz shakes her head emphatically. *"We're getting closer, though,"* she promises.

"Patti borrowed clothes from her," proposes Chris.

"Ah!" Finally, a suggestion the teacher deems worthy of writing on the board.

Whenever Liz's back is turned, she cannot interact. During the moments when she is cut off from her students, evidence of their waning interest appears. Patti and Tamara pass covert notes in purple ballpoint. Their written language reads like a hybrid of English and the faulty sign language they see used by so many of their hearing teachers: "R.C. told me that drop the plan the party at his house. He thinks because that we don't like him. He told me I told him. It is not true . . . Yes, R.C. talk me by yesterday. But today during math then he ask me something wrong?" They chatter across the page in scrawls that creep, urgent and lopsided, up the edges.

Liz is still writing on the board. Sofia grimaces. *"This is boring,"* she avers, without voice. Chris watches her without reacting, then lifts the corner of his upper lip — in the hearing world a sneer, but in ASL a sign of agreement. He wears a peach-colored T-shirt with "Deaf Pride" emblazoned across the chest, newly purchased from the school store.

"I'm glad we got that one instead of the one that said 'Deaf Power,'" remarks Sofia, looking at him in turn. As comanager of the store, she was involved in the decision about which shirt to order from Gallaudet. *"Power sounds like better than hearing people. Pride sounds more equal."*

Tamara, glancing idly over the lists of pronouns on the board, is suddenly seized by a new question. She starts drumming the table for the teacher's attention, uttering her name in clipped squeaks. Liz finishes writing and turns back toward the class.

"Tell me, tell me," Tamara implores, jiggling both knees in tandem, *"what's the difference between 'she' and 'hers'?"* She fingerspells each pronoun on a different hand, ending with the last letter of each frozen stiffly before her, a tableau of impatience. Her manner expresses the general web of frustration threatening to overtake the group. The students rivet their attention on the teacher, waiting to see how she will explain this one.

With a single hand shape, Liz unravels the mystery of possessive pronouns. In ASL, possessives all share one basic sign: a flat hand, flexed at the wrist, fingers closed. By pushing the heel of the hand in different directions, the speaker distinguishes between *mine, yours, hers, theirs,* and so on. Liz shows the students how to plug this hand shape into sentences when they're trying to decide whether or not to use a possessive in English. This is easy; this they know. The discovery of a new link between the languages appears to give them a second wind, and Liz takes advantage of the momentum to carry on, guiding them deeper into the labyrinth.

Twenty years ago, even if it had not been forbidden, few teachers of the deaf were able to conduct a lesson this way, using ASL as a bridge to English. They received their degrees without knowing even a few rudimentary signs, let alone having proficiency in the language or any understanding of its grammar and syntax. Ten years ago, the situation was little better. Teachers might have used signs in the classroom, but only as manual codes for spoken English, a string of disjointed nouns and verbs loosely pinned to speech, harboring no interior structure or reason. Recently, colleges have begun offering courses in ASL, but usually as an undergraduate elective rather than a requirement for people studying to become teachers of the deaf.

Liz's ability to draw on ASL for teaching English grammar is rare. Her boldness in doing so is rarer. Even as ASL edges into social studies, math, and science lessons, the old idea that using ASL is antithetical to learning English lingers ominously in most English classrooms. The other English teachers may or may not use ASL; it certainly is not part of Lexington's official curriculum. It's just something that makes sense.

Downstairs, under the smart and crabby tutelage of Adele Sands-Berking, James works on his college-entrance essay. It's the last period of the day, and it's wet outside, with great metallic sheets of rain rippling past the window, but warm in here, in Adele's box-shaped yellow classroom. On the back wall, chunky letters cut from construction paper spell out the advice GOOD READERS MAKE PICTURES IN THEIR MINDS. A pair of gold-rimmed spectacles perch elegantly on James's nose; they are new, obtained after much prodding from Adele. Through them he can see what people say without needing to squint.

Right now Adele is saying, *"This is a very good start. Very good start, James."* She sits in a kid's chair right beside him at the table and holds what exists of his draft — one neatly printed paragraph on yellow legal paper: "I is Interested in Archessurial Drafting because I took Art and woodwork class for two years and also I'm interest to build bridges, house, etc . . . that how I'm interest and I want to improve the city."

The way James writes is no measure of his intelligence. It is a measure of how difficult it is to master an oral language without audition. No hearing person, not even someone who is illiterate, would say, "I'm interest to build." Hearing people do not need to be taught the proper construction, "I'm interested in building"; we acquire that knowledge through exposure, without effort. Adele understands this, and James suffers no loss of dignity in her eyes. Outside of Lexington, however, he will probably always bear a stigma because of the way he uses English, no matter how hard he and his teacher work together now.

Adele points to his opening. *"'I is,' James?"* she queries, with indignation that may or may not be feigned. He uses his eraser, writes in "I'm."

"You cheater. What's that really supposed to be? I what?"

"Am?" he fingerspells.

"Yes. This is very formal, James; no contractions." She waits while he makes the change, then tackles the next error, and the next, and they slog through the entire paragraph, correcting grammar and spelling and punctuation. Adele helps him clarify concepts as well; they decide that he means carpentry rather than drafting, furniture rather than bridges.

"F-U-R-T —" James gets stuck in an attempt to fingerspell the word before writing it down.

"Fur-nih-chur," pronounces Adele, trying to help him sound it out.

"I have no hearing aid," he protests.

"Well, thank you, James. That makes it easy."

"I lost it," he tells her defensively.

"Okay, look: fur," she repeats out loud, breaking it down.

"F-U-R," he spells.

"Nih," says Adele.

"N," spells James.

"Nih," she repeats.

"N" is still all he gets.

"I." She gives him the missing letter, then, "Chur."

"T-U-R-E," he finishes, plucking the last four letters from memory.

When they finish editing the first paragraph, Adele launches him into the next part of the essay, in which James is supposed to describe himself, his experiences and attributes. *"Remember last year when we talked about supporting your ideas with examples? You're trying to convince them to accept you,"* Adele explains. *"Why are you special?"*

The question gives him pause. James's guidance counselor, after all, has advised him to apply to Camden County College in New Jersey, which offers a two-year vocational program for deaf students. Getting accepted should be a cinch, and James could learn a trade, but he wouldn't earn a degree; he has a hunch that this program is geared for students who are not in fact very special. Pat Penn, the cook in the dorm, has advised him to apply to Morehouse, the college where her own son goes. The idea of a black school appeals to James, but the thought of taking the SATs and competing with hearing students is daunting; in truth, he knows Morehouse is probably out of his league.

The essay he is working on today is for neither Camden (which requires no essay) nor Morehouse (which he has yet to contact); it is for his application to the National Technical Institute of the Deaf (NTID), at the Rochester Institute of Technology, upstate. Created by an act of Congress in 1968, NTID is easier to get into than a hearing university or even

Gallaudet, its liberal arts cousin; still, it is highly respected and offers the advantages of a sizable deaf community within a larger hearing college. The fact that NTID's application entails writing a personal essay raises it in James's esteem — not that he has any great affinity with essays, but it seems an indication of the school's selectiveness, and suddenly this seems important.

Now, in his last months at Lexington, feeling himself on the brink of being passed along into a future he cannot fathom, James sits up and takes notice. Within the Lexington community, he has been protected, respected, and admired. Outside these doors, what sort of deaf adult will the world perceive him to be? For James, who long ago found it in his own best interests to abnegate his power of self-determination, the answer to this question depends on who will be advising him, helping him, speaking for him. Somewhere beneath his measured nonchalance, he has registered the significance of this next step. He will surface once to aim himself, then surrender to the current again.

After pestering Adele into giving up her prep period — he himself is forfeiting woodshop to be here — James finds himself this afternoon, of his own accord, in the unlikely setting of an English room. He submits himself to Adele's prickly guidance and the awkward medium of written English for the sake of a voluntary essay. Now, having orchestrated all this on his own, he reclines like the blinded prince, entrusting his next move to the person in command.

"Many kids are applying," she is telling him, her long white fingers knitting an obstacle, a dare. *"Why are you special, why accept you?"* Sometimes when Adele is talking to deaf students, her speech slips into shorthand, a condensed English gloss of her signs.

"I don't know." James shifts in his chair, places one heavy brown boot under the table with a thunk.

"Yes, you do," Adele insists. *"I know. You know. Tell them."* They face each other as though squaring off, the teacher with

her thick blond hair chopped off below the chin, her pointed features frank and challenging, the student with his arms crossed and his neck held slightly back, the new gold glasses forming halos around his placid eyes.

"*Sports,*" Adele prompts, smacking the table. "*Sports! What about being captain of the wrestling team? And you're involved in another very important activity this year, what is it? Come on, you know.*"

"*Black Culture Club?*" he ventures slowly. Wrestling was last year; this year he's too old. And the Black Culture Club has met only a few times; in spite of being its president, James hasn't been very involved.

"*Yeah! So that tells them you're a leader, you're president of the club. Also means what else? That your culture is important to you. Need to show them why you'd be a good addition to the school. Why do they need someone like you?*"

"*Not me,*" he scoffs, but without removing his eyes from her face; he absorbs her words with skeptical fascination.

"*Yeah. I'm serious, James.*" Adele, glowering, reaches over and tenderly picks a scrap of masking tape off his shoulder. "*It says you're an athlete. And a leader.*" She pretends to be on the admissions committee, reading his essay. "*Mmm, mmm-hmm! An athlete and a leader! Wow, involved, interesting person! Complete person!*"

She becomes Adele again, fixes him with a strict blue stare. "*They want students who will do something important with their lives. And you will. I know that. And you know that. Right?*"

The noncommittal smile, the dubious gaze, have finally been shed; Adele's relentless faith has stripped James bare. The January rain strums at the gray windows, two narrow panes. For a moment here inside, with the comfortable mess of papers and colored chalk, the teacher in her crisp white blouse so tall and powerful, James borrows her confidence, shares her certainty. His face has gone sober, his lips have drifted slightly apart, and he answers seriously, crooking one fist at the wrist: "*Yes.*"

Then he glances at the sheet of legal paper, half filled. *"So I'm supposed to tell them I'm important to them?"*

"Well, you don't have to say exactly that," Adele responds tartly. *"You don't have to say, 'You're a jerk if you don't accept me.'"*

James bursts out laughing, his cockeyed chipped tooth shining, and shakes his head, passing a gold-ringed hand over his jaw.

"Okay, work on this," she orders him. *"You have twenty minutes to beef this up. I want this much by the end of the period."* The side of her hand slices down near the end of the page. This teacher will never stop busting his chops; James counts on it.

"Impossible," he protests, but without any heart; this is just to get her goat. He picks up the pencil, grave again. His future may hinge on how well he can portray himself in this headache called English. When he begins to write, his penmanship is painfully neat.

This is the morning of fluttery stomachs, extra No. 2 pencils, lips chewed raw. Down in the basement, in the breakfast room, the usual mischief and gossip are absent. Cocoa grows cold; bagels and jelly become bright forgotten centerpieces, replaced in front of the students by Regents review books, over which heads are anxiously bent.

In New York State, the Board of Regents gives two types of exam: the Regents exams, which students must pass in order to graduate from high school with a prestigious Regents diploma, and the Regents Competency Tests, which they must pass in order to graduate at all. At Lexington, students often graduate with a third option, something called an IEP diploma, which is awarded to those students who complete the Individualized Education Plan established for them by the school but do not pass the RCTs. IEP diplomas, offered only by special education programs, provide a way of acknowledging years of hard work. Awarded onstage amid all the roses and flashbulbs of commencement, they signify tremendous accomplishment for many students and their families. However, in the outside world, they carry about as much weight as play money.

On average, 60 percent of Lexington students graduate with IEP diplomas. That means that fewer than half graduate with regular academic diplomas. Only a handful even attempt to take the Regents exams; about one or two a year qualify for Regents diplomas. The RCTs, given in six subject areas — reading, writing, math, science, global studies, and United States history — are the standard fare. Reading and writing are the worst. The others are hard, but these two seem designed to try the students in their most vulnerable places.

The auditorium, with its dank shadowy aisles, its blue velvet curtains imposing a kind of leaden formality, seems a suitable site for this event. A message on the overhead projector hails "Good morning! Reading RCT . . . You need: a pencil, a lapboard, concentration." Pencils and lapboards line the apron of the stage; concentration is fostered by the presence of the high school supervisor, who solemnly patrols the front of the room.

James arrives, attired in matching tan denim pants and jacket, a black-and-gold baseball cap, all his gold rings. He takes a seat at the rear of the first section, on the aisle. This is a social spot; on their way to the stage, girls bend down to kiss him on the neck and boys clasp his hand for luck. But his primary reason for choosing it is easy access to the interpreters. It is a key spot. James knows because he has taken the test before, as a junior, when he failed by six points.

He cannot fail today. Even if he completes his personal essay, he needs an academic diploma to be accepted by a college. In order to get an academic diploma, he must pass this test. It feels like a bargain to him, a deal offered by hearing people. If he can prove himself here, in their language, then when he leaves Lexington he will gain the security of their continuing approval.

Now the seats are filling in; forty students are spread out, one per row. Dispersed among them are a few alumni who graduated with IEP diplomas in years past. Some return every year to retake the exam, still trying to win academic diplomas, the key to college and better jobs.

The high school supervisor steps onstage to explain the rules, which are projected beside her as she signs and speaks.

"No talking to each other," she begins.

"Freedom of speech!" wisecracks a stocky, pink-faced boy in the front row, his beefy hands held up above his head so students sitting behind him can see.

"Not here," she retorts, catching his unvoiced comment with the sharp eye of a veteran staff member. *"Freedom of silence!"* Her hands complete the austere arcs of *silence* and linger a moment in space, draping a visual hush over the auditorium. She goes on, explaining the rules for interpreters.

"Staff may sign the passage. Staff may watch you sign. Staff may read aloud — some students may have enough hearing that it helps them to hear the sentence out loud. Staff may not give answers."

The RCTs are available in twenty-nine spoken languages, from Mandarin to Lao to Amharic. The State Board of Regents also allows the test to be translated into sign language. Unlike the other twenty-nine languages, ASL does not get a standard translation (something that could be accomplished with a videotape). Instead, teachers at schools for the deaf double as interpreters.

"No egging staff on to tell you the right answer," the supervisor warns with spirit. She mimes the part of a pleading student, desperate and smarmy. A few students chuckle. *"I know you are skilled at that. Forget it!"* She signs the admonition with two hands for emphasis.

At eight-fifteen, the proctors begin handing out the test. It consists of seven multiple-choice questions for each of ten reading passages. There is no time limit; students may continue working on it all day.

Within minutes, hands start appearing above the seats.

Some pop up urgently; others levitate slowly, patient and resolute. The nine proctors are in hot demand. They move from summons to summons like contestants on a bizarre game show, interpreting passages, jogging on to the next waving hand.

James struggles through the first passage, about the rangeland of the American West, underlining, as he practiced in English class, the parts he doesn't understand. Heavy black marks grow along the page like a rash. He holds his arm in the air until it begins to prick, then drops it halfway, his elbow resting on the seat. *"Not enough teachers,"* he complains to himself. *"Lousy."* Finally he uses his voice, and the high school supervisor comes over and rests her hand on his baseball cap.

"Do you need this on to take the test?" she teases.

"Yes," he says grimly.

"Okay, where are you, which one?"

He points to the first paragraph.

"James! You're going to be here till midnight!"

"No," he contradicts aloud, without impudence; it is a statement of fact.

The supervisor signs the first paragraph in English word order, interpreting "ranchers" as *people who take care of animals* and "overgrazed" as *eat too much.* A chorus of whistling hearing aids swells and diminishes like crickets in the chilly, high-ceilinged room.

"Again," James says, and she obliges. He asks her to sign the questions now, with each of their multiple choices. After she has moved away, he continues to study the questions, rings flashing as he fingerspells to himself. After a bit, he sighs and erases something with vigor.

Across the great room, the hearing proctors call to each other.

"Betty? What's the sign for 'result'?"

"Maria! Could you interpret for her? I don't know all the words."

"How should I sign 'integrity'?"

"What about 'meanders'?"

"How do you do 'fluids'?"

And from a deaf proctor, *"We're really allowed to sign all the words for them?"*

"Yes," he is told by a hearing teacher.

He shrugs. *"I thought this was a reading test."*

At eleven-forty-five, bag lunches are wheeled in on a big metal cart from the cafeteria. James doesn't budge; he is in the midst of working one-on-one with an instructional aide. She sits backward in the chair directly in front of him, breathing the minty smell of her chewing gum all over the page as she reads upside-down. He is on the fifth passage, the one about the human skull. Around them, other students wave their hands in the air, but James won't relinquish the aide; he holds her with his focus, with his need.

Students take apples and sandwiches from the cart. Proctors go off to lunch breaks and are replaced by others, who roam the aisles, squat and kneel, and climb backward over seats. Students drum fingers on the wooden lapboards, drag palms across their brows, crack their knuckles. Gradually they finish and turn in their computerized answer sheets with neatly blackened ovals. Other students come in; the science RCT begins. James works on. He is one of only eight students still working on the reading test. A teacher makes him stop to eat something. He slides a dry ham sandwich from its wax-paper envelope, takes one bite, and, reading, forgets to chew.

James is picky about interpreters, always looking around to see who is standing nearby before he raises his hand, then monopolizing his favorites for as long as he can. Since there are no specific guidelines from the Board of Regents and the teachers' signing styles are so diverse, interpretations vary from person to person. On one side of the room, a teacher gets to a word she doesn't know how to sign and fingerspells P-A-T-R-I-L-I-N-E-A-L. On the other side of the room, another teacher gives the conceptual equivalent in ASL, signing *on the father's side of the family*. In each case the student accepts what is offered.

The effort to understand deaf people's own mode of communication is in its infancy. Educators are just beginning to acknowledge that the suppression of sign language might rob deaf children of the opportunity to learn, to experience, to understand. But efforts to mitigate the problem may be resulting in further injustice. After all, the cover of today's test booklet states, "This is a test to find out how well you read." Does interpreting English into ASL really test a student's reading ability?

Educators have been failing deaf children for centuries. The history of deaf education has been marked by a single goal: to get deaf people to communicate like hearing people. Does an increase in the number of deaf students who pass the test do more to assuage educators' own sense of frustration and failure than to serve the students themselves? If a separate standard exists for deaf students, does this put them at a disadvantage when they graduate and enter the hearing world?

By one-thirty, James is one of the last three students working on the reading test. Adele Sands-Berking has arrived for her proctoring shift. James, arching his back and yawning, spots her sitting cross-legged at one corner of the stage, interpreting for two juniors sprawled on their stomachs. Adele has always advised her students to get teachers whose signing they're most familiar with to interpret for them. James palms the apple from his bag lunch and ambles over to sit on the stage steps.

He waits as the juniors finish, then edges up to Adele. He nods a brief hello and slides the test booklet toward her: the passage on Venezuelan mesas. His eyelids are drooping; he looks sullen, but Adele knows it is only fatigue. She signs for him. *"Again,"* he says. She repeats it; he circles an answer. They move on. When he misses one, Adele mutters, "No, honey," to the back of his head.

By now James is the only person working on the reading

test. He has been here for six hours. All these bodies, for all these hours, have done little to warm the huge room. James sits hunched in his tan denim, skimming his pencil over the page as he studies and restudies the passage.

His apple is resting on the stage. Adele scoops it up and polishes it on her knee.

"What are you doing?" James asks, distracted from the test.

"You've never heard of giving an apple to the teacher?" She is trying to make him smile.

James rolls his eyes. He retrieves the apple and sticks it in his jacket pocket. He has no time to play.

11

Number-One Home

Sofia tries to look on her newly assigned task of selling yearbook ads as an honor. After all, she is only a junior intern, not even a full-fledged member of the yearbook staff. Ordinarily this would be Jasmine's duty, but Jasmine, the senior in charge of advertising, is absent today. So, having suddenly noticed that February is upon them, with pages and pages of ads yet to be sold, the yearbook adviser has dispatched Sofia to the local shopping plaza to rustle up some business.

She sets out from school with a copy of last year's yearbook and a stack of advertising order forms tucked under her arm, her pink quilted jacket unzipped. Winter feels worn through today. A dry Christmas tree lies stripped on the curb across the street, an old plastic jug of antifreeze lolls in the gutter, and the pavement wears a dull coat of patchy white salt. Catty-cornered from the school squats the shopping plaza, its hindquarters huge and daunting with concrete loading docks and slatted metal doors that slide straight up to reveal the gaping bowels of the supermarket. Sofia hurries past a group of men shouting to one another as they unload crates of pineapple from an eighteen-wheeler. Up the block and around the corner, she comes upon the somewhat less forbidding fronts of the shops and reminds herself to bolster her courage.

Lexington's yearbook staff comprises nine of the brightest, most dynamic senior class members and two junior interns. Sofia knows that being selected as one of the interns is an honor in itself; to be entrusted with her present mission, standing in for Jasmine, is almost too heady for words. In addition to being the advertising editor of the yearbook, Jasmine is cocaptain of the cheerleading squad, a choreographer for the dance troupe, and the senior class secretary. She wears her hair in a studied mane, with lustrous brown waves slopping over one eye. Sofia used to be a little bit intimidated by her: glamorous Jasmine, poised and respected, her Mona Lisa smile radiating a mysterious assurance. Within the context of Lexington, she is formidable. But outside Lexington, from the vantage point of the Jackson Heights merchants, Jasmine is just another deaf girl, just another one of those kids whose speech they cannot understand.

Sofia inherits the task with mixed feelings. Because she knows she has been picked for her capabilities, it is beyond her to think of refusing it. But a twinge of reluctance slows her after she crosses Thirty-first Avenue, stalls her for a moment on the sidewalk. The sky above the shops is a fervent blue. Late-afternoon light glances off the antennas and windshields of parked cars. Wind slaps the ends of Sofia's long hair against her face, and with tempting abandon it dances leaves and empty potato chip bags down the street. She draws in a sharp cold breath and swings open the door to the laundromat.

A young woman with curly red hair and chapped red hands stands behind the counter counting out piles of change from her apron pockets. She wears a puffy down vest as a guard against drafts and looks up at the cause of this current gust with a long-suffering shiver.

Sofia approaches the counter, mustering her most professional air. "The manager," she says, and says it again.

Both Sofia and the red-haired woman concentrate hard on Sofia's articulation. Having no way of gauging how much noise the washing machines may be making, Sofia aims her voice for a moderate volume. Her speech is richly nasal; the edges of the words are loose, elastic.

On the second try the red-haired woman nods — a successful transmission of meaning. "He don't come in during the day" is her answer, which she delivers in a clipped Queens rattle, simultaneously looking down at her configurations of coins.

Because of the downsweep of the woman's head, Sofia misses this statement. She tries to guess what was said, cross-referencing the woman's body language with her own mental list of possible responses, but she does not have enough clues to form a hypothesis. She tries a different tack.

"Would you like to please support Lexington School and yearbook?" she asks, smoothly sliding last year's yearbook onto the counter. It is opened to a spread of advertisements placed by local shopkeepers. The red-haired woman has not entirely understood Sofia's words, but scanning the visual information before her, she is able to deduce the purpose of the visit.

"They're not here," she tells Sofia again. "The manager's not here."

Sofia watches the woman's mouth closely. The woman does not flinch from such unnerving attention but patiently repeats the message, winding dry, cracked lips around her Queens accent. Sofia understands. She proceeds to phase two, peeling a sheet from her stack of advertising order forms.

"Will you give this to the manager? If he wants to order an advertisement, please to call this number." Sofia points to the telephone number. Her speech has become incidental; the order form, the prop, relates the story.

"I'll give this to the manager," the woman suggests, her

curls obscuring her face as she bends over to read the form. Sofia hesitates, not sure what the woman said or whether it constituted a dismissal. Straightening, the woman creases the paper in quarters and sticks it into a rear jeans pocket. "I'll give it to him," she repeats, nodding at Sofia, who smiles now, dips her head in thanks, and pushes back through the swinging glass door.

One down, thirteen to go. She will be late getting home again this evening.

It has been a hard week. Sofia has been swamped with schoolwork, studying for midterms and the Regents exams and the Regents Competency Tests. She has been working overtime on the yearbook and putting in her regular hours at the school store, and she has been talking with Louann Katz, her guidance counselor, about life after graduation. The junior class is beginning to take field trips to colleges that have programs for deaf students. Now, just when Sofia has started to feel at home in her class at Lexington, she must begin making plans to leave. With the encouragement of her guidance counselor and teachers, she has set her sights on attending Gallaudet University, the world's only liberal arts college for deaf students. Sofia is thrilled by the idea of living in an environment where everyone is deaf, but the prospect is scary as well as exciting. All at once the future is impinging on the present. And to make things worse, she has been quarreling with her mother.

Last Friday Sofia stayed at school all afternoon, working on the yearbook. She went home to find her mother bustling about their cramped kitchen, fuming as she prepared the Sabbath dinner. Mrs. Normatov chastised Sofia for staying at school so late and called her selfish for not coming straight home to help.

"I'll help you now," Sofia offered, switching into Russian, as she does automatically upon entering the apartment. Wearily, she took up her role of good daughter, shucking her shoes and bookbag by the front door, presenting herself ready for duty. But her mother was already deep in her foul mood, and now it spread to Sofia as well, so that as she carried plates of radishes and stuffed grape leaves to the table set up by one wall of the small living room, a hard seed of indignation was germinating.

Perhaps this seed was what provoked her, during Sabbath dinner, to ask the question that escalated the conflict. She waited until after the little cup of sweet red wine had been passed around. Her father had closed his worn brown Bible and set it next to his plate; he had torn off chunks of bagel, dipped them into the dish of salt, and passed them around to his family members. The rituals thus completed, everyone had been about to begin the meal in earnest when Sofia spoke.

"Mother," she had asked, pitching her clearest Russian syllables across the table, "when I graduate, will you let me go to Gallaudet?"

"Nyet" came the reply. As flat as that.

"Why?" Her question, charged with frustration, incurred the family's silent warning: "Hush, Sofia, don't antagonize Mama, not on the Sabbath." Anyway, she knew why. Gallaudet University is in Washington, D.C., five hours away by car, too far from the strongholds of the family and the Russian Jewish community. Education is fine with Sofia's parents inasmuch as it prepares her to be a successful, productive adult in the hearing world. But if she were to go to Gallaudet, if she were to migrate fully into a world of deafness, she would be lost; she would lose her sense of obligation to the family; she would become Other.

The simmering tension between school and home is the crux of this conflict, and has arisen with increasing frequency this year. Last year, while Sofia was still a greenhorn in the high school, she was more available to take on chores at home: cooking, cleaning, tending to her baby nephew and younger sister. But this year she has school commitments virtually every afternoon. She talks freely and passionately about deaf pride, asserts her right to use sign language rather than speech, has even begun to challenge her mother's expectations of her. Her Lexington friends don't have so many responsibilities at home; her Lexington clubs and activities demand more of her time; as a deaf person, she is entitled to develop her ties to the deaf community.

The Normatovs have seen Sofia grow calmly but powerfully defiant. Suddenly everything is about Lexington, about deaf culture and her precious new language, ASL. It is difficult for a parent not to harbor some resentment toward the school. The very institution to which Mrs. Normatov has felt such gratitude, such bottomless deference, has become a rival for her child's allegiance, and now evokes mistrust and jealousy as well.

The tension weighs heavily on Sofia, too. As strident as she appears to her family, she is privately racked with doubt. A tremendous sense of family loyalty and her own emerging identification with deafness ride on her shoulders, pressing into her their respective burdens of guilt and desire. How can she balance a commitment to her family's culture with the pull she feels toward deaf culture?

During the Sabbath dinner last week, Sofia dropped the subject of Gallaudet and draped herself in silence for the remainder of the meal. Later she cleared the table and washed the dishes with equal taciturnity, not once leaving the din of her own unvoiced thoughts. She was not sulking; she was thinking.

After supper, Mrs. Normatov remained alone at the table, a cup of hot tea and a plate of fruit and almonds set before her on the clear plastic tablecloth protector. With deep contentment she selected apples, pears, and kiwis, first peeling the skins in long coils, then slicing the fruit into disks. These she urged on her husband, her daughters, her sons-in-law, who were playing cards and backgammon on the big gold sofa, browsing through photo albums, and laughing at the baby, who danced with a toy chicken in front of the television. Although they declined, Mrs. Normatov pressed the fruit on them anyway. She smiled in amused vindication when they eventually polished off the treats, a molar shining gold in the back of her mouth.

Sofia was too tired to try to catch on to the conversation or to ask one of her older sisters to explain. She felt torn, split, incapable of reconciling the two portions of her life. She observed the after-dinner fare being passed around, her mother binding everyone together with uncanny will, feeding them what she could offer. Sofia was both shut out and drawn in by the easy banter ricocheting about the room in a blend of Russian and Farsi, incomprehensible to her but familiar just the same. That night the thickness of family feeling seemed a force impossible to resist. She would accept this path, resign herself to the loss of Gallaudet.

Later, after the married sisters had departed and the parents had gone to bed, the little sister followed the big one into the kitchen. The Sabbath candles, left burning on the counter, had melted near the vanishing point, reduced to two soft bits of light floating in pools of wax. On the stove, two tremendous pots sat over low gas flames. One was filled with rice, the other with bahsh, a Bukharan dish of water, potatoes, eggs, and a tea bag to give the food a sepia tone. This is the traditional lunch fare on the Sabbath in Samarkand. The food would cook overnight, as no one may turn the stove off or on during the Sabbath.

The Normatovs follow the no-work rules of Sabbath with some flexibility: Sofia began doing the dishes. She washed them very quietly for a deaf person (deaf people stereotypically being pot-bangers and silverware-crashers), suggesting a conscientiousness born of years of coaching by or admonishments from family members. Irina watched her sister's hands dip in and out of the hot soapy water. The apartment was dark and still except for here in the kitchen, this spot of warmth. The high window next to the refrigerator was a cube of pitch. Irina stole a handful of rice from the pot on the stove and licked the grains from her palm, waiting for Sofia's hands to be finished so they could talk.

But Sofia was tired. *"All right now, it's late. To bed,"* she ordered after only a minute of chat. One Sabbath candle was out, the other a wan blue filament. She herded Irina toward their bedroom. But nothing with Irina could be this easy, and the younger girl suddenly became churlish. She would do anything to prolong this time together.

"You're not really deaf," she accused.

This was an old routine, and Irina was just an immature kid. Why, then, did Sofia let it rile her? *"Yes, I am!"* she snapped back.

Irina saw that her first strike had hit its target precisely; all she had to do now was aim gentle blows around the edges. *"Nooo, you're only hard of hearing."*

"I am not, I'm deaf!"

"You can hear!" Irina taunted.

"Without a hearing aid I'm deaf! I couldn't go to Lexington if I wasn't deaf!"

All her life, Sofia has been taught to use speech, language, residual hearing, and lip reading to compensate for her deafness, to broaden her choices and opportunities in the hearing world. But no matter what level of proficiency she achieves with these skills, they manage to fail her in one way or another. They either fall short of gaining her real access to the hearing world or they distance her from the deaf community, which looks on the too-enthusiastic development of these skills with some suspicion: does she idealize hearing people, is she rejecting her own deafness?

"I don't believe you," Irina persisted. *"You're not deaf. You speak too well!"*

Later that night, the only one in her family still awake, Sofia, in tears, called a friend. Through a watery blur she watched the words her own fingers typed in electric blue letters across the TTY screen: I FEEL MY NUMBER ONE HOME IS SCHOOL SECOND HOME IS FAMILY I FEEL I GREW UP

AT SCHOOL FROM AGE THREE TO NOW I MUST BREAK THE
HABIT AND LEARN TO LOVE FIRST HOME THEN SCHOOL.

Sofia's next stop after the laundromat is Pat and Joe's, the deli
where Lex kids flock after school. It is late enough in the
afternoon for it to stand peaceful, nearly deserted. Sofia enters and goes straight to the cash register, her order forms at
the ready, her index finger stuck into the yearbook at the
page with the advertisement placed by this establishment
last year. She decides to show the cashier the material first,
without any verbal introduction. The cashier has been snack-
ing from a bag of fried sesame sticks; she licks her fingers
and rubs them on her pants before examining the wordlessly
offered paraphernalia. Sofia glances idly at the rack of chewing gum and batteries.

"I give to manager," the cashier determines out loud. She
scrapes a waist-length hank of black hair over one shoulder
and looks at Sofia for approval. Sofia, sensing this shift in
attention, brings her gaze back to the cashier and waits expectantly, oblivious to the response that has already been
made. They look at each other, locked in this puzzled stalemate, until the door swings open and the woman from the
laundromat breezes in to trade her coins for bills.

"Oh yeah," she says, assessing the scene. "Just give it to
the manager," she advises the dark-haired cashier, blithely
swinging behind the register and clanking her apronful of
money on the counter. "Take the form, it's for their yearbook." Nodding follows, and multiple exchanges: yearbook
for order form, quarters for bills, welcome for thanks. The
transaction completed, Sofia leaves Pat and Joe's without
having used a word of English.

Sofia has been practicing the art of translation since she
was sent away to the school for the deaf in Leningrad at age
three. She is a learned practitioner of the skills of communication, seasoned enough to know that regardless of what
means are employed, the interaction is successful if the

message gets across. Interpreters (both professional and impromptu), gestures and mime, notes and diagrams, signed and spoken languages — for Sofia there is no hierarchy, no sense in valuing one method of communication more or less than any other. Despite all the haranguing of the hearing and deaf establishments, all the stormy theoretical debates over ASL and English, in real life most deaf people must be agile code-switchers, ready to employ various combinations of all these methods at any given time.

On a recent afternoon, Sofia was fishing around in her jacket pocket for some change to lend to her friend Sheema when she came up instead with the cap to a bottle of Rolaids. Sheema exploded with the mirth produced in many adolescents by any reference to intestinal gas. Her gentle brown eyes narrowed quizzically as she tried to grab the cap from Sofia's hand. *"What're you carrying around that for?"* she gibed, at once teasing and curious.

"Shut up, you," returned Sofia easily, jamming the red plastic cap back in her pocket and going a little pink. *"My sister sent me to the drugstore for it, and I brought the cap from the old bottle to show the guy."*

"Oh!" Sheema nodded in commiseration. *"Wait, let me see it,"* she demanded, sticking her hand out for the bottle cap. Sofia retrieved it and plunked it into Sheema's palm. *"R-O-L-A-I-D-S,"* fingerspelled Sheema. "Rolaids." She tested the word orally, found it odd, and made a face. *"Better to show the cap,"* she agreed, nestling it snugly back in her friend's pocket.

Now Sofia heads for the bank, whose main doors are already closed. An earnest young man at the walk-up window accepts an order form through the money slot. Sofia hurries on. The Chinese restaurant is next. The early drinkers in overcoats appear rooted to bar stools, and an old cop show plays on the television set mounted over their heads. Sofia wrinkles her nose; cigarette smoke hangs visibly in the air around the bar. She launches her pitch: "Would you please like to sponsor our yearbook?"

The manager comes toward her, wiping his hands on a white cloth and squinting furiously. "Yellow book?" he queries.

She has no idea what he is saying. It is a clash of accents. For all her American speech lessons at Lexington, Sofia still trills her r's in the Russian way, giving the word "year" two syllables. The manager of the Chinese restaurant transmutes the r's to l's, and once again Sofia finds herself staring, bewildered, at someone who is staring in equal bewilderment back at her.

"Yearrrbook," she repeats, but as this proves no more illuminating, she extends the book toward the man. The smoke is stale, raunchy. She does not know whether the television sound is on or off, so she cannot modify her voice accordingly. She lets the man discover for himself why she has come, and waits uncomfortably, trying to breathe without exactly inhaling, taking the air in little shallow sips.

Eventually, the manager accepts an order form without making any promises. Sofia is relieved just to be back outside, breathing the cold, gasoliney air of the parking lot.

With ten shops left and the afternoon darkening, Sofia zips her jacket and speeds her step. Some of the managers are in and some are not; some are friendly and some are impatient; some shove pencil and paper at her, refusing to try face-to-face communication. One will make no attempt to communicate at all but shoos her from his beauty parlor as though she were drunk or deranged.

Sofia often gets saddled with tasks such as these because she is so capable and responsible. Her reliability is less remarkable for her deafness than it is for her age. But in tandem with her verbal acuity and relative ease in functioning in the world at large, it makes it easy to forget that she is a teenager, with all the typical growing pains of adolescence. Instead people call on her to perform an unusual array of tasks. Perhaps the most demanding and conflict-ridden of these is the rearing of Irina.

Charming, maddening Irina is Sofia's special charge, and both sisters know it. Their relationship is unusually close and fiery. The seven years between them are insufficient to guarantee Sofia unchallenged authority, yet their parents have habitually assigned her responsibility for Irina; as a result, a kind of elimination dance has ensued, with the two sisters perpetually retesting their liberties and limits.

When Irina is kept in class during lunch to work on her reading, it is Sofia who takes time from her own day to visit the supervisor's office and demand, *"Are you punishing her for being confused?"* And when she is informed, *"No, it's because she's not doing her homework,"* it is Sofia who pushes aside her own homework and works with Irina in the evenings to make sure everything gets done.

When Irina wakes in the night, wanting a snack or comforting because of a nightmare, it is Sofia she goes to, Sofia who cares for her. They communicate in their own silent language, without disturbing the others. It is Sofia whom Irina asks for a poem at bedtime, Sofia who indulges, signing *"Moon Near Stars,"* the ASL poem she wrote for English class, its liquid rhythms spinning from her fingers like a visual lullaby.

When Irina stays after school to rehearse for the dance show, it is Sofia who waits around to take her home on public transportation. And when Sofia goes out with her deaf friends, it is Irina who increasingly insists on going along, despite Sofia's efforts at dissuasion. Through her big sister, Irina has glimpsed a portal into the deaf community, and with steel-jawed efficiency she has clamped on, determined not to be left behind.

Sofia's relationship with her deaf sister is full of implications about her own deafness. To Irina, Sofia is often a hero: Sofia can make herself understood in Russian, can stand up to their mother and articulate for them both. Irina was only eight when the Normatovs emigrated; she never reached Sofia's level of fluency in speaking or lip-reading Russian. It falls to Sofia, then, to serve as the interlocutor for Irina with the hearing family members.

But if at such times she is Sofia the Hero, she can be Sofia the Betrayer as well. Because of her ability to bridge the gap within the family, the family sees it as Sofia's duty to do so; therefore, they perceive withholding this service as the worst kind of treason. When she declines to advocate for Irina, when she refuses to assume the duties of a parent, it invariably upsets everyone. Sofia is the only one who can be the bridge, and until she submits to that task once again, the atmosphere around the apartment is thick with grousing and blame. In fact, Sofia has begun to wonder how much of her parents' objections to her going to Gallaudet actually stems from their anxiety about being left to rear Irina alone.

Last Saturday, in the aftermath of the almost-fight during Sabbath dinner, Sofia raised the question quite bluntly, asking her mother, "What would you do if I left, if I were gone? How would you communicate with Irina?"

Mrs. Normatov responded with equal candor. "Can't you teach her to be more like you? To have better speech, better Russian, be more mature?"

Sofia considered this and answered truthfully, "No, I can't. It's too hard."

It was a rare exchange, untinged with anger or defensiveness. They had the living room to themselves, and rested there in the bleak gray light that filtered through the curtains, a frothy cream-and-gold fabric drawn against the winter afternoon. In the absence of tension, Sofia felt that the room was charged with possibility.

"Mama, tell me," she begged, "how did it happen when I was born and you found out I was deaf? How did you find the school in Leningrad? Tell me the whole story." She already knew bits and pieces, but she had never heard it in full, and she needed it now, all at once, straight from her mother's lips.

Mrs. Normatov became brusque in an attempt to shake off

the request, but Sofia persevered until she relented. She had been sixteen when she wed her uncle Iluysha, a match that was not unusual in their culture. She had hoped for a large family, a great brood of at least eight children. She gave birth to Adalina, her first, when she was eighteen, and Nadezdha two years later — two perfect daughters. Three years later Sofia was born, and if there was any disappointment over having yet another girl, it was canceled by the blessing of a third healthy baby.

Sofia was two years old when her mother noticed that something was not right. If the baby's back was turned and Mrs. Normatov called to her, she didn't respond. She told her husband, who replied, "Nonsense!" and repeated the experiment himself. Perhaps he took a step as he called, sending a vibration through the floorboards; perhaps the baby caught a flash of movement out of the corner of her eye. In any case, that time she responded. "There, you see?" Mr. Normatov soothed his wife. But she would not be comforted.

A visit to a local doctor shortly thereafter proved her right: Sofia had a hearing impairment. However, in Samarkand they could not get access to an audiologist or the technology that would allow for a detailed diagnosis and recommendation for treatment. It was Mrs. Normatov's grandmother, Mr. Normatov's mother, who told her what she must do: "Put her in a special school."

For Jews living in the Asian part of the Soviet Union, this was no easy feat. Fueled by the grief and guilt that most hearing parents first experience upon learning that their child is deaf, Mrs. Normatov sought answers through a labyrinthine series of connections. After months of letter-writing, she finally found someone who would agree to help: the friend of the husband of a sister of a friend. This man was a Jewish doctor, a hearing specialist in Leningrad. Mrs. Normatov left Ada and Nelly with her grandmother and took the baby north, only to be told by the doctor that the best thing would be to leave Sofia in Leningrad, in the oral school, where she would learn to talk.

Mrs. Normatov did as she was told. She returned to Samarkand in a severe depression, feeling tired and aged, defeated, dried up. When Irina was born deaf, seven years later, her mother simply sent her along to join her sister in Leningrad. After that Mrs. Normatov made sure that she would bear no more children.

Sofia received the story from her mother, who cried as she told it, in the muted shadows of late afternoon. For the first time, it included the true, bitter ending, the part of the message that goes "Having no children is better than having deaf children."

"I don't blame you" is what Sofia summoned herself to say to her mother after the story was finished. "I don't blame you. I know you went through a lot. So have I. And I'm proud to be deaf. You need to accept that."

A few days later, Sofia was in the room when Mrs. Normatov asked Irina to hang her clean clothes on the drying rack. Irina complied, and when she was through, Mrs. Normatov surprised both daughters by signing, *"Thank you."*

Irina's large eyes went round behind her glasses. She leaped toward her mother in amazement and lavished kisses on her cheeks.

Sofia rose and gazed at her mother. "That's the first time I ever saw you sign!" she marveled. "You did that so beautifully — where did you learn?"

Her mother, pleased and embarrassed by all this fuss, smiled over Irina's head at the older girl. "From you."

12

Train Go Sorry

James has been here before. Twice he has stood on this curb, faced the steep, brambly embankment across the street, and waited for the bus to jail. Visitors are not allowed to drive onto Rikers Island. They must wait for the city bus, pay full fare, and ride for three minutes over to the island, which lies just across the bridge. James can't see it, because of the way the road dips out of sight, but he can see the gulls circling in the dull greenish sky, and he knows that not far beneath them lies the Rikers Island Channel and just beyond that the prison where his brother has been incarcerated for almost a year.

He remembers the exact day it happened, the second Saturday in June. It was Great Adventure's seventh annual Deaf Awareness Day. James made the pilgrimage to New Jersey with some Lexington friends and spent the day downing hot dogs and Mountain Dews, winning cheap, lumpy stuffed animals, looping the loop, flirting with danger, letting the rides spin him upside down. He was swallowed up in the amusement park, so bright and improbable, with its neon-colored slush in paper cups and girls in skimpy halter tops streaking by, everything wild and safe at the same time. When James and his friends fired water guns across the baked asphalt of the parking lot, it was only in play, nothing but sweet relief from the heat.

At home in the Bronx, his kid brother Joseph was also hanging out with a group of friends. They had a gun too. Theirs was a real one. They used it to stick up a woman in the elevator of their own apartment building.

That night, after James got home, he saw his brother for the last time. The walls of their apartment, slick with humidity, seemed to harbor the residue of recent quarrels. James felt the tension but couldn't piece the story together, and no one took the time to explain it to him directly. When he awoke the next morning, Joseph had already gone to hide at the apartment where their father was staying. Mr. Taylor made him turn himself in to the police a few days later. By the time someone bothered to look James full in the face and explain the whole story with clear, steady lips, his brother was gone.

James keeps a picture taped inside the door of his locker at school. Snapped on Easter Sunday last year, it shows the two brothers against the wan yellow exterior of their building, each in a tough homeboy squat, elbows braced on knees, hands open, prepared. They wear sweatshirts and baseball caps. James, on the right, meets the camera with his impervious gaze, devoid of feeling. Joseph, on the left, smaller, stockier, poses with a deep scowl, half hidden by the shadow of his cap. Their bodies are angled slightly toward each other.

In their neighborhood, Joseph is feared and respected. He has been in and out of school, family court, group homes. He is lighter than James, his skin the color of cinnamon; his eyes are flat and narrow, his body taut with muscle. Girls are drawn to him like iron filings to a magnet. He has a baby son by one of them, a friend of his sisters'. He is seventeen.

James says he thinks Joseph is funny. Funny and crazy.

When he speaks of his brother, he shifts into a childlike character, becoming increasingly animated. His eyes grow round and shiny, his grin somewhat forced. He speaks as though describing a fictional outlaw, a figure both revered and remote, whose actions can be interpreted only within the context of the strange and separate world he inhabits.

James once seemed destined for a place in his brother's world. One summer when they were kids, fourteen and twelve, James helped Joseph set a car on fire. It had been a tedious afternoon, glaring, bone-white. When Joseph found the can of gasoline, what came next seemed natural. Joseph egged his older brother on to douse the car, but it was Joseph himself who dared to light the match. The second the thing caught, a cop car came cruising down the avenue, and both boys tore off, slamming along the soft pavement, their lungs aching from the chase. James leaped over the wall by the commuter rail tracks, shinnied down a tree, and hid. Joseph ran slower and got caught. That was his first arrest; there were two more, for a joy ride and a fight on the subway, before he landed in Rikers.

The story was funny, made a good anecdote. James relates it today with a kind of rote mirth mixed with something else: the uneasy luxury of distance. Both brothers have traveled a long way from home. Now, with James at Lexington and Joseph at Rikers, as the crow flies they live less than a mile from each other. But one mile doesn't begin to cover the distance between them.

Rikers Island is only a five-minute drive from Lexington, but it is Valentine's Day — more than seven months after Joseph's arrest — before James ventures out on his first attempt to visit his brother in prison. He stands outside the concrete bus shelter, eyes watering in the wind. Thin snow trims the embankment across the street. At least a dozen others wait with him, though it is still early, eight A.M. The parking lot behind their backs is already jammed, cars slung in at awkward angles.

James stands frozen like a sentry, his handicapped rider card (which entitles him to half-fare) and sixty cents in his fist. He notices that the other people waiting are virtually all women, mostly black and Latina. Some hold infants so swaddled they might be sacks of flour. Others hold shopping bags bulging with food packages wrapped in foil. Some look straight ahead, with cloudy eyes and nappy hair and drawn, ashy faces. Others tap out little keep-warm dances in their spike heels, checking frequently to see whether the bus is coming; these wear party dresses, tight and sequined, and mulberry lipstick and door-knocker earrings. James can smell their perfume.

Beside him, a small girl grabs at her mother's stiff, chapped fingers and tries to rub them warm between her own bare hands. She chatters cajolingly, all baby teeth and darting eyes. Her mother does not look down but snaps a reprimand in a harsh plume of frosty breath and yanks herself free. James shifts a pace away.

When the bus comes they all cram on, choking the aisle with bodies right up to the white line. As they are waved through the checkpoint and across the bridge, past a sign advising YOU ARE NOW ENTERING RIKERS ISLAND PRISON COMPLEX and over the sun-jeweled channel, James can see the tip of La Guardia Airport and great silver jets ascending from the city. The bus deposits its load on the other side, and James follows the other passengers into a long, low building divided into glassed-in waiting areas, each corresponding to a different section of the complex. James has his brother's location, C-74, written on a scrap of paper. He finds the matching waiting area, takes a seat in the last vacant chair, and glances at the television mounted on the wall. He recognizes the show: *The People's Court*. There are no closed captions; he rubs his eyes and looks away.

A huge corrections officer wearing mirrored sunglasses and a hat with earflaps makes the rounds, checking picture IDs and handing out stiff white cards. James studies the procedure, eyeing his fellow visitors with a control that could easily be mistaken for aloofness. He always takes care not to look too affable, for this could be construed as a sign of weakness. Neither, however, does he want to appear overly tough, which could be read as a challenge. Both invite trouble. He has perfected a safer, amorphous expression. From behind this mask he searches for clues.

The guard comes to him last. James turns over his handicapped rider card and his student ID. After a brief inspection, the guard hands them back with a separate white card on which is printed "Inmate name," "Inmate number," "Dormitory name." James skips to the bottom, where he finds a space for "Visitor." After filling in his own name there, he deduces that Joseph must be the inmate. The rest of the information he copies from the scrap of paper in his pocket; although his mother gave him Joseph's address months ago, this is the first time he has used it. Not one person from his household has yet made the trip down from the Bronx to visit Joseph in jail.

Forty minutes later, the people in C-74 begin shuffling to their feet, responding to some invisible summons. James follows suit, lining up to have his hand stamped, passing through a metal detector, and then going through the rear door into a parking lot, where they are all herded onto an orange bus and driven to another building, fifty yards away. The bus stops and the door folds open. Once again James follows the rest as they corral themselves between a set of metal railings outside the door. From here he can see other buildings, all of them dull brick and gray cement, squat and regular, their roofs fenced with rolls of barbed wire.

Another corrections officer opens the doors and lets the visitors inside, packing them into a wide vestibule, where they are held for a second check-in. This guard walks through the crowd with a jaunty step, making an announcement; James detects a bit of showmanship. The other visitors laugh as the guard gives his spiel, and James reads the lips of the woman in front of him: "Uh! A comedian!" She chuckles, her lip curling back to reveal a gold vanity cap, and her companion nods her head in agreement. James, not privy to the content of the man's speech, retains his placid mask throughout.

One at a time, the visitors are permitted out of the vestibule. After several minutes, James gets near enough to the front to examine the procedure through the doorway. When his turn comes, he has the information card ready to turn over to the guard behind the counter, and he knows to empty his pockets: a keychain, coins, his lean black wallet. The guard punches the card in a kind of time clock. Then he reads James's Lexington School for the Deaf student ID.

"What are you doing here?" he quizzes.

James peers at him. The guard has a mustache and an odd way of pursing his lips when he speaks; James does not get all the words. He draws upon context and instinct to hazard a guess, compensating for the vague generality of his reply with the clarity of his speech: "My brother."

"How old are you?" continues the guard, apparently satisfied with that answer.

James hesitates, thrown by the non sequitur.

"How old, how old are you?" the guard repeats, pressing a hand against his own chest as if that will somehow provide elucidation.

"Nineteen — nineteen!" James, comprehending the question after the tiniest delay, rushes in obediently with his answer, speaking at the same time as the guard, who now treats him like an imbecile, using broad gestures to instruct him to pull up his pants legs and the stomach of his sweatshirt. Doing so reveals a band of red long johns at the ankles, an undershirt tucked into jeans. The guard tersely informs James that he may wear only one shirt, only one pair of pants, and he points toward the bathroom.

When James emerges several minutes later, stripped to his Air Jordan T-shirt and jeans, with his jersey, sweatshirt, jacket, and long johns rolled into a bundle and hugged to his chest, there is more waiting to do. Many of the visitors have already been assigned lockers for their loose possessions, and these people line up in their stocking feet, waiting to pass through yet another metal detector and beyond, where their husbands and sons, their boyfriends and brothers, must be. The rest sit in hard plastic chairs bolted in rows to the floor. They watch a snowy television, mounted and caged high on the wall. They feed their babies from bottles, or slap them for whining, or just hold them, the sleeping ones, like warm, heavy loaves of bread. They are all waiting for their names to be called.

Three hours after leaving Lexington, James is finally sent by one of the guards to the big counter beneath the television set. The peeling Formica comes up to his collarbone; he stands tall and waits for further instructions. He is so numb from the morning of waiting and lining up and not asking questions, from the rules and submission, that he is scarcely nervous.

The guard who finally addresses him does so without making eye contact. James has to focus with all his might to receive the message, which, in contrast to all the hours of waiting, is delivered with marvelous economy. "Joseph Taylor? He's in court today. You can wait for the bus back to the reception building; they come every half-hour."

James understands what has happened in a single phrase: *train go sorry.* This is what deaf people say about missed connections, lost opportunities. Sometimes people gloss the expression as *train gone sorry* or *train go zoom;* in any case, it is the ASL equivalent of "you missed the boat." The story of James's life has been the story of the missed connection, the train that has left the station, the boat that has set sail without him.

A hand extends briefly over the counter, gesturing back toward the bolted seats. James knew which days of the week (Thursday, Friday, and Sunday) and which hours (seven to noon) he could visit Joseph, but he didn't know about the arbitrary nature of last-minute court dates. Yet no disappointment or frustration registers on his face. He does what the man said and takes a seat.

Next to him, a young woman uses a toothbrush to comb her child's wispy side curls, smoothing them with her finger and a dab of Vaseline. A young white girl using the pay phone wipes her tears delicately, mindful of her black eyeliner. Up at the counter, a gray-haired woman argues with the guard, who is sending her away because her son has already reached his two-visitor limit for the day.

James pays none of them any attention. He slouches in his seat, hugging the bundle of garments to his chest, smothering yawn after yawn. From the way he sits, no one would ever guess that this is his first time at prison.

The second time James attempts to visit Joseph is in early March. It is the same day as the Honors Breakfast at Lexington. James made honor roll again this quarter, as he has done consistently ever since taking up residence in the dorm a year and a half ago. This good news is compounded by the recent posting of RCT results, sent down from Albany: James passed his last two tests, reading and U.S. history, thus clearing his path to an academic diploma. He postpones his departure for Rikers Island until after the ceremony; he would deign to miss today's classes, but not the Honors Breakfast.

At half past eight, students begin collecting outside the small dining room — a basement room, windowless and close, its walls painted cream and liver brown and hung with only a framed print demonstrating the Heimlich maneuver. But the students' mood amply compensates for the unfestive decor, and the food, an extensive buffet of bacon and eggs, waffles and syrup, bagels and cream cheese, jelly, juice, hot chocolate, coffee, and tea, arranged in serving trays heated by violet flames, and the paper tablecloths spread neatly across the everyday tables — all of this evokes such pride and delight that the room is transformed. These are the top high school students, and James sits among them.

He is one of the first to arrive, but rather than claiming a spot in the buffet line, he chooses a seat at a table near the door, where he can watch the others take up paper plates and royal blue napkins and help themselves to food. A pretty girl with egg on her lip passes by James's table and asks why he isn't eating. He shrugs mildly and assures her that he will. Another girl, standing far back in the line, waves for his attention and cries a chipper "Yo, James!" with excellent speech. He flashes her his chipped-tooth grin, tips his head a notch, and stays where he is. A guidance counselor greets him, urges him to join the line. He nods compliantly; still he remains content to sit.

He was up late last night, talking with members of the dorm staff about his oldest deaf friend, Paul Escobar. They are still together — both seniors at Lexington, both living in the dorm — but now they are also apart. In the dorm, James is the recognized leader; Paul regularly gets suspended for breaking curfew or fighting. James will graduate with an academic diploma; Paul will stay behind and repeat his senior year. And James has earned a spot at the Honors Breakfast this morning, sitting among the top students, the ones shiny with potential. Paul is absent. So are most of James's other black male friends.

In some ways Paul is like James's younger brother, with his rigid jaw, his short fuse, and his jailhouse chic (he favors a style of pants on the cutting edge of street fashion: barrel-legged and sagging off the hip, in homage to inmates, who are not permitted belts). James willingly stayed up late last night, conferring with staffers who thought he might be able to talk to Paul, get through to him. But in truth, the link between James and Paul has eroded. James has traveled far to gain a place at this breakfast, in this room of promise. The relationship he can now afford to share with Paul resembles that which he has with his brother Joseph, based mostly on a fondly remembered but distant past.

James has not shed all trappings of that past. He claims vestiges still, in gait and adornment; they are important for survival on the streets of his neighborhood. But survival in the classroom calls for a different set of behaviors and appearances. James's greatest contribution to his own survival may be his instinct for adapting himself to different cultures.

Last year he penned a rap song for his English class and staged it, complete with dance posse, in the auditorium for the entire school. The audience adored it, demanding encore after encore. *"Deaf can do it / Have no fear / Deaf can do it / Except hear!"* went the chorus, whose phrasing, if slightly awkward in the English gloss, flowed beautifully in sign. The performance scored with teachers and students alike; it blended palatable, nonthreatening amounts of black culture and deaf pride.

But quips from teachers and counselors remind James that his past remains fresh in their minds. He gets flak for not wearing a hearing aid and suspicious inquiries for wearing a beeper. His current status as an honor roll, college-bound senior still seems tenuous, largely conferred on him by those who are hearing and white. They will recognize his intelligence and groom him for a place in their world as long as he will reciprocate by conforming to their social needs.

James has accepted the conditions of this arrangement without complaint. But inside he has begun to wonder, to chafe. This spring, after taking part in a cultural awareness workshop at Lexington, he tapped into his frustration and resentment to write an essay articulating the feeling that he is being held hostage to a set of biased expectations.

> Some teachers often used two different attitude between Black and White students. For example, when Black students raise they hand up to answer and White students raise they hand up the teacher pick White student to answer the question first. That not fair to the Black students. Another example, when White students ask teacher to repeat the question teacher accept and repeat the question but when Black student ask teacher to repeat the question the teacher show

their attitude and say "pay attented". That happen to me. Also some counselors encourage mostly white student about college but not me.

Teachers and Staffs have to stop think negative about Black and Spanish students without know who they are. Students like to dress up to show that they support their culture or the way they like. Some staffs and teachers should have a group meeting with different cultures and learn about each other cultures.

At the Honors Breakfast, James watches all the others fill their plates before him. He has earned the right to be here, a privilege important enough to make him delay his second attempt to visit his brother in prison. But he cannot bring himself to partake in the festive mood of his classmates, packed shoulder to shoulder around the other tables, sopping up syrup and jelly with their bread, their hands crackling with news and witticisms, all of them reveling in the special treatment. To be here, James has traveled farther than they have from his past, and what he left behind still sets him apart. Thoughts of Paul from the night before and thoughts of Joseph from the morning ahead quietly sandwich him in his own space by the door.

A little before nine, when the buffet line has dwindled to nothing, James stands and fills a plate for himself. Then he joins a table with a couple of black sophomore boys, keeping his jacket on while he eats bagel and egg. The presentations begin and he watches for his name. When his turn comes, he goes to the front and accepts his certificate. He will take it home this weekend, give it to his mother.

For now he creases it inside his leather jacket, and it rides with him all the way to Rikers Island, this sheet of calligraphy tucked against his ribs, a promise of future, a voucher for success. It remains concealed within his garments all the way across the channel and through the metal detector and past the guards and up to the desk at C-74, where he is again informed that his brother is in court today. No one knows it is there; no one can guess what James has accomplished, what he has survived. All they see is a young black man who seems a little out of touch, a little slow to understand.

Late in the spring, he tries for a third time. He has come early, so early the sky hangs low like a canopy of ashes and the streetlights are still on, melonlike globes in the haze. Once again the bus, the bridge, the metal detector, the emptying of pockets, the waiting in line. Only today it happens that when he is called, the guard behind the counter slides him a large white card and a special pen. James signs his name in two places with some sort of invisible ink. Then he gets a locker, deposits a quarter to make the orange key come out, and stores his jacket, sweatshirt, watch, wallet, and all his jewelry except the JAMES stud in his ear.

A hand-marked sign tells exactly what may be brought in: "1 Pamper, 1 Bottle, 1 Pants, 1 Shirt, 1 pair of socks." A longer list beneath it tells what is forbidden: hats, cigarettes, money, watches, gum, candy, tokens, headbands, bows, material strips, jackets, bracelets, hanging earrings, sunglasses, chains ("except one small chain with religious significance").

James feels someone rub his arm. He turns and there is a short woman saying something with a moderate degree of urgency, her eyes fixed on his feet. James looks down and sees a large and nimble cockroach traversing the tongue of his shoe. He stamps once; it falls to the floor. Twice; it is crushed. James nods politely at the woman. She nods back. He sees she is standing in her socks, dangling a pair of red sandals by their straps. James removes his shoes too, purple-and-white Filas, and waits behind her in line.

One by one the visitors are summoned through a second metal detector. When it is James's turn to step through and around the corner, he finds himself facing two female guards at the bottom of a stairwell. They are used to dealing with people who don't understand English, and with bored gestures they direct him to stand on the third step, untuck his shirt, run his fingers around the waistband of his purple nylon sweats, pull up each pant leg, unroll the cuffs, pull down his socks, bang his shoes together and hold them upside down, and open his mouth. Then he is sent upstairs, where he comes out into a large room appointed with chairs facing each other across dozens of short square tables. At many of these stations, visitors sit opposite men in gray or mustard-colored jumpsuits with DOC, for Department of Corrections, stenciled boldly across the backs.

The guard at the top of the stairs makes James open his mouth again; she looks straight in, then waves him behind a wooden partition into a small holding area filled with other visitors. Instead of taking a seat, James leans his elbows on the partition and scans the great room beyond. It is not raining, but a kind of oily spring wetness has caused drops of moisture to cling to the iron bars that cage each window. Through these few square panes, pale gray light is permitted to mix with the light from the bald fluorescents. The visitors, having left their watches in the lockers below, sit in bolted chairs, caught in a helpless stupor. The guard, a woman with long copper fingernails, directs a dead look at the far wall when someone asks her the time. After a languid pause, she utters a response, but James doesn't catch it. He can't stop yawning.

James begins to think there has been a mistake; maybe Joseph is in court again today. He has been in the holding area for more than an hour — longer than anyone else — when finally he is called. A male guard leads him out onto the floor and deposits him far across the room at a table with two empty chairs. James sits in one and looks around.

He is struck again by the fact that nearly everyone is black or Latino. He doesn't see any white people, except a few of the guards. Around him, couples clasp hands across the tables as they talk. They run their hands over each other's forearms. If the bodies start inching too close, a guard materializes and separates them like a chaperon at a parochial school dance. Two inmates are led right past James out of the visiting room; one has a pink scar across his cheek, the other's cheeks are pink with lipstick smears. James tips his chair back against a pale green pillar and stares past them, out the window, out of this room, until he feels a commotion and turns to the front of the room. A new batch of prisoners is being brought in.

James sees Joseph before Joseph sees James. He is still tipped back on two legs of the chair, arms folded over his chest, and he watches Joseph coolly, without signaling to him. The other inmates have located their visitors and dispersed themselves accordingly. Joseph, ten yards away, surveys the room indifferently, then spins back to the guard desk in a short fluid move. James sees him shake his head. The guard says something; Joseph turns again and glances casually, slit-eyed, from face to face, until finally he lights on James. Then there is a tiny flicker of recognition before his features snap shut and he looks away again, apparently engrossed in inspecting the rest of the room while he weaves slowly, almost incidentally, toward James's table. Only when he is standing over James does he reach down an arm, still without looking, and the brothers grip hands in a neat three-part shake.

"I thought you were Daddy," Joseph accuses, by way of greeting, after he has claimed the vacant seat.

"No."

"Well, it's the same fucking name." James is really James Lee Taylor III.

Joseph makes no effort to moderate his speech or maintain eye contact. But he is James's brother, and even when James misses specific words, he understands the meaning. A smile tiptoes across his face; he is smiling at his brother's nerve, at his crazy, reckless, self-damning bravado. He keeps the smile off his lips, keeps it small and wary and constrained in the fringes of his eyes. He smiles because any alternative is unthinkable.

Joseph spends a considerable amount of time attending to

the rest of the room, tossing a terse nod at one inmate, cutting his eyes contemptuously at another ("He's scared of me," Joseph brags), waving to a third with the back of his hand, fingers splayed in a clawlike salute ("He's my son," explains Joseph, grabbing his left pectoral in a gesture intimating the depths of this jailhouse kinship. "My son."). He tells James that he refuses visits from family and will come out only if the name on the slip is that of a girlfriend, but James knows that his mother and sisters haven't ever tried to visit. "I thought you were Daddy," Joseph repeats. "I wanted to see what he wanted."

James tells Joseph about the babies at home; two new nieces have been born this spring, one named Onisha and the other he's not sure of, he hasn't quite been able to decipher it on anyone's lips, but he thinks it's *M* something. He tells Joseph about taking driver's ed and getting his learner's permit. After failing twice, he passed the written test at the Department of Motor Vehicles just this week. He has been accepted at Camden County College and will start its summer orientation program in July, but he doesn't tell Joseph this.

Joseph tells James about the fights in prison, fights all the time, over the television and the phone and the food line, even over coming from different boroughs. He tells James he fought a man just because he was from Brooklyn. He cut him, Joseph says, he cut him in the jugular, and the man had to be taken to Kings County Hospital and Joseph went into the lockup for ninety days — one bed, one sink, one toilet, and solitude for twenty-three hours a day; they let you out to shower and you get your food under the door; it makes you crazy, he says. He tells James that his lawyer is scared of him, afraid to come close to him. He says he's in trouble now because he lied to his lawyer. He says the inmates make knives out of anything — this chair (and he reaches beneath himself and strokes the metal leg), your glasses (and he half reaches out toward James's face). He tells James he could make a knife out of anything, tells him he knows what he's doing.

James jerks his head back and laughs shortly. "You're bad. You're a bad boy now," he says, as if it's a joke.

"No. I'm good."

"You look different from before," says James. "Ugly."

Joseph stares at him. He wears the mustard DOC garb. Outlined by the thin cotton, his stomach muscles lie in rigid bars. His eyes keep flicking away, checking out movement, watching his back. His skin looks dry, yellowish.

"Jail make you ugly," says James.

Joseph looks at him hard. "Jail don't make you look ugly. I look nice."

Joseph asks James for money four or five times, tells him to leave cash for him at the window downstairs. It's one of the few signs he knows: *money, girl, home, eat.* "Don't come visit me if you don't bring money," he tells his brother. But James already knows he won't be back.

The strange thing is that all those years of growing up, it was James and Joseph together with the neighborhood boys, getting in fights, playing hooky, stirring up trouble. Not until James moved into the Lexington dorm did he really sever ties with the homeboys and their dangerous schemes, although they will never be completely foreign to him. Even that day last June, that Saturday afternoon when a group of boys pulled a gun and committed armed robbery — who is to say that if James weren't deaf, he wouldn't have been there too? James himself believes that if he were hearing, he might be in jail now beside his brother.

It is past noon, time for James to leave.

"You stay here and I'll go home," says Joseph, so quietly he seems serious.

"No," James retorts lightly, mock appalled. He stands and stretches his back, ready to depart.

But there is something else Joseph wants to say. He makes the sign for *home*: all five fingertips bunched together and touched lightly next to his mouth. The way he signs it, it could also mean a kiss on the cheek.

"Home is nicer than jail" is the message he delivers. He says it seriously, instructively, as though it is a realization that has come to him lately, something he wants to be sure James understands. "Home is better than here."

James shakes his brother's hand goodbye. He knows. It was Joseph who had missed the boat this time.

13

Whose Apple Pie?

Oscar is sitting cross-legged on the floor of his office underneath the little plastic basketball hoop, a picture book propped against his shins. His guests, four elementary school students, have plunked their knapsacks and jackets on the couch by the window and positioned themselves in front of him on the nubby brown carpet. Even though Oscar has greeted each by name, they act very formal, almost prim. One boy has his hands folded in his lap.

Oscar looks severe. Not especially so this instant; just in general, around school, he has a reputation for looking severe, a touch somber. It's the eyes, set so deep below the wide forehead, the prominent brows. And it's the teeth, what Oscar calls his Bronx teeth, by which he means unmitigated by orthodontia, the lowers tucking into one another crookedly. It's his stature as well; he's six-two, lean and broad-shouldered. Some of the littler children think possibly he is the president.

It's not that they haven't seen him get a pie in the face (he did so in the spring dance show) or dress up in green tights and tunic and play a forlorn, bewildered Robin Hood (he did so in the senior class play). It's not that fifteen minutes ago they weren't giggling at him onstage, as he acted foolishly addled in the staff skit that touched off the elementary school's Literature Week. It's that within the world of Lexington, this seven-acre red-brick world on the edge of Jackson Heights, home to their extended family, Oscar is the head. *Cohen*, they call him. His name-sign, a *C* hand shape tapped against the shoulder, combines his initial with the sign for *boss*. He is the patriarch. And also, he is so tall.

The whole elementary school has been split into storytelling groups. The four children assigned to Oscar sit hushed and reverent, chins up, throats elongated. It is early March; the world is just beginning to go soft and muddy, with old snow slopping from the junipers and crabapple trees outside the window. They wait for him to begin the story.

"Do you want me to speak or sign?" he asks first, doing both. Some of the children in the elementary school have not learned to sign, because of resistant parents or a natural aptitude for oral communication or a simple lack of exposure. Many others benefit from a combination of auditory input and signs. *"Both? Okay,"* Oscar agrees to their shy nods.

The book is *Tar Beach*, by Faith Ringgold. Really *Tar Beach* was a quilt first, with panels stitched together to compose a single story, a dream-story about a girl and her brother, who fly from their Harlem rooftop and soar above the city at night. Later the words and images of the quilt were made into a picture book. When Oscar explains this, the students wriggle closer and peer at the pages.

"Beautiful pictures," says a smallish boy with an Afro shaved into a fade.

"Yeah. They're beautiful." Oscar holds up the page and shows it slowly around. He reads, and the children's bodies relax. A girl with lavender glasses rests her chin on her knees. A boy with a black velvet yarmulke stretches out on his side.

"*What's the sign for W-A-T-E-R-M-E-L-O-N?*" Oscar stops to ask, having come to that word in the text. On Knox Place, his family would have fingerspelled it. One boy shows his own made-up sign: he mimes eating a wedge. Another shows the more widely used sign: *water* plus thumb and middle finger thunked against the opposite wrist, *melon.* "*Thank you,*" Oscar says to them.

When the story is over, he asks, "*So what does 'tar beach' mean?*"

"*Roof,*" says the boy with the yarmulke.

"Star beach," the boy with the fade pronounces musingly.

"*Not S-T-A-R,*" says Oscar. "*T-A-R.*" He fingerspells it slowly. They find an illustration and look at the tarred roof.

"*You know, black stuff, smells,*" explains a large boy with long eyelashes. The smaller one nods in comprehension.

"*Do they swim at this beach? What do they do?*" asks Oscar.

"*Fly!*" This from the girl with the lavender glasses.

"*Do you think that family is rich or poor?*"

"*Poor.*"

"*What kind of work does the father do?*"

"*Construction,*" answers the large boy. They turn to a picture of that. The book explains that the father couldn't always get work because he wasn't in the union, and he couldn't join the union because he was black. The children ask what a union is.

"*Workers form a club,*" Oscar explains. "*They have to pay dues, and they try to improve the organization where they are working. In Lexington we have a union. The teachers have a union called the TA and they try to improve the working conditions at Lexington.*" He sits there on the floor of the superintendent's office suite, facing an audience of rapt ten-year-olds, and warms to his subject as though he were a labor organizer crouching with migrant workers in the shade of a peach tree. This is the great joke, the paradox that has haunted Oscar ever since he became principal in 1976: the administrator as agitator.

Over his desk, a photocopy of an old cartoon hangs in a cheap blue frame. It shows a school principal flanked by a group of teachers brandishing picket signs and a group of board members in three-piece suits, each churlishly demanding, "You used to be a teacher — talk some sense into them!" The print was given to him by an old friend, a deaf teacher, during Lexington's teacher strike of 1979. It is a relic from the days when Oscar, uneasy in his relatively new role as management, would leave home early and slip into school before dawn so as not to cross the picket line.

In those days, Lexington's function as a spiritual hearth for the deaf community was more pronounced. The dorm housed 150 students; their lives filled up the building and gave it a visceral charge. The umbrella organization, Lexington Center, and its affiliates that serve the outside community had not yet been created; Lexington was still a single organism, a family tree whose limbs were all connected to the same roots.

In those days, Oscar wore corduroys to work, and his old denim jacket that flared at the hips. He strove for unity and peaceful solutions. Another print that hangs behind his desk — the one of Martin Luther King standing before a photograph of Gandhi, with King's famous quote about the descending spiral of violence and only love being able to drive out hate — also dates from his early days as an administrator. Then he believed that he could best accomplish things by being patient and taking a moderate stance.

So while at home he taught his children the importance of workers' rights, when the teachers at Lexington went on strike he skirted the picket line and showed up mute and strained at the negotiating table. And while he got obvious pleasure from teaching us to sign at home, when my sister and I found ourselves with a can of green paint one dull afternoon and inscribed "Hi Signers!" on the bumper of his car, he demanded that we scrub it right off. Wounded by his uncharacteristic outburst, Reba and I had no inkling of the oral-manual debate then raging at Lexington, nor of the controversy our salutation could have sparked in the school parking lot. Today, when I remind my father of this story, he looks stricken, mortified. But there it is: in the early stages of his career, in his efforts to accommodate opposing sides and bring them together, he sublimated his social ideals.

Things have changed since then — both within the community and within Oscar. At Lexington, voices have become more disparate, needs more complicated. The family tree has twisted and thickened, become enhanced and encumbered by new growth. The family has branched into factions that now include the center board, the school board, the parent association, the deaf parents group, the black parents group, the Hispanic parents group, the deaf teachers group, the union, manual students, oral students, foreign students, alumni. Reconciliation among all these groups will not come easily.

And Oscar has grown weary of playing the facilitator, eliciting the compromises. Last year he turned fifty, or half a century, as his children are wont to remind him, and his sense of time has telescoped. He is less patient, less cautious now. A new print, a gift from his wife, has gone up beside the desk. It features a quote by the civil rights activist Fannie Lou Hamer: "The history we've been getting never happened, baby, and never will."

A bald irreverence, an impatience with distortion, have taken hold within Oscar. The agitator is no longer content to work gently, slowly, beneath the surface, but has risen with new urgency. In the eight years since Oscar became superintendent, the composition of the school board has gone from twelve white people, of whom eight were men and only one was deaf, to a group of sixteen, of whom seven are women, four are deaf, three are black, and two are Hispanic. He has established the black parents group, the deaf parents group, and the Black Deaf Children Project. Last year he brought in a psychologist to do ongoing group work with deaf and hearing staff members, exploring the barriers and conflicts that exist between them. Oscar is taking greater and greater risks, with increasing candor, and discomfiting some along the way.

The discomfiture may derive in part from the fact that he is so obviously in earnest. After all, opposing prejudice and injustice is the implicit responsibility of any good citizen; maintaining this stance is no less than expected. But Oscar has the temerity to disinter issues from his own back yard, bring them to the table, call them by name. Before board members and teachers, in Lexington's auditorium and at national conferences, in periodicals and on videotape, he has dwelt on particulars, speaking of the gross disparity in academic statistics among Lexington's different ethnic groups and acknowledging that hearing authorities have long justified their hegemony by keeping deaf people helpless.

Some find it unseemly that a man in his position, a white, hearing, middle-aged, middle-class professional, should raise these issues with such apparent probity. He is either dangerously naive or annoyingly self-righteous, an idealist who refuses to play by their rules. Among this group, many of whom make up the Lexington Center board, Oscar has provoked enmity, and he sometimes wonders whether his days as superintendent are numbered.

But for now he is sitting with four elementary school children, and he is gentle with them. Age and gravity have made the skin on his face loose and mobile, so that as his features shift while chatting about *Tar Beach*, he appears ingenuous, almost childlike. *"You know,"* he says, *"it looks like a very simple book, but when you start thinking about black people, white people, rich, poor, discrimination, the union, dreaming . . . it's really a book you can think about for a long time."*

This is Oscar in his element. He leans toward the children, tie hanging forward, pen and eyeglasses protruding from his breast pocket. The children watch his face; his brow wrinkles up like an accordion, and his eyes are wide with the offer of a question. He asks the children, *"Do you ever dream like the girl in the book?"*

Oscar leaves the house by six-forty each morning, backing out of the gravel drive in a wide arc, and steers east across the Tappan Zee Bridge. He switches on National Public Radio, heads south on the thruway. He has made this commute five, sometimes six, mornings a week ever since moving to Nyack seventeen years ago.

He finds it not unpleasant. Depending on the time of year, the mountains across the Hudson hunker down against a purple sky or are backlit by streaky ribbons of dawn. His briefcase, bulging with books and folders, legal pads and articles, maybe a piece of cold chicken wrapped in foil, is slung on the back seat, out of sight. He cannot attend to the items in it now; he faces a whole guiltless hour of time to himself, and his mind is free to tarry over as many ongoing projects and dilemmas as it likes, or none at all.

Once, bent on making more efficient use of his commuting time, he bought a little tape recorder in order to dictate thoughts that struck him while driving, but the habit never really took. More recently, Lexington purchased him a car phone (making him the target of merciless ribbing from members of his immediate family), which renders his commute somewhat regularly a matter of business. But when the phone is dormant and the radio news turned low, Oscar dwells in the sovereignty of his own thoughts. Often this is the most productive time of all.

Once he arrives at school, he may be approached with any number of problems — "We need to borrow your necktie for senior yearbook pictures"; "One of the kids' mothers had her purse snatched and she needs car fare home"; "A big German shepherd has gotten into the main lobby." And he will relinquish the tie, extract thirty dollars from his wallet, see to the dog. In the natural mayhem of a regular schoolday, underlying politics and principles are obscured, forgotten.

In the haven of the car they rise to the surface. The dramas of the day arrange themselves against the larger backdrop of the field as plainly as scraps of fabric laid out along the dashboard. Here Oscar mulls over the connections, considers the relationships. His mind works piecemeal, as a quilter does. The pattern that emerges is one of paradoxes, inconsistencies. The most puzzling of these is that while Lexington has held the longstanding belief that English should be both the language of instruction and the ultimate goal for its students, after more than a century the school is still unable to teach its students to read at grade level, and children of deaf parents, who have been exposed to sign language from birth, tend disproportionately to be the student leaders and achievers.

Recently, Albany decided that ASL satisfies the foreign language requirement in high schools. There is great excitement among deaf people over the potential job opportunities this will create — even though most of them will not be eligible for these jobs, since few deaf people hold the qualifications the state requires for teacher certification.

Then there is Lexington's implementation last spring of mandatory sign language classes for teachers who do not meet minimum levels of proficiency, which yielded indignant reactions from the union and from those teachers who were told when they entered the field that signing to children would prevent them from ever learning English.

And perhaps most urgent to ponder, there are the Lexington students themselves, newly awakened to the idea of deaf pride from their mandatory deaf studies class, who resent their parents for never having learned to sign; and the parents who were told when their babies were diagnosed that the most loving thing they could do was not to learn sign but rather to speak and speak and speak to their children.

Now, with "Morning Edition" playing on the car radio, Oscar thinks of how effortlessly he absorbs information about the world, of how he will walk into Lexington this morning with a wider breadth of knowledge, a greater ability to make connections, than his deaf colleagues. Of course, they can receive similar information through the newspaper or television, but that entails carving out an extra portion of time and spending less time doing something else.

How to compensate for that? His deaf colleagues will always have to work harder to keep up. They will always have to make sacrifices and choices that hearing people do not. Given deaf people's limited exposure to information, can there ever be parity? Like Tantalus in Hades, reaching for the apple that remains eternally just beyond grasp, educators may be pursuing the impossible.

The inequities, after all, begin accumulating at birth. Even the small pool of deaf children with deaf parents — children who grow up signing and who live in language-rich homes — are at a disadvantage. Even they are deprived of myriad opportunities for communication that hearing children have. While hearing children are being pushed in their strollers, they can hear their parents talking to them from behind. While bent over coloring books, they can overhear phone conversations, and while lying in bed, they can eavesdrop on disputes going on in the next room. In instances of both direct address and peripheral contact, the sheer quantity of interactions is far greater for hearing children. It is difficult to conceive of any circumstance in which a deaf child could receive comparable amounts of exposure to language.

These are not the biased opinions of hearing chauvinists. They are facts that affect children's development. But many deaf people contest these facts, as well as the idea that deaf people are disabled. The National Association of the Deaf rejects the representation of deaf people as having an impairment; it characterizes them instead as having enhanced vision.

If we lived in a society that did not regard hearing people as the norm, these differences might not constitute deprivations. In fact, in a society that regarded deafness as the norm, it is likely that hearing people would be at a disadvantage. But hearing people dominate our society; it is hearing people's gaze that determines reality. Within this reality, deaf people are disabled.

No matter how Oscar looks at it — from every angle, in every season, his feet working the clutch and the gas, one hand absently kneading the cords at the side of his neck as he spins south along the Major Deegan and north along the Palisades, through traffic jams and puddles, blue winter mornings and violet summer nights — the fact remains inescapable: deaf people are disabled. They will always be at a disadvantage. In order for that to change, society's definition of "normal" would have to change.

Perhaps the weight of this disadvantage accounts for the importance of congregation within the community. It breeds a special need for coming together, sharing information. Through contact comes knowledge, and the transmission of culture. Deaf people use their special schools and clubs to gather vital missing pieces, not only in terms of education but also in terms of group identity and self-esteem.

But for all of the tensions festering among various groups within Lexington and the deaf community, the greatest threat may lie outside, from the advocates of mainstreaming, who believe that this practice constitutes more equitable treatment for deaf people. As mainstreaming contributes to the dissolution of schools for the deaf, it may cause more harm than good. For many deaf people, parity with hearing people can be approached only through separate schooling.

Of course, here in America — and Lexington is nothing if not in the thick of the melting pot — segregation is supposed to be reviled. The mainstreaming movement is backed by the full weight of democratic ideals. The irony strikes Oscar with sudden vividness, comes to him with hopeless clarity. Mainstreaming may be as American as motherhood and apple pie. But whose motherhood? Whose apple pie?

I. King Jordan, the first deaf president of Gallaudet University, arrives on the eleven o'clock Trump Shuttle. Oscar meets him at the airport. It is early April and the day, neither warm nor cold, glistens with a pearly dampness.

King flew up from Washington this morning to participate in an educational leadership seminar that Oscar organized at Lexington. The whole question of "whose apple pie?"

fermented in Oscar's mind all winter and grew into the premise for this seminar, called "Mainstreaming Deaf Children: When Reality Conflicts with Social Policy." This afternoon deaf and hearing people from around the city will converge in Lexington's auditorium to hear a panel of experts explore the topic.

The panelists include two deaf and two hearing people. Besides King, who is perhaps the most renowned, having achieved a kind of folk-hero status during the Gallaudet uprising, they include the chairperson of the Congressional Commission on the Education of the Deaf, the assistant commissioner for special education in New York State, and the director of special education in New York City; the moderator is a former deputy commissioner for the New York State Education Department. It took some effort to assemble all these people on one afternoon, and Oscar was gratified when the project finally came together. Now, when so many schools for the deaf are bogged down in political strife, he would like to see Lexington provide a forum that will keep the issues in focus and generate intelligent discussion. Rather than trying to provide the answers, Lexington will try to frame the questions.

"So how are you?" Oscar signs once they are in the Lexington van and headed toward the school.

"Good!" King replies, cheerily emphatic, and then, *"Sort of,"* he qualifies, chuckling, tipping a flat hand back and forth. They both use simultaneous signs and speech. King, a tall, thin man, frank and personable, lost his hearing as a young adult; his English has the clarity and inflection of a native speaker. *"And you?"*

Oscar parrots King's response, gently oscillating one hand. King laughs. *"These are exciting times — perhaps a little too exciting."*

"There's a Chinese curse, 'May you live in interesting times.'"

Again King laughs appreciatively, the rich sound of recognition. Both men are deeply embroiled in deaf politics.

With a mixture of warmth and concern, they brief each other on the ride. They touch on the current status of the ASL-only rule at Gallaudet; after a barrage of complaints, it has been suspended and the policy is under review. They discuss the J.H.S. 47 movement, the protest of the New York Board of Education's decision to split the only city school for the deaf in two, with a new principal to run the elementary division. The deaf community has interpreted the change as a step toward closing the school and mainstreaming its students; it has held public demonstrations and gone to the press with cries of injustice. Oscar and King talk about the brewing tension over the hiring of a new superintendent at Saint Francis de Sales, the school for the deaf in Brooklyn; letters from the deaf community urging that the position be filled by a deaf person have not met with a favorable response. They mention Lexington's own imminent vacancy; a new president must be elected for the center board this spring, and the vast majority of the board's members do not appreciate suggestions that the time has come for Lexington finally to have a deaf president.

Everywhere indications of anger and frustration crop up, on both sides, on all sides. Oscar and King commiserate knowingly. They are not close friends, but they are plagued by similar polemics, each kept abreast of the wider situation by various sources along the same grapevine.

Beyond the rain-spattered windows of the van, the scenery uncoils: the droning gray rectangles of Jackson Heights, the sidewalks lined with a mishmash of interesting trash — rolls of carpet, fireplace fenders, old coffee tables and lamps piled topsy-turvy along the curb, as if in evidence of mass home improvement. But the neighborhood never changes. Blocks from Lexington, King brightens. *"Congratulations on Atlanta!"* he says. *"I heard that went very well."*

He is referring to the Black Deaf Experience Conference that Oscar cochaired last month in Georgia. The first of its kind, it drew more than 340 people from all sectors of the deaf community, from all over the country, for three days of presentations, public hearings, and focus groups. Preparations are already under way for a Hispanic Deaf Conference, to take place next fall in San Antonio. Slowly, the different perspectives are being brought to light, shared among the different groups.

"I think that's the main issue we're facing now," continues King. *"The problem is, politics keeps us so busy that we can't . . ."* He trails off, hands lingering helplessly, inexpressively, in front of his chest. It's as if the energies of the community are being pulled in opposite directions: toward challenging the paternalism of hearing authorities and toward understanding the differences within the deaf community. Some militants see the latter as undermining the former.

"We have to do both," says Oscar. The two men are quiet for a moment under the weight of this precept.

"That's right," agrees King. The van pulls into Lexington's lot. *"We have to do both."*

The seminar convenes in the auditorium after lunch. Student government representatives, turned out in touching finery, act as ushers. The panelists sit at tables covered with royal blue cloths and outfitted with microphones and pitchers of icewater. Three interpreters have been hired for the event: one onstage signs to the audience, one in the front row signs to the deaf panelists onstage, and one with a microphone voices questions that are signed from the audience. Both deaf panelists speak and sign for themselves.

Points are made by both panelists and audience. Deaf children can't hear, several speakers reiterate; they must be in an environment where there is visual information. Mainstreaming won't provide enough of that. There will be a loss in terms of quality of services, and a more insidious loss in the absence of role models. Years ago, someone comments, relating an adage familiar to many in the room, young deaf children assumed that when they grew up they would either become hearing or die, because they never saw deaf adults.

But overturning the popularity of mainstreaming won't be easy, other speakers caution. After all, mainstreaming came about because some handicapped children were being excluded from public schools. Advocating special schools can be construed as reverting to harmful segregation. And for many, the stigma remains intact: children who do not succeed in mainstream programs are perceived as failures.

The discussion continues for three hours. Oscar has made it clear that the purpose of the seminar is not to spiral into a debate with winners and losers, and this it never does. Various sentiments are put forth, and they accumulate, arrange themselves into a sprawling, multifaceted montage. Oscar himself sits quietly in the front row. As he has become more aggressive in his actions, organizing public exchanges of ideas and information, he has become more thoughtful about his status as a hearing man who has no trouble being heard. His greatest contribution now may be to provide forums in which other voices have eminence, and to spend more time listening.

The last question comes from one of the student ushers, a tall, raw-boned, gangly senior. He stands, his skinny necktie wobbling against his Adam's apple, and phrases his question solemnly. *"As more students are placed in mainstream programs, our culture will decline. We have pride in our culture and want to pass it on to future generations. Don't you see this as a concern?"* He reclaims his seat without taking his eyes from the stage, so as not to miss any of the reply.

"That's the responsibility of the deaf community, not the schools." The panelist from the congressional commission chooses to field this question. *"The worst mistake the deaf community could make is to give that responsibility to the schools. The deaf organizations themselves should assume responsibility for transmitting the culture."*

But I. King Jordan signals that he would like to field the question, too. First he pours icewater into his glass, innocent of the effect created by the proximity of his microphone: it sounds like a string of pearls being dropped on a dresser, amplified a hundredfold throughout the room. For the hearing people, it provides an unintentionally dramatic preamble to his final comment. *"I take the position that you don't teach culture, you absorb it,"* he says. *"The center of the deaf community has always been the schools. The importance of their role cannot be underestimated."*

During the Deaf President Now movement, the Gallaudet students coined a new visual expression that has become the deaf cultural equivalent of clapping hands. Silent, glimmering applause — arms raised, fingers splayed, wrists oscillating — was widely, instantly adopted by deaf communities everywhere. It is easy to forget how recently this tradition was created, so ingrained has it become. Really, it is a perfect example of the way deaf culture thrives in and emanates from the schools.

Oscar looks over his shoulder now to gauge the response to King's last statement. All over the darkened auditorium, arms are lifting silently into the air, hands shimmying back and forth, like pale underwater creatures responding to an invisible current: a sea of deaf applause.

14

Moving the Boundaries

I went to him for language lessons. Sign language lessons, I wanted, but that first night in his windowless office at New York University he drew a Chinese ideogram on the back of something and asked me to copy it.

My whole childhood I had heard stories about Alec Naiman. While still in high school he'd gotten his pilot's license; upon graduation, he had traveled around the world; he had studied in China on a fellowship and driven a taxicab in Manhattan; in the New York State Court of Appeals, he had won the right to serve on a jury by using an interpreter. Every so often, word of his latest exploit would come to my attention, and in this way I grew up with a constant, if peripheral, awareness of him.

I did not know him personally. He had been a student at Lexington when my parents began teaching there, and his parents and mine had become close friends. Alec was fourteen years my senior, and generally off exploring any of a number of distant countries by the time I learned to talk. But over the years his name was invoked with enough frequency and in such a way that it acquired a faintly consanguineous quality, and it was on the basis of this connection that, when I was twenty-one, I asked him to tutor me in American Sign Language, although I had not seen him since I was a child.

That first night I sat in his office, rain-damp and shy, and stared miserably at the Chinese character before me, unsure of the purpose of this little test. My raincoat, which I had not removed, dripped over a stack of workbooks on the floor. I picked up a pen and copied the figure.

"Not bad," said Alec, picking up the paper when I had finished. Speaking aloud, with no signs, he proceeded to point out all the details I had missed. I nodded with what I hoped looked like humility. I needed a tissue, badly. He said something else. I couldn't understand his speech. I nodded again, and wiped my nose on the back of my hand.

After that first night we met once a week. On these winter evenings, after almost everyone else had gone home to supper, Alec and I faced each other across a heavy wooden table in Shimkin Hall and dispensed with English. The rule was no voice, no mouthing of words. The only sounds came from the hissing radiators, a vacuum cleaner humming out by the elevator, and us: the click of teeth, the damp patter of lips, the muted percussion of hands.

"*Don't worry about vocabulary,*" Alec advised right away. "*You've got a good base there. Concentrate on grammar.*" In ASL, grammar occurs in the eyes, the brows, the tilt of the head, the lips. We practiced *near* and *far*.

"*Where's the water fountain?*" he queried.

It was near. I pointed in the general direction of the hall. He showed me how to make it precise: eyes narrowed, lips pressed tightly against teeth, shoulder raised, chin tucked in, wrist near body as one finger traced a tight angle — "*Just around the corner to the right.*"

Mindful of the Chinese ideogram with all its essential lines and dashes, I tried again, attempting to replicate each of his movements with equal grace, but managed only a feeble imitation. "*I'm so* hearing," I lamented in mock despair.

"Let's break it down," Alec suggested. *"Watch just my mouth."*

He would indicate either *near* or *far* by moving only his lips, and I was to say which. *Far* lips were pursed and sometimes parted with an intake of breath; *near* lips mashed together near the teeth. I sat back and watched, chewing the embarrassed smile from my own mouth as I interpreted his. He had a black mustache, rather winsome and offhand, and now it tucked in. *"Near,"* I signed. He gave a short nod. To his entire string of examples I then responded in quick tempo: *"Far far near far near near near."* Alec nodded yes.

This proved a portentous early lesson; as we evolved into conversation, we nearly always talked of travel. Alec told me about his experiences working on a farm in Australia, packing shoes in a warehouse in New Zealand, smoking opium in China. In turn, I told him all the places I wanted to explore. He showed me how to make mountains and forests, carve meaning from space, open up new territory with my fingers. He made pictures of my very thoughts. With the uncanny accuracy of a compass, he seemed to know where everything belonged, and I began to absorb the conventions and behaviors of ASL unconsciously.

Still, between thought and expression my hands often failed me. Once, faltering for the means to channel what I meant to say into signs, I let my gaze drift to the place where ceiling met wall, my hands still working as my face tilted away.

"Leah." Alec shook his fingers gently within my peripheral vision until I looked back. *"Always maintain eye contact while you're signing to someone."*

And when I dropped my eyes for a moment to study an unfamiliar sign on his hands, he chided, *"Remember always to watch the eyes. Use peripheral vision for my hands; the eyes are most important."* I blushed and pressed my fingers to my cheeks and earlobes, cooling them inarticulately. (I thought the university was unconscionably overheated; I had noticed that my face was always warm during our sessions, my palms a bit damp.)

Each time we met I slipped deeper and more easily into this place with no words. There were moments, watching him, when I no longer mentally translated what he said into English but lapsed into unmediated comprehension. As a non-native user, I would always be somewhat clumsy in expression. Still, I found myself able to converse more intimately in sign, without all the euphemistic vagaries of English. Threads that had previously bound my thoughts to the rigid, linear grid of English loosened and came undone; I began to trust what I could see. Tactile and explicit, with language passing like liquid between us, we engaged in uncommon communion.

The winter evenings yielded to spring evenings, flush with the heady sweetness of warm winds, of plaintive street musicians and lengthening dusks. I took plums and apples to our sessions. We spoke of exploring other cultures. Alec showed me the signs for Japan, Austria, Egypt, Thailand. He promised to take me flying someday.

In April I left New York to travel around the country. At the end of our final session, I gave him a flat package wrapped in colored paper. Inside was a map, a Peters Projection of the world. On this map, all the continents appear shrunken or distended into unfamiliar shapes. Europe and Scandinavia, for example, are compressed into neat lavender parcels, while Africa and South America stretch across the water like giant mustard-colored cocoons.

The Peters map is a redrawing of that which we thought we understood. However ridiculous or blasphemous the altered landmasses seem, they are, in fact, cartographically superior to those we've grown up believing. On this map, impossible distances shrink. Boundaries shift.

I enclosed a card. "Thank you," it read, in a message that I hoped was clever and subtle. "See you around."

*

It was a hot night in Central Park, late June, the duskier end of a crazily long dusk. We sat around on a couple of bed-sheets outside the Delacorte Theater — a dozen graduate students, Alec, and I. The students had brought crackers, cheese, grapes, sardines, wine, pickles, cherries. In two days, Alec would lead the group abroad, where they would earn college credits by studying deaf rehabilitation in England and Sweden. For now, they laughed and drank and practiced their sign language while waiting to go into the theater. Alec had managed to get the whole group tickets for *Twelfth Night*.

There was an interpreter with us as well, a woman who would accompany the group abroad. She was the first inter-preter I'd ever met socially. She had generous features, pale, quick eyes, and lots of teeth, and she and Alec talked effort-lessly and abundantly, signing beyond my skill. He had taken his shoes off. Awed and jealous, I drank a cup of wine and turned to watch the soccer game in the dusty meadow behind us.

Shortly before we were to go inside the theater, a large man with whiskers came on foot down the bicycle path, swinging a cowbell. Alec looked up right away, and we all followed his gaze. The man wore a T-shirt that did not quite cover his stomach and carried a basket on which was fas-tened a sign: WISHES $1. We watched as he wended his way among the picnics laid out between the trees, soliciting wish-ers. For the said price, a customer could make one wish; when he or she was finished, the man would ring his bell, presumably ensuring that the wish would be granted. Alec sort of yelped at the man to get his attention and removed a dollar bill from his pants pocket.

We had been seeing each other around all month, Alec and I, ever since I had gotten back from my travels. He had taken me flying nearly every weekend, in a small plane with blue-and-white wings. He rented it from an airfield out in New Jersey. We'd meet at the field early in the morning, and while Alec signed papers in the office I would wait outside, watching other planes take off. They were as neat and plump as sparrows. One minute they bustled along the runway, models of practical efficiency; the next they were airborne, luminous and miragelike in the haze. Eventually I'd hear a screen door smack and there would be Alec, sloe-eyed and bearish, standing behind me. He'd flip his cigarette onto the gravel, give me a nod, and head toward the field.

I was proud not to get sick in the air. Alec went in for acrobatics, making the plane tilt and sink so that the ground spiraled. *"It feels so strange!"* I told him breathlessly after the first time. *"Look, why are my hands shaking?"*

He said something about centripetal force, something about blood rushing to the body's center. I had a terrible time understanding him in the airplane. For one thing, the noise of the engine obliterated what little voice he sometimes used; I hadn't realized how much his speech gave me clues as to what he was saying. For another, he wore dark glasses to block the glare; I could not see his eyes.

"I've never felt anything like that." I was still lightheaded.

"Were you scared?" he asked.

"No. I trust you."

He smiled then, quite a pleased smile, and pulled up on the throttle.

I did trust him; his control, his ease with the whole contraption, was evident. There was nothing up there to listen for. He watched the whole sky, pointing out other planes and helicopters long before I made them out. He had had his first lesson when he was twelve, his first solo at sixteen. Every cent he had earned, his allowance and birthday money, had gone toward breaking gravity's hold.

He showed me pretty things. We flew into New York Harbor and circled the Statue of Liberty, right up close to her huge green face. Boats glittered like bits of chewing gum wrapper beneath us. We flew along the beach at Coney Island and up the East River, crossing bridges, now the size of cake decorations. We found my parents' house up the Hudson River and dipped our wings while my mother stood in the yard and flapped a yellow tablecloth.

"Do you mind my being up here with you?" I asked him once. *"I mean, is it — it's not your private place?"*

"It feels nice to share it," he said kindly, but I don't know that we were sharing it. He was the most alone person I had ever met.

One night after flying we drove back across the river to Manhattan and walked into the East Village for blintzes. We talked incessantly along the way, with me periodically interrupting myself to ask him the signs for things (*"How do you say squirrel? What about stereotype?"*) and him periodically grabbing my elbow to steer me clear of various obstacles (fire hydrants, oncoming traffic). I was not yet accustomed to conversing in sign language while walking on a crowded city sidewalk, and even after more experience it seemed as if he were forever rescuing me from crashing into things whenever we went out.

At supper Alec spoke a little of his former wife. He had been married for eleven years to a hearing woman from New Zealand. He had met her while managing a youth hostel over there and they had come to live in New York. Soon after the divorce she had gone back to her country. They had had no children. Alec rarely talked about it; I didn't ask. Something like 90 percent of marriages between deaf and hearing people end in divorce. That night in the restaurant he said he would think twice before marrying another hearing woman.

But so much of his life existed in the hearing world. He had left Lexington after five years and graduated from a hearing high school. Really bright deaf students were supposed to do that: mainstream, assimilate. At the time, Lexington was entirely oral, so he hadn't even learned to sign until he was in his twenties. He read voraciously, everything from Shakespeare to Kerouac to the *Bhagavad-Gita*. His college degrees were from a hearing university. And all of his fluency in English did nothing to help him fit in with the deaf community.

The first sign Alec ever taught me was *strong-deaf*. *"He's deaf,"* he signed, indicating an imaginary person off to his left, and then, pointing at an adjacent phantom, he repeated the sign with great emphasis.

"Ahh . . . you mean like the first person is just hard of hearing and the second is really very deaf?" I suggested.

He smiled and explained that it had nothing to do with degree of hearing ability; rather, it was about attitude, a measure of political and social involvement in the deaf community. *"If you want to learn ASL, you should know these cultural idioms,"* he advised. Then he showed me another, this one the antithesis of *strong-deaf*, the cultural equivalent of Uncle Tom: *think-hearing* — literally, one who thinks too much like a hearing person, functions too much in the hearing world.

This one I recognized immediately, because I had seen it said about Alec.

That hot night in Central Park, Alec did not make a wish. He turned to the interpreter. *"Call him over. Ask for a poem."*

"A poem?" She laughed.

"Just call him over. I know him."

The Wish Man was currently preoccupied with a sardine-and-cracker sandwich that one of the graduate students in our group had prepared for him, but he made his way rather unsteadily around the circle when summoned by the interpreter.

"He wants a poem," she said, pointing at Alec, who grinned up at the man and dropped his dollar into the basket. The graduate students hushed expectantly. The Wish Man looked at Alec for several seconds, then cleared his throat and launched into an original recitation, very loud and fast and furious, imbued with impressive sprays of saliva.

The interpreter made a valiant attempt to keep up with the lyrics — something about John Lennon, psychedelics, Superman, and hippies — but there were so many words to fingerspell and such erratic phrasing that she stumbled and made faces as the poem continued. Still, her hands pieced the verse together with a kind of lucid intelligence. Alec glanced up occasionally at the Wish Man, at his damp red face and meaty, gesticulating hands, then back at the interpreter. With a final moist wheeze the poem ended, and the students sort of mopped their brows and shook one another's hands and someone poured the Wish Man a drink.

Alec thanked the interpreter. I touched his sleeve and waited for him to turn. *"You said you know him?"*

"Not really."

"But how did you know to ask him for a poem?"

"Oh! I mean I always used to see him, growing up — he'd always be in the park. Sometimes here and sometimes down in Washington Square. He's an old city character."

We watched him wander off with his basket and cowbell and cup of wine.

Late that night, after the play, Alec and I waved the graduate students goodnight. We watched as they headed east out of the park. Then he and I went west, disappearing into the shadows of the night-bushes and reemerging on the street to hail a cab.

Two days earlier I had finally told Alec how I felt about him. With my mouth I had said, "I think about you a lot." I remember dimly noticing that my hands betrayed me, signing, *"I think about you all the time."*

We had been sitting on the hot trunk of his car, illegally parked near Washington Square, having just spent the day together and now about to part. It was that hour of the evening when all the buildings turn gilt and violet, blazing with ambient light. *"Is there music playing somewhere?"* Alec asked suddenly. A low-rider, stuck in traffic, shook the block with its pumped-up stereo, and the vibrations had caught Alec in the back of his legs. I pointed the car out to him.

He told me he was wary. W-A-R-Y. I broke the cardinal

rule and watched his fingers. They traveled toward me in the sign for *attraction*, circled away spelling *W-A-R-Y*, and hovered there a minute. I stole a glance at his face; he was squinting furiously into the throngs of Villagers, and I looked away to give him privacy. When he spoke again, it was to invite me back to his apartment.

Now, two nights later, we were headed there together for the second time. Warm black wind rolled in the open windows of the cab. It was too dark for talking; we sat apart.

"I still don't understand what made you go."

We were back to that again. I was being stubborn, Alec secretive. We were in his living room, sprawled in the late afternoon light, drinking glass after glass of cold tap water. Heat and hunger and hours of catching up had left me restless, and I'd gone back to pestering him for a better answer as to why he had done it.

We had not seen each other since *Twelfth Night;* it was now the end of August. He had returned from Lebanon two days before. After finishing up with his graduate students, he had flown to Cyprus. From there, in defiance of a prohibition against U.S. citizens traveling to Lebanon, he had sneaked into Beirut by boat and spent five days interviewing deaf Lebanese on videotape. He hadn't told anyone of his plan; not until he arrived safely back in New York did he explain where he had been.

"I wanted to speak with deaf people living in the war, to get their stories on camera —"

"Yes, yes, I know," I interrupted. *"You wanted to bring their stories back on film so that deaf people in this country could feel a real connection with their experiences. But I mean why — what* in you *made you want to go?"*

He stared intently at the carpet, which was as usual covered with a sea of papers and boxes and books, copies of periodicals for the deaf, precarious towers of travel brochures and investment brochures, tattered air letters, smatterings of foreign currency, ashtrays, socks, videocassettes, and maps.

"Was it because — Alec, was . . ." I knew he could see me signing from the corner of his eye, but he did not turn: a maddening habit. I had to reach across and touch him. *"Were you attracted to the danger, was that part of it?"*

"No." He looked away again, drank from his glass, rubbed his palm across his chin. He had not shaved since Lebanon. *"There's another reason, but I'm not comfortable discussing it with anyone right now,"* he said at last, and then, brightening, *"Tell me more about your plans."*

In the morning I was to drive seven hours upstate to the National Technical Institute for the Deaf, in Rochester. I had been offered an internship in the college's theater department; I hoped that a semester's immersion in an ASL environment would tip me over the edge into fluency. I wanted to become an interpreter.

"You already know about my plans. You know all I know." I was embarrassed to talk of my aspiration. I was afraid he would think me overconfident, or else one of those newly devout hearing people, pie-eyed over deafness, who seize on sign language like a new way of being. *"Do you — you must get so irritated talking with me."*

"What do you mean?"

"My signing. It's so awkward."

"Not at all." He looked at me as though I were mildly demented, and I realized at once how accustomed he was to communicating with hearing people who didn't even speak English, let alone sign language. Alec himself never used ASL with me outside our lessons, but rather a mixture of signs and spoken English, the latter being dominant. He barely voiced, but mouthed the words with a little breathy sound and signed along in English word order. When he wanted to use an English word that had no exact correlate in sign, he always simply fingerspelled the first letter of the English word as he pronounced it rather than signing a conceptual equivalent. Sometimes he signed whole sentences this way. It was like speaking only in acronyms, while I struggled to match the string of initials with the words he shaped on his lips.

Our language was neither English nor ASL. It fell somewhere along the spectrum that links the two. Later I would learn that this is not uncommon among deaf people, but in the beginning I was confused by it.

When I spoke with Alec, I did the opposite of what he did. Intent on signing every bit, I constantly modified the English phrases in my head to fit more neatly into signs. It wasn't until much later that I realized the folly of this. Alec's native language was English, as he was the first to proclaim, and he was perfectly capable of appreciating all the rich and subtle connotations of specific English word choices. While someone fluent in ASL could convey the same complex and finely nuanced message in sign language, I was certainly not this person. By so diligently packaging my thoughts into phrases that I could sign, I robbed them of their original value and presented Alec with badly watered-down versions, although he assured me that my signing was not tiresome. *"You seem very clear to me."* He drained his glass. *"Want to go for a walk?"*

We dressed our feet and went outside. Alec bought a carton of orange juice from the market across the street. It was not yet evening. People drank beer on their stoops.

As we strolled around the block, Alec's rubber thongs neatly smacking the hot sidewalk, I puzzled over his journey, over the aspect of it that he had decided to keep mysterious. He and his interview subjects had gotten on very well by exchanging bits of American and Lebanese signs; whatever communication barriers arose, the common bond of deafness overrode them. I thought: If my signing were better, I would know the perfect question to ask. I thought: If I were deaf, I would understand the part left unspoken. Or he would tell me.

Around the back of the block, a woman swept the patch

of concrete between her building and the sidewalk. Within the iron rail that protected her little garden grew a tree whose gnarled trunk branched quite low, with several limbs curving out from the crotch and twisting upward like a cupped hand. I stopped. The tree seemed small and large at the same time.

"Do you know the name of that kind of tree?" I asked the woman.

She leaned on her broom and looked up into it. "Sure, it's a tree of heaven."

Alec turned to me with his nose and brow bunched inquisitively.

"She said the tree is called a tree of — what's the sign for H-E-A-V-E-N?"

He put the brown paper bag with the orange juice between his knees and, clenching it there, showed me the two-handed sign for heaven. Palms down, his hands rose one over the other until they split apart and made an opening.

"Do that again," I demanded. He obliged, the bag going back between his legs, his hands again churning upward and separating.

"Okay?" he asked.

"Okay."

He retrieved the bag a second time and we nodded good evening to the sweeper and continued down the block. In front of the second-to-last building, a woman in a housecoat watched our approach. As we neared, she leaned out over the railing and beamed coyly at Alec. "That was cute, the thing you did back there with the bag."

I started to tell Alec what she had said, but judging from the blush spreading across his face, he had read her lips accurately.

"You could have handed the bag to me," I told him as we kept walking.

He deadpanned back, *"It's part of the sign."*

I didn't understand immediately. It took my brain a few

seconds to make sense of his language, and in this interval Alec might have apprehended a polite, desperately blank expression working across my face. By the time I got it, and laughed, he had turned away.

Sitting in a Burger King on upper Broadway, Alec asked, *"Did I ever tell you the story of Abraham and Isaac?"*

"I'm not sure," I said, although this was untrue.

He had told me the Bible story only a few months earlier, just after getting back from Lebanon. I had been idly surveying a scramble of documents on the floor near my feet when I spied a little navy blue book stamped with gold. *"May I?"* I asked, plucking it from the heap, and *"Go ahead,"* he had said, shrugging. I flipped the passport open to his picture and read beside it, "Alec Abraham Isaac Naiman."

"That's quite a name you've got there," I said. *"That's really your name?"*

He nodded and put out his cigarette. *"Do you know the story, in the Bible, about them?"*

"Yeah," I said. *"How does it go again?"*

So he had told me how Abraham heard a voice claiming to be God. This voice commanded him to take his youngest son, Isaac, to the top of the mountain and sacrifice him. Abraham, who loved his son, did as he was bidden. He took him to the top of the mountain and raised his knife to slit Isaac's throat. Just then an angel came and stayed his arm; Abraham had proven his faith and Isaac was spared.

But, said Alec, the point is, how do we know it was really God talking? How do we know Abraham wasn't hearing voices? He might have been insane. The angel might simply have been Abraham changing his mind, or coming to his senses.

I pressed his passport to my chin and peered at him doubtfully. *"That's really the point, in the original story? How it's meant in the Bible?"*

He looked surprised. *"That's how I've always interpreted it."*

We eyed each other, puzzled. I had thought the story of Abraham was intended as a model, a perfect example of absolute faith. To Alec, it was a cautionary tale: be suspicious of that which cannot be verified. Do not trust unseen voices.

I let his passport fall back to the carpet.

He told me the story again a few months later, across an orange plastic table in that crowded fast-food joint. I was down for a weekend from my internship at NTID. We seemed destined to do this: keep catching up with each other during those brief times when we overlapped in the same city. In a way, it was best. Alec did not want anyone to know we were involved. The deaf community is small, as people say, and news travels almost impossibly fast within it.

Even later that year, when I moved back to New York and we saw each other more frequently, we stayed inside almost exclusively, making little forays for Chinese food and videos. During these expeditions, I was terribly conscious of not speaking for Alec. I found that if salespeople realized I was hearing, they would direct everything to me, addressing Alec in the third person and expecting me to speak for him. My initial solution was not to talk at all, just hang back and let Alec handle everything. Sometimes he had to repeat himself two or three times, but he always made himself understood.

I realized, however, that in relinquishing my own voice, I had chosen a subordinate position. It seemed dishonest, as well. So I began speaking for myself, and occasionally, when a cashier shot a beseeching glance at me, I piped up for Alec. I tried to do it swiftly, unobtrusively. Sometimes he would whip around and watch my lips, checking that I got his message right.

The rest of the time we spent in his apartment. Only the security guard knew. The signaling device that should have linked the downstairs buzzer to a light bulb in Alec's apartment was perpetually broken, so I had to go through a little routine with the guard each time I visited. "Remember me from last time?" I would ask. "The person I'm visiting is deaf? He can't hear the buzzer?"

"Oh, yeah. He know you're coming?" the guard would ask.

Alec and I would have just spoken on the TTY, capital letters marching stiffly across a strip of black screen, electric blue words glowing like the numbers on a digital clock. It always thrilled me how Alec could make those messages tease and flirt, pause for comic timing, twist into grins and grimaces and pensive sighs, even once sing me happy birthday. "Yes, he's expecting me," I would reply.

The guard would nod and sometimes keep me waiting a minute while he studied me. "You can do that sign language, right? That's cool. I saw some a that on *Sesame Street*. He your boyfriend? How'd you learn that?" When he was satisfied, he would press a button behind the counter, letting me through the glass doors.

Up in Alec's apartment I felt folded into a world as separate and private as if we were in the airplane. Hours of talking with him left me not with a memory of actual words and phrases so much as with an indelible, dreamlike sense of what we had discussed. They also left me exhausted. Talking with him, engaging with him in this peculiar blend of the physical and the cerebral, required deep concentration.

If our hands were busy, we couldn't talk. If the lights were out, we couldn't talk. If we were not facing each other, we couldn't talk. And so I learned to be more alert, to listen with my peripheral vision and the back of my neck, to respond to a glimpse of motion, a shift of weight. To get my attention, Alec might sign on my body instead of his. *"What are you thinking?"* he would ask, his finger on my temple. There were times when I could not get his attention; if he chose not to look, I was effectively silenced.

Once, while making an earnest point in the middle of a debate, I caught him staring at me with an inscrutable smile. He lolled against the end of the couch, propped on one elbow, and although watching me intently, he clearly was paying no attention to what I was saying.

"What!?" I demanded, quite annoyed.

Unruffled, he continued to smile. *"I was just thinking,"* he mused, *"that your signing is looking so natural, like a deaf person's."*

I melted.

But no matter how good my signing got, it wasn't enough to dissolve the boundary between us. Alec was beginning to align himself more strongly with the deaf community. He collected shelves of books and videotapes on ASL, deaf history, deaf politics, deaf culture. He talked interestedly about the movement in the 1850s to establish a separate deaf state in the western part of the United States. He talked about the patronizing attitudes of the hearing community, about the dearth of deaf teachers and role models in schools for the deaf, about hearing parents who deprive their deaf children of exposure to deaf adults.

I knew what was coming that day when Alec repeated the story of Abraham and Isaac in the grease-laden air of that Burger King. I let him repeat the story even though I had heard it before. I listened keenly to the way he told it, to the slant, hoping to decipher something new, a deeper shade of meaning — some elemental clue as to the difference between us, why it wouldn't last.

As the story unraveled, I became aware of a short man in an army jacket weaving among the tables with a sort of thick-shoed shuffle, silently proffering small yellow cards. A few people gave him money, which he accepted with a glassy nod. Eventually he reached our table and placed a card on Alec's tray. It was printed with the manual alphabet and read, "Learn the Language of Deaf-Mutes."

Alec had been talking in his most Englishy fashion, blending speech with fingerspelled initials. Like many profoundly deaf adults, he never wore a hearing aid; it was likely that the man assumed he was hearing. Without interrupting his story or looking up, Alec handed the card back and dismissed the man coldly. I blushed and ducked my head, jabbing at my milkshake with my straw. The man hitched up his pants and moved on.

Deaf organizations and their leaders have waged a battle against deaf peddlers at least since the end of World War II, when the National Association of the Deaf established a Committee for the Suppression of Peddling. They believe that the image of the peddler exchanging alphabet cards for donations perpetuates the worst stereotypes about deaf people: they can't communicate; they can't hold jobs; they are simple, stupid, seamy, incapable of moral reasoning.

I thought Alec's behavior was rude and condescending, and I was ashamed. But when I looked up, the scene had shifted. Glancing away from Alec for a sliver of a moment, I registered something else. A group of teenage girls were getting up from a nearby table, laughing. As they dumped their trays, I saw a yellow alphabet card flutter to the floor. And I understood that most people there would carry home with them that day the impression of only one deaf man, and I understood that it wouldn't be this one sitting across from me.

15

Light after Dark

It is 5:45 in the morning and the junior class is gathered near the student entrance, inside the bus room, eating Dunkin Munchkins from a large cardboard carry-out box. They have left their sleeping bags and knapsacks in the lobby, piled haphazardly against one wall in anticipation of the chartered bus. The large-paned windows reflect the vaporous shapes of sleepy teenagers. It is far too early for all this confectioner's sugar, all this cinnamon and honeyglazed chocolate; the students seem united in delicious conspiracy, the doughnuts and orange juice fueling their buzz of excitement.

Sofia, licking her fingers, notices how many of her classmates have dressed in sweatshirts emblazoned with various Lexington insignia. She goes into the hall and digs through the pile of luggage until she locates her own bag, from which she wrestles her navy blue Lexington Volleyball 1991 Champions sweatshirt. This she exchanges for the pale raspberry sweater she put on earlier. Then she loosens her hair from its scrunchie, lets it tumble down her back: an older look. By noon today, she will be facing her possible future.

Each spring, Lexington's social studies department takes the junior class on a two-day field trip to Washington, D.C. Ostensibly, the trip's purpose is to enliven the eleventh-grade curriculum — U.S. history — with visits to an impressive array of government buildings, museums, and memorials. But for many of the students, that purpose is eclipsed by another, more personal interest: the agenda includes a visit to Gallaudet University. Their overnight accommodations will be right there on campus, albeit not in the college dorms but with the high school students who live up the hill, at the Model Secondary School for the Deaf.

The Lexington kids can hardly be faulted if the allures of the Capitol, the White House, and the Supreme Court pale beside the thought of staying overnight at Gallaudet. More than just the home of the world's only liberal arts college for deaf people, more too than the home of MSSD and the Kendall Demonstration School, which educate deaf children from around the country, Gallaudet is the epicenter of deaf power and deaf pride.

It is also the place where Sofia hopes to continue her studies after Lexington. She slides the scrunchie up on her wrist and zips her bag shut. Outside the student entrance the sky is going pearly gray, and now a teacher comes swinging through the lobby door: *"The bus is here! Tell everyone to come."*

They filter out to the parking lot, shove their bags inside the gaping, lit holds of the bus, and climb aboard. This year's junior class is small — only twenty-three students to begin with, four of whom can't make the trip — so there is plenty of room, and they stake out territory, exploring the little toilet and the overhead storage compartments, playing with the individual lights and air vents over each seat, claiming spots toward the rear portion of the coach. Here in the dark, homely neighborhood of Jackson Heights, the interior lights give the bus an officious, alien glow: it might be a space capsule, about to propel the students into a foreign zone. They sink into gray and burgundy plush, use the arm levers to tilt themselves back.

A figure intrudes at the front of the bus, tall and dark-suited, stooping a little as he travels partway down the aisle. It's *Cohen,* as they tell each other, reaching around to shake the shoulders of classmates who did not see him come aboard: *"Hey, look, pay attention, it's Cohen."* In the back, they press fists into cushions, elevating themselves, and crane their necks to see over the high backs of the seats.

"Have a great trip," Oscar says slowly, having arrived early at work and come to see them off. He pauses, takes in the students, and smiles at their damp hair and scrubbed faces, on which excitement wrestles with sleepiness. They watch him attentively, patiently. He has nothing in particular to impart, but feels a sudden warmth, a sorrow almost, at how grown-up they look. *"Say hello to the president for me,"* he says. They laugh. They tell him, *"Okay. We will."*

When Oscar leaves, the teachers, seven of them, board the bus and pass out shiny blue-and-white folders. Inside, the students find stapled trip booklets with maps and schedules and, naturally, homework questions. They glance over the folders perfunctorily, then jam them between the seat cushions. At 6:15, when the eastern rooftops are all touched by a thin yellow glow, the bus rolls imperiously from the lot, leaving Lexington behind.

The travelers have arranged themselves along certain definite lines. The hearing teachers sit up front, along with a handful of students from the lower academic grouping. The rest of the students, Sofia and her crowd, spread across the back of the bus. The single deaf teacher, Janie Moran, sits smack in the middle.

Another way of identifying the subdivisions is by language. Those in the back of the bus use ASL, or rather, they do not use it so much as revel in it, sass and tease and fool in it, flick it over the backs of their seats and around the corners. Just as each generation of hearing kids invents its own vernacular, the Lex kids use a particularly teenage brand of ASL, encoded with slang signs. Even those students with strong speech skills cast off their English here. They kneel, sit backward, dangle across the aisle, contort and bend their bodies in every way to see the conversation. Secrets they sign at the hip, or conceal beneath a jacket or behind someone's back. Jokes they deliver standing up; still, someone invariably cannot see the whole thing, and seatmates copy-sign the missing components for each other.

Those in the front of the bus do not know ASL. The hearing teachers know various amounts of sign language, but they could neither express themselves in nor fully understand the language being used so rapidly in the back of the bus. The four students who sit up front do not know ASL either. They communicate with signs, but without the fluency, the grammatical structure, or the extensive vocabulary of their classmates. They are what used to be called "low-verbal" or "low-functioning." Once people would have said they had "minimal language skills," but now, largely owing to the efforts of deaf activists, these phrases have become archaic and are on their way to being rendered obsolete, with the likes of such offensive labels as "deaf-mute" and "deaf and dumb."

Now, within Lexington, these students are called "six-one-one," a descriptive term that refers to state-mandated special education ratios for instructional grouping. Based on their Individualized Education Plans (IEPs), no more than six of these students may be grouped in a classroom, and that classroom must be staffed by at least one teacher and one instructional assistant (as opposed to the students in the back of the bus, whose IEPs designate them as twelve-one-one or twelve-one).

Two decades ago, Lexington broadened its curriculum so that it could accept deaf children with multiple handicaps, learning disabilities, and serious emotional disturbances. In 1974 it started the Secondary Individualized Learning Center (SILC). The program was housed in a part of the building separate from the regular high school, and grew to account for about a quarter of the total enrollment before it was dissolved in 1990 and its students were incorporated into the rest of the high school. Now, although about two dozen students continue to be educated separately in self-contained classes, the rest of the former SILC students have been integrated educationally and socially with the other students.

Of course, the students themselves know who is who. Now, instead of saying, *"He's a SILC kid"* by way of explanation for some out-of-kilter behavior or inability to comprehend, they'll say, *"He's six-one-one."* Most of the students have no idea what "six-one-one" literally refers to, but the implication is clear. They tilt their heads, squint their eyes in a pinched sort of apology, and mean this: *He's low-functioning. You can't really communicate with him.*

They say it not unkindly. Even in the throes of adolescence, as preoccupied as they may be with trying out their own forms of expression, fighting their own battles to be understood — not only by parents, teachers, and other authority figures but by hearing people in general — they are not without compassion and do not intentionally ostracize these students. Some of them will even step in to interpret when they notice a communication breakdown; they will piece together meaning from a classmate's signs, rephrase it in more familiar syntax for the teacher, and relay the teacher's answer back, converting it into simple signs or even gestures.

ASL is not a gestural or iconographic language any more than English is an onomatopoeic one. But sometimes mime and gestures are used with people who are fluent in neither a spoken nor a signed language. Within the field of interpreting, some deaf professionals specialize in facilitating just this sort of communication, between deaf people who have no complete language system and hearing interpreters who know ASL but do not possess the cultural background to operate in this languageless zone. Many Lexington kids, particularly the more agile code-switchers, will intercede in this way — and very sweetly too, without giving the impression that they are acting out of any but the most basic human decency. After all, each of these students knows what it's like not to be understood; any opportunity to alleviate misunderstandings is embraced as a matter of course. Still, given a choice, they would rather socialize with people fluent in their language, and on the bus they naturally gravitate together.

It is Janie Moran, stationed midway, who evinces final proof that language, more than either deaf/hearing status or teacher/student status, is the predominant factor in the way the travelers have dispersed themselves. Although part of the time she converses with another teacher, sitting across the aisle, she is the sole staff member who mingles with the ASL crowd at the back of the bus. They adore her.

She is one of only three deaf teachers in Lexington's high school, and the closest in age to the students. The course she has recently charted holds great appeal for many of them. Before getting her master's degree in social studies education from Columbia University, Janie was an undergraduate at Gallaudet, where she participated in the historic campus takeover. Before that she was a Lex student. Old yearbook photos show her looking just the same, with straight dark hair and round, florid cheeks, her expression a mixture of shyness and faint rebelliousness. She was a leader in student government and a star athlete; she even qualified for the Deaf Olympics the year they were held in Los Angeles. There's a picture of her in Oscar's office, posing with a volleyball in front of the five famous interlocking rings.

Janie is a heroine, smart and successful and ASL. When used as an adjective, ASL implies more than just fluency; it connotes an entire outlook, almost an ideology. To the students, it means this: Janie always understands them the first time. Her meaning is always clear. She teaches in ASL, doesn't use her voice, and doesn't wear a hearing aid. In fact, when she was a high school student at Lexington, she refused to wear her aids; if a teacher insisted, she stuck them in her ears but kept them switched off. She was suspended twice, once for cursing in speech class and once for scrawling on the back of the speech room door a common and vulgar suggestion about what the speech teacher might care to do to herself.

Sofia and the others have not heard these stories, but they understand empirically who Janie is: a strong, signing deaf woman. They treat her with a mixture of deference and horseplay — deference because of their respect for her as a teacher, coach, role model, and adviser to their chapter of the Junior National Association of the Deaf; horseplay as a kind of flirtation, an expression of their affection and desire to be close to her. On the bus, they engage her in conversation both silly and serious, repeatedly steal and hide her jacket, even borrow one of her sneakers — something to do with a game of Truth or Dare (Janie elevates one eyebrow, decides against specific inquiries, and relinquishes the shoe with a wry shrug).

Eventually they hit the highway; the rhythm of the bus works its spell and the students begin to doze. When they wake up, farms are skimming past the windows. They look quiet, unpeopled, their silos and fences solemnly upright against a pale sky. Sofia gazes out the window, gazes at the American land, receding, gentle and sober; even spring seems grave in this expanse.

Tamara, her seatmate, stretches awake and inadvertently sticks an elbow into Sofia's arm. Sofia protests and they pretend to bicker for a moment, then Tamara totters back to the toilet, after Sofia, in hilariously graphic ASL, advises against it with the prediction that the movement of the vehicle will cause water to slosh up on Tamara's bottom. Janie and a student are playing chess in the aisle, crouched intently over the pieces, which jiggle on the gameboard. Everyone is waking up hungry. The doughnuts, after all, were three states ago; they don't count.

At nine-fifteen the bus pulls into a rest stop in Maryland. The students and teachers scatter around the building, dodging into bathrooms, the gift shop, various sections of the food court. Sofia orders breakfast at Burger King, pays the cashier, and steps aside. It is the sort of fast-food line where the customers are issued receipts with numbers; the number is called when the food is ready and bagged. Sofia's number is pale on the slip, barely legible, and while she studies the faint ink, she misses the fact that they are calling out not numbers but food items. So her breakfast sits on the counter in a white wax-paper bag, unclaimed, as Sofia continues to watch the lips of the server, on the lookout for her number.

It is the cute hearing boy behind her in the line — boy or man, she can't quite decide — who taps her shoulder and says, "Did you have the bagel and cream cheese?" and directs her to her bag. She thanks him and blushes, because he's smiling very nicely at her, and then she joins Tamara at the condiments bar, where she pours a miniature bucket of half-and-half into her coffee and wonders what the difference is between sugar and Sweet 'N Low — one of those details she would certainly have picked up by now if she were hearing. She dumps a packet and stirs and spills and mops the spill, Tamara urging all the while, *"Come on, come on! The bus!"*

They are subjected to a short scolding for being the last ones to reboard, but they barely feel it, sipping coffee on a chartered bus, rolling south on a spring morning, knowing that tonight they'll be sleeping at Gallaudet.

Since they have an hour still to ride, Janie comes back and organizes a game. It's one most of the students know already, having played it before with kids from other deaf schools when they've stayed overnight for athletic tournaments. They split into two teams of eight and face each other, kneeling on the seats or standing wedged among them. There are three possible ways to stand: like a deer, with hands up for antlers; like a hunter, with hands out for guns; and like a person, with hands pressed down in a neutral position.

Each team confers for about two seconds, signing low behind a seat back, and picks one of the three. At the referee's signal, each team snaps into its role. Hunter wins over deer, deer over person, and person over hunter. It's silly, fast-paced, and entirely visual — no English necessary, only heightened camaraderie, the ability to respond instantly as a group. Janie plays among them, easily crossing the usual teacher-student boundary. Thumbs to temples, she stands like a deer, forfeiting not a shred of authority. Regular shrieks of laughter rip from the back of the bus, and the hearing teachers look around, amused and perplexed.

As if of its own volition, the game changes. The teams metamorphose into a single staggered circle. The students stand roughly shoulder to shoulder, knocking and swaying together, and each person picks a country. A rhythm is established, lilting and quick. Thirty-two eyes, keen and bright, rove around the ring as the players send their signs around, calling on each other: *"Germany to Italy . . . Italy to France . . . France to Poland . . . Poland to the Dominican Republic . . ."* Whoever interrupts the rhythm is eliminated, and the students are gleefully exacting: *"No way, you signed Poland on your chin, that's wrong . . . You did France up by your forehead; sit down."* They whittle the circle down to a champ, then get to their feet and play again, this time with animals instead of countries, and then with colors, and then with foods (*"Spaghetti to orange . . . orange to egg . . . egg to soda . . . soda to potato . . ."*).

Sofia gets to laughing so hard her eyes water. Crimson seeps across her cheeks and her breath comes out in high, helpless snuffles. As her shoulders shake with merriment, she inclines her head toward her knuckles in order to obscure her face. She tries to stifle the sound, tries to come from behind the mirth and swallow the laugh, seal off the feeling in her chest. It's force of habit. Many deaf people have been told all their lives, by hearing relatives and teachers, to rein in their laughter, that it sounds strange, ugly. Even when spared verbal reprimand, they are accustomed to being sent quick, disgusted looks. In this way, they come to understand that hearing people monitor their own laughs, adjust their muscles to make the sound come out in a certain acceptable way. And laughter becomes one more luxury that hearing people control.

"*Soda to potato . . . potato to chicken . . . chicken to gum . . . gum to milk . . .*" Hands are tensed, poised, all eyes trained on the signal being passed, and when Sofia messes up on *milk*, she yelps, rolls her eyes, and joins the ranks of her friends who are already out.

They lean over the backs of seats and watch the harried proceedings of those still competing. All of them are giggling now, it's all right: everyone here is deaf. They release their breath in natural, tumbling explosions. In this place, there is no one to hear the sound. Each one is entitled to laughter, free from reproach.

The Lexington students arrive at Gallaudet shortly before noon. They leave their jackets on the bus and step down into a mild wind. Magnolia buds, swollen fat and half cracked open, stud the trees with pink; the dogwoods have put out their white saucer blossoms; the grass smells like sugar. There are few people around, since classes are in session, but those they do encounter — professors on the footpath, staff members in the visitor's center — are all signing.

In the visitor's center they encounter an exhibit about deaf people and the Holocaust. Sofia falls behind the group. She walks close to the wall, studying the documents and photographs. One poster shows a simple figure forming three signs, *Force Can't Baby,* and beneath that, in English, "Forced Sterilization." Sofia bends her neck to read the accompanying document mounted above her on the wall. It is a letter, translated into English, addressed to deaf Protestants of the Third Reich, explaining why deaf people must not question forced sterilization but submit to it for the improvement of the race.

For Sofia, who breathes a little patch of mist on the glass, her jaw set, her eyes steady and very dark as she reads, the letter strikes several chords at once — her own experiences with anti-Semitism, the discrimination she has experienced as a deaf person, and, most jarringly, the connection between the Nazis' efforts to prevent the birth of deaf babies and her own parents' decision not to risk having another deaf child. The sum of this knowledge is disturbing and oddly stimulating at the same time. Already, between deaf studies class and the gentle probing she has done at home, Sofia is coming to know her own story in broader contexts and on deeper levels. If she goes away to college, her understanding will expand even more. She can feel how new information will separate her from her family even as it defines her more clearly.

When she goes, if she goes, her whole picture of herself will be altered against this new backdrop: a college campus, a place of learning, populated by culturally deaf adults. Her personal history will be recast in relation to theirs; it will intersect with others past and present, fall within a grid of common histories, a scaffold on which she could stand, on which she could put her weight. And it would hold her up.

The idea is so large and heady it makes her feel suddenly wild to think it. Sofia scrambles after the others, catching up as they head out into the lilting noonday breeze and across the quad. They enter a large, sprawling building, which seems designed for them, expressly tailored to deaf people's needs. A great section of the second story, up next to the snack bar, has been cut away, creating a kind of wide circular balcony above the pit of a first-floor lounge, so that students can spot each other and converse easily across the levels. Everywhere, sight lines are open. The Lexington group skirts the perimeter of the lounge and enters the campus bookstore; there is just enough time to shop before lunch.

"We should get that for the school store," says Sheema, tapping a fingernail on a display case. She and Sofia appraise the merchandise with entrepreneurial interest. Beneath her clicking nail, an assortment of ASL jewelry sparkles on a narrow glass shelf: tiny gold and silver hands molded into the hand shapes for *I Love You* and *Friendship*, attached to posts for pierced ears or with little loops soldered on so they can be worn around the neck as charms, or with backings for brooches or tieclips or cufflinks.

Tamara, standing farther along the counter, breathes on the glass, then wipes the fog with the side of her fist. *"Look at these,"* she tells them, surveying rows of bookmarks, ink stamps, key chains, all cut with the same ASL hand shapes. Displayed on a lower shelf are flashers that can be attached to a doorbell or telephone ringer, and the latest, sleekest, portable TTYs (or telecommunication devices for the deaf, TDDs, as these trimmer models are properly called). There are travel alarm clocks that vibrate instead of beep and can be slipped beneath a pillow. (A long time ago, the students have heard — the story may be apocryphal, but they like it just the same — deaf people depended on a more organic alarm clock: if they wanted to rise from bed at a particular hour, they simply drank the commensurate amount of water immediately before retiring.) There are even baby criers, which are attached to a crib and trigger a light in the parents' room when the infant wails. (Not very long ago, deaf parents rigged string from crib slats to their own toes and relied on the transmitted vibrations to know when their babies were stirring.)

Behind them, one of the six-one-one boys is asking another student to explain something. *"What does this say?"* he wants to know, holding out a baseball cap and gliding his finger gently across the embroidery above the bill.

"Gallaudet," she tells him. Even though it's a proper noun, the university's name-sign is uniform with deaf people across the country, a standard part of the ASL lexicon.

"Ohhh . . ." The student has a large face with an easy, rounded jaw, which now drifts open. He looks at the racks and racks of college sweatshirts, T-shirts, boxer shorts, jackets, sweaters. *"All of those say the same thing . . ."* He is just now realizing where they are.

Some of their other classmates have paused outside the

store to read the bulletin board: "Hearing Ear Dog Class Beginning"; "Sign Up for English Tutoring Now"; "Used Vibrator on Sale, Cheap." This last item might raise eyebrows at a hearing college; here, within the context of the environment, it is understood to mean a tactile signaling device. Other classmates are already standing in line at the checkout counter, confident that whatever souvenirs may beckon from gift shops during their forthcoming museum visits, nothing will top what they have found here.

The Gallaudet bookstore has everything. Besides the jewelry and the hi-tech assistive devices there are the books: books on deaf culture, on sign language (American and international), and on deaf educational and sociological issues; literature by and about deaf people; picture books for deaf children. Posters and bumper stickers carry such slogans as "Deaf people can do anything except hear." The stock seems thrilling testimony to just how deaf-oriented the campus really is.

Now the teachers are rounding up the Lex kids and herding them out of the bookstore and upstairs to the snack bar for lunch. Sofia has heard that everyone who works at Gallaudet must know some sign language, and it's true: the hearing people behind the food line all seem able to use some. The students purchase burgers, pizza, and french fries, pump little swamps of ketchup onto their plates, and find a cluster of tables unoccupied by college students. Over their lunch tables, a couple of mounted television sets broadcast soap operas. Nobody pays them any notice until the commercials come on. Almost all of these bear closed captions, and their white block letters draw gazes upward.

As the students eat, they busily point out people they know: this one graduated from Lexington two years ago, and this one's sister is on the basketball team at the American School for the Deaf, in Hartford, and this one was at that party at the international deaf club in Brighton Beach. Sofia even recognizes another Russian immigrant, Eugenia, a young woman who graduated from Lexington a few years ago. Eugenia's mother is the one who told Sofia's mother about Lexington. Gallaudet attracts students, professors, and researchers from all over the world, but the community is so intimate that within five minutes of sitting down, Sofia has had three people she knows stop by her table to say hello.

After lunch, the students pile back into the bus and go dutifully tramping around Washington. Two o'clock is the Capitol building; three o'clock, the Supreme Court; three-thirty, the Library of Congress; four o'clock, the American History Museum; five-thirty, the Lincoln Memorial. At this last stop, while the students clamber up the steps, Janie sits by the Reflecting Pool. The weather has been very fine all day; now, with the sun easing down, the air turns suddenly blue and bracing, the stone steps cool beneath her.

All day long it has been Janie who has engaged the students, Janie who has most consistently informed and taught, who told them as they advanced on the Capitol that when a green light shines in the dome, it signifies that Congress is working on an issue of great importance; Janie who continued to talk with them when they were stuck in traffic, sharing an old Irish superstition that was part of her childhood, recapitulating details of her involvement in the Deaf President Now movement, dispensing trivia about the workings of the nation's capital; Janie who pointed out landmarks from the bus. She has been constantly reorienting the students, giving them their bearings. Now, while she sits by the pool, resting her eyes on the coppery water, choppy now with an evening breeze, students come to stand by her.

"Was it here that Martin Luther King spoke, or at the Jefferson Memorial?" one boy asks.

Janie points out the spot from which Dr. King made his "I Have a Dream" speech. *"Why do you think he spoke here?"* she asks the student.

"Because Lincoln had a role in ending slavery."

She nods, satisfied; he has made the connection.

Other students drift over; they have just come from the

Vietnam Memorial, where they saw someone holding a sheet of paper against the wall and drawing on it. *"What was he doing?"* the students want to know. Janie explains that he must have been making a rubbing of someone's name — a brother or a father or perhaps a friend who died in the war.

More students gather on the steps around her. They hug their arms around their waists and position themselves so they can see her sign. They bring her no specific questions, but having spied the congregation, having seen Janie dispensing information, they have wandered over, always hungry for more. Sofia sits on a lower step, holding her hair out of her eyes with one hand and regarding her teacher.

In class, Janie is drill-sergeant tough. Her signing takes up the entire space in front of the board, where her strong hands illuminate concepts, structuring each one with logic and clarity. Any attempt at side conversations (which students carry on in blithe silence in many hearing teachers' classrooms) is thwarted instantly and emphatically, by Janie's kicking a table leg or slapping her palm on the offending party's notebook. One moment she is pulling up a chair and sitting among them; the next she has materialized across the room to whip down one of the roll-up maps or indicate a point on the time line that curves around two walls.

Squinting into the wind, anchoring her hair at the back of her neck, Sofia looks up at Janie, who is signing against the backdrop of all those white steps and pillars, talking about presidents and amendments, looking a bit tired but utterly comfortable and knowledgeable. Once, in Russia, Sofia thought she might grow up to be a seamstress or a factory worker. Then, in America, she began to set her sights on becoming a lawyer. But now, just lately, she has been thinking perhaps she will be a social studies teacher.

That night, when Sofia lies burrowed inside her sleeping bag in a dorm lounge at MSSD, she thinks of the college that lies so close, somewhere in the darkness on the other side of the hill. She thinks how this environment could belong to her, *does* belong to her. And her excitement turns to guilt. This time tomorrow she will be back in Rego Park, at her real home. She knows it's her real home. She knows that. But it dawns on her now, in a bittersweet rush of guilt and relief, that she will not let her family prevent her from going to Gallaudet.

They will have to let her go. They will have to understand, and let her learn about her cultural family, and trust that she will not forget her biological one. She can love both. It is her right to love both.

Up here in the dorm lounge, a lamp still burns, but it does not bother Sofia. At her old school in Leningrad, the light switches were outside the bedrooms, and at a certain time each night the dorm matron would sweep down the hallways, aborting conversations as she brought darkness to each room. Now Sofia is dimly aware of mattresses all around her, bathed in light. Like a fleet of rafts, they support her classmates, some floating into sleep, others propped on elbows, still awake, still talking.

16

Interpreting

During the short time that I worked as a freelance interpreter, it got so all I loved every day was the commute: the D train, most mornings, across the East River, the waves looking as if they were hammered out of sheet metal, the barges, the abandoned cars under the highway, the sun pulsing through the girders with such force that I had to lift my head from the pages of my book. Or at night, riding back to Brooklyn wedged between a man in a trenchcoat smelling of snow and pickle and a couple of women speaking Russian, each consecutive uptown bridge arched and lit like angel wings — in these moments alone I felt present, corporeal. The rest of the time I spent submerged in the lives of others, hollowed out so that I could cleanly conduct their messages.

Those were lonely months — really, I worked solely as a freelancer for only two months, but they have swollen in my memory to consume an immeasurable, nebulous mass of time. I seemed to be always in motion that winter, shuttling by train and bus around the boroughs with my paperback, my crossword puzzle, my appointment book, bound into a kind of requisite solitude by the interpreters' code of ethics. In scores of rooms I removed my coat, spoke and signed other people's words for them, put the coat back on, fished for a subway token, and headed to the next job, never having given my name or shaken hands: less a person than an instrument.

Interpreting was something I had dreamed of doing ever since I had learned there was such a job. When I was small and lived at Lexington, I had relatively little exposure to interpreters. The only professional ones I ever came into contact with were those who appeared infrequently on TV, framed in floating ovals in a corner of the screen. At Lexington, whenever a situation that called for an interpreter arose, a staff member would volunteer to step in informally — usually someone like my father, a hearing person who had grown up with deaf parents in a signing household. Interpreting took the form of incidental asides, and was so unobtrusive as to be unnoticeable.

In those days, interpreting was still barely recognized as a profession. Although the Registry of Interpreters for the Deaf (RID) was first proposed in 1964, it did not begin certifying interpreters until 1972. Even then, the idea of treating interpreting as a profession caught on gradually. Until 1972, no official standards or code of ethics had ever existed; few interpreters ever received remuneration for their work, and the quality of service varied dramatically from interpreter to interpreter.

All of this constituted a grave disservice to deaf people. The lack of professional standards not only led to many incompetent people performing as interpreters, it also helped perpetuate several stereotypes among hearing people, chiefly that sign language could be picked up easily, that it was therefore a simplistic, primitive language, and that deaf people who signed were limited in their ability to comprehend and express abstract thoughts. Never mind that the interpreter may not understand the deaf person's sophisticated use of ASL; never mind that the interpreter may not be experienced enough as a signer to convey the subtleties of the spoken English message. Almost always, when an interpreter does a poor job, either by voicing a deaf person's signs in muddled or simplified language or by rendering a hearing person's speech in unintelligible signs, it is the deaf person who comes off looking a bit slow, a trifle dull in intellect.

It is no coincidence that RID came into being around the same time that researchers were first lauding ASL as a legitimate language and that deaf people were beginning to view themselves as a minority group with a civil rights agenda. Interpreters play a significant role in how the hearing world perceives deaf people. The professionalization of the field of interpreting translates into increased credibility and respect for deaf individuals as well as their political agenda.

I neither knew nor cared about any of this when, at age thirteen, I encountered my first live interpreter. It was during a ceremony where my grandfather was to be posthumously honored, along with a few other hall-of-famers, by the Eastern States Athletic Association of the Deaf. In front of the podium, in a straight-backed chair, sat a woman in a silk blouse the color of pine trees. She interpreted the first speaker's speech into sign language. Her hands were a bit plump, luminous against the shiny green. She had a great mass of hair like dark curly noodles and eyes ringed with lashes like punctuation marks, and everything about her was energetic. She was like a synapse, with impulses firing across her body.

I could not follow what she said, although I did recognize a few of the signs, nor was I particularly interested in the content of the man's speech. It was the picture of her sitting there, creating a juncture where two languages converged; it was the dance of white against green, her movements laden with meaning; it was her ability to join, the way she was drawing together all the people in the room, that we each might know exactly the same things as the others.

For a moment my skin felt taut under a queer kind of pressure and I understood that nothing in the room — not the chandelier nor the sherbet melting in the cup before me nor even the speeches paying tribute to the honorees — was any finer than this act of joining. And as I watched, the image slid in past my intellect and lodged itself somewhere deeper. Like storytelling, that incessant loving rush of explaining and repositioning and telling again, all for the sake of finding something shared, something mutually recognized — so interpreting seemed to me. It seemed a kind of goodness.

Then something went awry. Perhaps the interpreter was only in training. At any rate, she could not have been very experienced, for although the presenter's speech was not esoteric or hurried or cluttered with awkward phrasing, and it did not pursue illogical tangents — all potential pitfalls for many good interpreters — she began to fall behind the speaker, and as she did she grew flustered, and as she grew flustered her signs grew stammering and halting. Before long it became clear that she was no longer providing even a rough-hewn interpretation of the speech.

I felt for her then, as she went from being an instrument of understanding to a mute block, an impediment responsible for a communication deficit. (The presenter must have been the only one in the room who failed to notice the problem; he proceeded apace, while all the deaf people at the luncheon lost more and more of his speech.) The interpreter glanced about miserably. Her shirt seemed suddenly too bright and lustrous; her eyes, her hair, everything that had enhanced her expressiveness while she was conveying meaning now served only to underline her incompetence.

My father then exchanged places with her, on some unseen signal, quietly, modestly assuming her seat, picking up threads of the speech with his long blunt fingers. As the interpreter slid into the vacant place beside me at the table, her cheeks were mottled with red; I felt mine burn as well. We watched my father interpret the rest of the speech. With his lanky slouch, his craggy face, his deep-set gray eyes, he appeared far less spectacular than the woman had, as well as far more relaxed, and if no particular art graced his movements, no particular tension afflicted them either. He had grown up in the language, and his signing looked effortless, natural. But I was not misled; I would never be able to lay claim to the language as my father could. Signing, for me, would require practice and effort.

Next to me, the woman in green sipped icewater and composed herself in a kind of steely embarrassment. Watching her watch my father, I felt humble. I felt a respect for that which I did not know. And I understood — even then, on that day when the desire to become an interpreter first took hold — that there were risks involved in positioning oneself between two languages, as a link between two cultures. I sensed that those risks might extend well beyond embarrassment, and I vowed always to be careful.

Less than a year after I first went to Alec for ASL tutoring, I began to support myself as an interpreter. I had just moved to Brooklyn, taken an apartment in a brownstone in Prospect Heights, and commenced looking for work, any work, although interpreting was about the last thing I considered doing, since I was convinced that my skills were as yet inadequate. But there was another reason I shied from exploring the possibility: I wondered whether I could ever feel comfortable in the role of interpreter. Not whether I could feel confident — this had nothing to do with ability — but whether I could feel honest. Ethically comfortable, I mean.

These doubts had arisen during the past three months, during my internship in the performing arts department at the National Technical Institute of the Deaf. I was housed with another hearing intern in an apartment just off-campus but spent most of my time at the college, conducting interviews for a booklet on deaf theater, taking classes in ASL, working in the offices of the performing arts department, viewing stories told in ASL up in the videotape library, and, of course, attending rehearsals.

The bulk of my internship consisted of working on the fall production, *Great Expectations*. The script had been adapted and translated into ASL by the director, a deaf man and a veteran of the National Theater of the Deaf. The play was staged for both deaf and hearing audiences: a primary cast, composed of deaf people, enacted the drama in sign; a secondary cast, of hearing people stationed like a Greek chorus on the aprons of the stage, provided simultaneous voicing. Many of the hearing actors were not proficient signers. A rehearsal interpreter was needed, and the director asked me to fill this role. Flattered, nervous, and against my better judgment, I accepted.

At the first read-through, more than two dozen cast and crew members packed into the rehearsal room. We began with introductions, the deaf people fingerspelling their names. I was supposed to voice them. I missed, I think, every single one. I could hear blood swishing through my ears, could feel something hot, like steam beneath my skin, rising halfway up my face. My hands, clasped loosely in my lap, formed a cold, sweaty pocket. I tried to steady myself and read the spelling fingers, tried to focus not on individual letters but on the shape of the word. I told myself that fingerspelling is the hardest thing to apprehend, and consoled myself by saying that proper names are the hardest of all, with no context, no way to anticipate or use cloze skills. And all the while I felt myself becoming tiny, shrunken, like my own clenched hands, into a sodden, chilly knot.

One of the hearing cast members was an interpreter at the college. When her voice rode, unbidden, over the silence, I felt both quashed and relieved. Later she apologized to me for breaching etiquette. I thanked her and assured her I was grateful. That afternoon I resigned the position of company interpreter.

In the end I became stage manager, and from the relative safety of that position, without conscious effort or even awareness on my part, my signing and interpreting skills quietly flourished. During rehearsals I presided over a card table downstage. From there, referring to a script threaded into a black loose-leaf notebook, I recorded blocking, prompted and cued actors, and took notes about props and sets from the director.

The director's language was ASL, which he used in its purest form, autonomous from English, never mouthing glosses to go with his signs. Only rarely, when his patience was sorely tried, did I hear him use his voice, and then it was simply a loose rasp, a sort of feathery growl. His signs, uncompromised by English, were a pleasure to behold. I found it so easy to understand him that it was several weeks before it registered that the notes I was jotting down in English had originated in ASL. All those times that I had written what the director said, I had been unconsciously, instantaneously interpreting between the languages inside my head.

I further realized how much I was grasping, not just of the direction but of the conversations that went on among deaf actors who were not busy onstage, when some of the hearing actors began to sidle up during breaks and ask me to interpret. I offered to oblige them as best I could, only to surprise myself by being able to voice whole conversations. At the same time, the ASL stories in the videotape library were making more and more sense. But the real breakthrough came when I began to get jokes.

As the deaf people I worked with gradually included me in their banter, I started picking up subtle scraps of their humor: the way one deadpan adjustment could convert an innocuous sign into a double-entendre; the way English and ASL could be blended to yield richly punning alloys; the way English words and phrases could be slyly manipulated so as to appear, in sign, nonsensical, inane. This last kind of joking was wickedly barbed, a counterhegemonic response to oppressive hearing people and the language they so righteously touted. I felt honored by the invitation to share in this joking, by the permission to laugh at it.

Finally, I began to detect another sort of humor, related to this last but more pointed, as well as more veiled. It took various forms but always targeted certain hearing people, who, I gathered, were perceived as trespassers who had trod into the deaf community lacking proper credentials. At first I thought "credentials" were a matter simply of language — good signers were accepted; bad signers were not. But I soon saw that this rule did not apply. One of the other hearing interns had come to NTID as a novice signer; she struggled with the most basic hand shapes, labored to string a few signs awkwardly together, yet within a few weeks deaf staff members and students had afforded her a certain warmth and trust, taking her under their wing and helping her with her signing. Moreover, another hearing woman working on the play possessed far more advanced signing skills, but the same people subtly snubbed her. I saw them poke fun at the way she signed, the way she used certain ASL conventions in the wrong context, or with peculiar emphasis, or just too abundantly. It was as though by flaunting her knowledge of certain superficial features of ASL, she were trying to ingratiate herself with deaf people. She didn't mean it to be condescending, but it was. Like a white politician trying to talk jive, it aroused suspicion and distaste.

For centuries, hearing professionals have assigned themselves the task of "rehabilitating the deaf" without ever troubling to educate themselves about deaf culture and language. Now that the culture and language have caught on with the hearing world — have become, in a sense, fashionable — new problems hover. While hearing people's interest could lead to positive outcomes for deaf people, it could also present a danger: that the culture and language will become tools with which hearing people can further control deaf people's lives.

By the time the play was performed and my internship ended, I was in a sort of moral quandary over the concept of interpreting. I recognized the need for interpreters. At the same time, I began to think there was something terribly strange and complicated about the job, in the power and dependency inherent in the relationship between interpreter and client, in the fact that almost all interpreters are hearing, in the idea of appropriating the language of an oppressed minority and exploiting it for financial ends.

I was twenty-two years old, feeling very raw in the skin of a grownup and prone to feverish investigation of my own actions as well as their motives and consequences against a larger social backdrop. The whole framework of deaf politics was looming gigantically in my mind. This new construct had jettisoned my old sense of place within the deaf community; I couldn't feel my way clear to a new spot.

What had seemed when I was a child like a natural act of goodness now seemed more complicated, tainted. I no longer viewed interpreters simply as agents of connection. I also saw them as members of the very group that had dictated the hierarchy of languages that positioned ASL last. Good interpreters function as cultural mediators; now I wondered how, as hearing people, they could fairly represent both cultures, when they must harbor an inevitable bias toward their own. Deaf people constitute the only minority group in the world forced to rely solely on interpreters from outside their culture. By taking part in this equation, how could I help but perpetuate this inequity?

By the time I moved to Brooklyn, I had been stewing over these dilemmas for weeks. My head was swimming. The apartment I had found, a basement studio on Prospect Place, was miserably cold (two of the windowpanes had been replaced with loose-fitting cardboard) and itchy (the previous tenant's cats left a legacy of ridiculously hardy fleas), and I was extremely anxious to secure employment. I decided to table the whole interpreting issue for a while and concentrate instead on getting a job.

There ensued the proverbial endless days of circling ads in the classifieds, placing telephone calls, mailing résumés. The whole time it rained, and I sat on the floor of my chilly apartment and scratched at flea bites and fretted. After a few weeks of this, when a friend told me he had heard of a place in Manhattan that screened noncertified interpreters and referred them for jobs, I was just desperate enough to call.

A certified interpreter is someone who meets the national standards established by RID, which administers an exam that includes both a written and a practical component. The latter tests voice-to-ASL and ASL-to-voice interpretation; it also tests separately for transliteration between spoken English and signed English. This part of the test is recorded on videotape and distributed nationally to RID raters, who may then award a partial or comprehensive certificate, depending on the candidate's performance. Many interpreters work and study for years before taking this exam; I knew I was a long way from being ready to attempt it.

Because of the national dearth of certified interpreters, agencies in several cities and states have established their own less rigorous screening procedures. People who pass the screenings may work through these agencies. They are paid less than RID-certified interpreters and are restricted from certain kinds of jobs, such as legal interpreting. Often they work for social service organizations. New York Society for the Deaf (NYSD), the place my friend mentioned, is the main agency in New York City that screens and refers noncertified interpreters. I made an appointment to have my skills evaluated; at least I could obtain some sense of how far off I was.

My screening was scheduled for a Friday. Thursday night I was something of a wreck and decided I ought to practice. I switched on the radio, stood in front of the bathroom mirror, and tried to interpret news broadcasts. It was devastating. I could not keep up with all the densely packed sound bites. My fingers cramped as I improvised frantic spellings for all the names of foreign countries and their rulers. The announcer's deep male voice prattled on assuredly. My hands went limp. I locked disgusted gazes with myself over the sink. This was a farce.

But when I rose the next morning, I mustered my will, put on a plain navy blue sweater (interpreters are supposed to wear tops that provide a clean contrast with the color of their skin), pulled my hair back, put on minimal earrings, and, because I had read that female interpreters should wear lip color to provide better definition for lip reading, applied lipstick, which I promptly proceeded to chew off. Still, dressing for the part helped me summon courage. At NTID I had witnessed interpreters changing for work in the bathrooms, donning their dark solid blouses, shedding dangling bracelets and distracting rings, fixing their hair and makeup just like actors preparing for a performance. It had always seemed a little bit thrilling. I set off to keep my appointment with a kind of fatalistic resolve.

NYSD's test paralleled RID's, coming in two parts, written and practical. The written portion asked what interpreter training program I had attended. Feeling rather bleak, I wrote down "none." But I gained confidence as I moved along, answering questions to do with the structure and history of ASL as well as RID's code of ethics. Although I had never actually seen a copy of the interpreting code of ethics, I had enough awareness to answer with common sense. "If someone curses, is it acceptable to clean up their language in the interpretation?" Of course not; the interpreter may never edit or otherwise distort meaning. "If someone asks the interpreter a question about the client, is it all right to respond?" No, that question, like everything else, should be interpreted exactly as uttered. "May the interpreter ever discuss, with anyone, the specifics of a job or particular client?" No, the need for an interpreter must never compromise a client's right to confidentiality. "If a client requests, may the interpreter give personal opinions or advice?" No, the interpreter's job is to interpret, period.

When I had finished the written test, I was shown a videotape of a deaf man at a doctor's office. I was to sign everything the doctor said and voice everything the patient signed, just as if I were the interpreter present. An evaluator sat in the room with me and made notes as she listened and watched.

It was not atrocious. The doctor didn't speak at the breakneck speed of the radio announcer the night before. The patient signed fairly short, simple phrases, and they were all in response to the doctor's questions, so I had a sense of what to expect. I didn't feel very smooth or professional, and I missed some of what the patient said (his fingerspelled address, for instance), but neither did I make a fool of myself, and when I had finished and the evaluator asked me to wait outside, I did so with a certain satisfied relief. I was sure I had failed the screening, but at least I hadn't been a total disgrace.

The evaluator called me back into the room a few minutes later. I sat opposite her with a small contrite smile and waited for the critique. She launched into a short list of what I had missed, showed me a better way to sign "up till now," told me that my voicing had a nice quality but I should try to project more, and said I could start working on Monday.

We sat through a short silence.

"You mean as an interpreter?"

"That's what you're here for, isn't it?"

I worked at vocational schools, sheltered workshops, mental health facilities, social security offices, outpatient programs. There were filthy buildings and poorly heated buildings and buildings with rats. The clients were young people learning mechanical trades, elderly people going for physical exams, immigrants attending clerical school, parents trying to collect unemployment benefits. I collided with each of them briefly, tried to be true to their words, then left them and went on to other jobs, cloaked in the disturbing ether of anonymity.

I cringe now to think of my early clients, of how inexperienced and muddling my efforts with them must have been.

One of the first rules of interpreting is that you can't interpret what you don't understand. I learned that lesson well on one of my first jobs, interpreting an instructional filmstrip in a class on refrigerator repair. I sat leaning into the ambient light of the projector and fumbling over possible ways to sign "induction coil" and "condensing unit." Not knowing what these things were and therefore at a loss to interpret for meaning, I was reduced to a harried transliteration, finger-spelling nearly half the words and making, I am sure, very little sense.

Gauging the degree of cultural mediation implicit in the role of interpreter could be daunting as well. Certain things were obvious. In hearing culture, if someone is looking away and you want her attention, you call her by name. In deaf culture, a perfectly appropriate way to interpret this is by tapping the person's arm; I had no qualms about this. But I was utterly lost when a deaf patient sobbed in his therapist's office while the therapist made sympathetic clucks and mur-mured, "I know . . . I'm sorry . . . I know." The man shud-dered, damply oblivious, his face sunk into his hands. Should I pat him, in order to convey the therapist's consoling words tactilely? I sat, unable to make up my mind, hands cupped uselessly in my lap.

The intimacy with which I entered people's lives seemed at odds with the professional nature of the work, the de-tached way I had to glide out again at the end of the job. I remember an old woman going for her first mammogram, the sight of her, so soft and vulnerable as she stood naked with her breast pressed between the plates of the x-ray ma-chine. I remember a middle-aged man in a day-care center for the emotionally disturbed, who sat eating cake and ice cream and doughnuts all afternoon, reminiscing sadly about a visit to a farm. I remember a young man in a sheltered workshop who told me conversationally that he had raped his former girlfriend. And because my role as interpreter made me an invisible, silent vessel, I carried their images and stories home with me each night, and each day felt myself absorbing more, growing swollen with glimpses of private lives I could never share.

After two months of this, I was asked to apply for a full-time position as a staff interpreter at the Program for Deaf Adults at La Guardia Community College, part of the City University of New York, in Queens. The structure of the job interview took me by surprise: the department's six staff members (two hearing and four deaf) took turns quizzing me about my skills and experience. The actual questions mattered less than the way they were posed. Each of the staff members adopted a different mode of communication — pure ASL; signs in English word order, nonvoiced; straight signed English with voice; words mouthed with neither signs nor voice; and other variations or blends. I was to respond by matching the style of the individual questioner. The interview reflected the nature of the job requirements; interpreters must be prepared to work along a continuum. I thought the structure of the interview made a fine game and thoroughly enjoyed myself.

A few days later, when I was offered the job, I readily accepted. I would meet other interpreters, would have colleagues. Colleagues — the word was deliciously appealing. The loneliness of freelancing had been difficult, but in truth it had also come to have a qualified appeal. It served to heighten perception. The cross-sections of all those lives, the daily interlacing of foreign and familiar, the play between intimacy and detachment — these things were in some way stimulating.

What really motivated me to accept the staff position at La Guardia was the conviction that my solitude as a freelancer was professionally irresponsible. I had learned a great deal from deaf clients over the past two months, but it seemed an impropriety to make them shoulder the burden of my professional development. At La Guardia I would have a

proper mentor: the coordinator of interpreting services, Bonnie Singer.

Working with Bonnie, admiring the grace with which she
made sense of things, her apparently infinite ability to bring
clarity between people, I relearned some of my early ideas
about interpreting. I also learned that the frustration and
self-deprecation that plagued me as a beginning interpreter
were more or less endemic to the profession, for Bonnie,
who held top RID certification, was perfectly forthcoming
about her own failings and the dissatisfaction she still sometimes felt with her performance.

For every language except sign language, the ideal interpreting situation has the interpreter working in one direction
only: interpreting into the mother tongue. At the United
Nations, for example, no matter how proficient interpreters
may be in their second or third or fourth language, they only
interpret *from* these languages *into* their first language, the
reason being that the most authentic and faithful interpretation can be rendered only by a native speaker. ASL interpreters are the only interpreters in the world who regularly, of
necessity, interpret from their native language into one
learned later in life (the possible exception being hearing
children of deaf parents). Coming into contact with Bonnie
and other interpreters at La Guardia, I learned that a certain
awkwardness with ASL never entirely dissipates.

Still, I made strides. From Bonnie I learned about lag time.
Rather than spewing signs directly on the heels of the spoken message, I learned to pause and trust my short-term
memory while I listened to enough of the message to grasp
the larger intent, so that when I did begin signing, I stayed
truer to meaning than if I had scrambled to produce something more nearly verbatim. I increased my ASL vocabulary
so that I had more choices to select from, to produce the right
nuance. I learned to be less literal in my voicing so that the
words I spoke rang more naturally in English.

At La Guardia I grew to feel comfortable with myself as an
adequate interpreter in many situations. I no longer thought

so much about political implications. What had been insurmountable in theory turned out to be moot in practice; polemics aside, when a situation requires an interpreter, it makes sense to provide that service as best you can. And I liked interpreting. I enjoyed the challenge, enjoyed thinking about language, making connections between the aural and the manual.

But I left my job there to go back to school the following fall. I knew I could never make interpreting my life's work. I couldn't bear the constant frustration of entering people's lives, feeling their private sorrows and confusion and rage pass through me in the form of language, yet remaining helpless, forbidden to interact, weightless as a ghost. Worse still was the frustration of being unseen, uncounted, as I performed my task.

The February after I was hired at La Guardia, exactly two years after I had gone to Alec for tutoring, I went to visit him for the first time in months. We rarely saw each other anymore, but we had remained friends, and I dropped by his apartment one afternoon to chat. He had just brought two glasses of water into the usual comfortable mess of his living room and was fumbling around for a pack of cigarettes when a buzzer sounded and the light bulb in the corner lamp flashed. He shot me a quizzical look and went to the door. There stood a very tall woman with lots of earrings and a purple knapsack.

"Hello! Yes, I got a note from you under the door this morning. It was a surprise," Alec voiced.

"Er . . . I think I can understand if you . . . it takes me a little while." The woman grinned hesitantly; she had a German accent.

Alec called me over. *"Do you want to interpret?"*

"Sure." We both knew they could have managed without me, but the woman's accent and relative unfamiliarity with English would have made it especially difficult; since I happened to be there, it made sense for me to expedite their conversation.

The woman turned out to be someone Alec had met during his European travels a few years back. Her name was Sabine. She was in town for two days on her way down to Central America. She had kept his address and decided to look him up.

"*Well, come in,*" he said. We made our way back into the living room, cleared an island in the sea of Alec-paraphernalia, and sat.

For the next three hours, I interpreted for Alec and Sabine. They smoked cigarettes and talked about travel and German politics. After the first two hours I got a little fed up with being a nonentity and tried to interject a comment or question every now and then, at which point Alec would frown at me and ask, "*Who's saying that, you or her?*" because of course I was signing everything Sabine said as well as my own remarks. So I gave up and went back to just interpreting, and by the time their visit wound down it was time for me to leave, too.

Outside, the afternoon was already dark, the dead end of winter. I headed for the subway with the same odd detachment I used to feel when freelancing. I knew I had just done a good job. Three hours is a long time to interpret with no breaks. When Alec had asked whether I would interpret, I had been flattered, had felt sort of proud and important to be his link. But at bottom, that was the trouble with interpreting.

I had always thought that interpreting might be my ticket into the deaf community, the logical way in which my adult self could belong. But it wasn't my self that was engaged. As an interpreter, I'm not really being *with* deaf people. I do not think there is any way for me to recover the relationship with deaf people I felt as a child. I am a hearing adult. English is my language. I belong to hearing culture.

I still interpret on occasion.

17

Long Goodbye

Oscar doesn't tell people that he thinks of leaving Lexington. The funny thing is, he never planned to be there in the first place. It just sort of happened.

When he was growing up in the Bronx, it never occurred to him that deafness could be any kind of career choice. Deafness was his parents and their friends and their clubs and their parties, a tapestry so familiar that he was nearly incapable of seeing it. Working with deaf people was nothing he ever considered, much less dreamed of.

After high school he halfheartedly meandered into Hunter College with the vague notion of maybe becoming a gym teacher. He wound up teaching science for a year at a junior high school in the Morissania section of the east Bronx, then heard about a master's degree program at Columbia University's Teachers College that trained teachers of the deaf. Tuition was free; the program even included a stipend to cover expenses. Figuring that he would make a reasonable candidate, he applied and enrolled. All of the student teaching took place at Lexington, which subsequently hired several of the graduates. In this fairly nondeliberate fashion, Oscar found himself, at age twenty-five, employed by his father's alma mater.

Now, on a spring afternoon twenty-six years later, he has been invited to appear before a ring of students who wish to interview him, as their superintendent, in their deaf studies class. And to the students, who know nothing of the round-about path that led him to this position or of the increasingly insistent tug he feels to leave, his name might as well be Mr. Lexington.

They are an energetic lot, these five high school prefreshmen, agitated and mildly aghast at the presence of such a distinguished visitor in their classroom, which is really a fraction of a classroom, a thin quadrant behind a rickety wooden partition. Oscar appears formidably large in this constricted space, wrapped behind the spatulate arm of a desk-chair, the dark legs of his trousers extending well into the ring of inquisitors, who manage to give the impression of hopping from foot to foot while remaining in their seats.

"What's your sport?" comes the first question — apropos of nothing, yet bearing a certain studied urbanity — from the boy on Oscar's left.

Oscar levels an equally debonair gaze at the student before responding somewhat drily, *"I'm the superintendent; that's my sport."*

The field of deafness seems to grow more complicated daily, with the emergence of new goals, new rules and stratagems, the continuing distillation of multiple opposing factions. Even within Lexington, some of the political sparring has truly taken on the pettier aspects of sport, and of this Oscar is contemptuous. Many of the current board disputes are unrelated to educational issues — they seem to be about little more than power for power's sake — and he resents the way these contests consume increasing amounts of his time.

This interview with the deaf studies class, however, is well removed from all those troubles, and Oscar makes an effort to shake his mind free, to devote himself entirely to these five students for the next half-hour. The location is a help, since this is the most makeshift classroom in the school, wedged into a hidden corner of the uppermost floor. It can be reached only by going through another classroom, and is strikingly unkempt, littered with half-dismantled collages and empty tissue boxes. Clearly, the chalkboard has not been washed in ages. It is perhaps the spot where one would least expect to find the superintendent, and gradually Oscar relaxes, submitting himself with genuine pleasure to the questions of the class.

The deaf studies curriculum concentrates heavily on self-identity and feelings about deafness. Students enter Lexington's high school with diverse attitudes about their own deafness and deaf people in general. Part of the class entails interviewing guests — mainly deaf staff members — to learn about their experiences growing up. In this way, the students are exposed to a host of role models, different from one another in terms of philosophy, mode of communication, and life choices but all successful deaf adults.

Oscar, obviously, is an exception. But if the students mind that he is hearing, they don't show it. They quiz him about the history of Lexington and find out that he used to be the basketball coach, a long time ago, at the old school in Manhattan. They get him talking about the Lexington Avenue building, which, he explains, didn't have a gym, only a courtyard. (This triggers a brief spat among the students over the proper sign for *courtyard*.)

"*I remember at the old school,*" Oscar continues peacefully when their quarreling has subsided, "*after lunch, going outside and playing basketball with the boys. Sometimes it would be snowing, and we would still play! It was a lot of fun.*" And then, reminiscently, "*My father used to play on the Lexington team.*"

The students sit quite still for a moment, eyes lingering on Oscar as if straining to make out an afterimage of his signs. Then they toss sideways glances at one another: *Did he say father?*

One boy gets up the nerve to ask. "*How . . . ?*"

And Oscar puts the question back to him: *"How?"*

His face drenched with skepticism, the boy makes the sign in slow disbelief, the side of his right index finger describing an arc from mouth to ear. *"Deaf?"*

Oscar nods. *"My father was deaf. And he was a student at Lexington School."*

The students give each other little surreptitious whacks, registering the profundity of this piece of information. It makes them queerly shy; they become skittish for a moment, silly, whack each other back. They look faintly pink, as though someone had just delivered them a compliment.

Oscar glances at his watch. It is time for him to go back to his office, and already his thoughts are returning, like haggard, dutiful soldiers, to the political strife that usurps more and more of his time. He wishes there were a way simply to do his job, to concentrate his attention on the students.

But he is so deeply embroiled that to extricate himself would probably require leaving the field altogether. This he cannot bring himself to do, not just yet, anyway, with so much at stake in the world of deaf education. Of course (and he acknowledges this with a grim jolt), if the antagonism between the school and center boards continues to escalate at its present rate, and if certain center board members have their way, he may be relieved of having to make such a decision.

In 1983, Lexington School for the Deaf restructured itself, splitting into distinct agencies, or affiliates — the school, the Hearing and Speech Center, the Center for Mental Health Services, and the Research and Training Division — and creating an umbrella organization, the Lexington Center, to govern the whole. Each affiliate was to have its own board, whose members would serve as well on the huge center board. The center board would also have a core of about ten center-board-only members.

It seemed an excellent idea, a way to broaden and

strengthen the services that Lexington could provide to the larger community, and in many respects this proved to be true. But from the restructuring there also arose conflicts. Most of these have involved tension between the center board and the school board.

Oscar had just become superintendent when the changes were made. During the next several years, he played a significant role in recruiting the new members of the school board. The tension, then, exists largely between what might be perceived as "Oscar's group" and the center board.

It is difficult to pinpoint the exact nature of the tension, which in turn makes the tension difficult to assuage. If it were brought on by concrete pedagogical differences, for instance, it might be possible to communicate in specific terms and reach some accord, or compromise, or at least mutual understanding. If it were brought on by *any* concrete differences, resolution might be possible. Instead, the tension seems wrought by more abstract matters: issues of power, domain, and control.

This spring the four-year term of Lexington Center's current board president, Dr. Carol Reich, will come to an end. Dr. Reich is the first president in Lexington's 125-year history who is not a white, hearing male. She has issued a statement to the mostly white, hearing, male board urging them to choose a deaf person to succeed her. The school board has officially endorsed her suggestion; the center board has not. This has become the latest in a series of instances in which the school board is perceived to be representing an affront to the status quo.

The animosity between the boards is intensifying. Within a year, the center board will have executed a coup, dismantling all the affiliate boards, including the school board, and subsuming all the members into one massive, fifty-five-member central board, thereby diluting the individual voices that sounded in powerful dissonance from the school board. Once Oscar was able to look on the board troubles as an unfortunate but peripheral part of his job. Lately, they have dominated it. And in the past few months he has heard strong rumors that members of the center board would like to see him removed. Even in the midst of all this unrest, he appreciates the irony in that.

At schools for the deaf around the country, hearing administrators are feeling vulnerable in their jobs, aware that deaf activists would like to see the positions held by deaf people. At Lexington, Oscar feels vulnerable as well, but in his case the immediate threat comes not from the deaf community, in which he has dwelt comfortably since birth, but from the old ranks of hearing authorities, who are trying to maintain their patronage in changing times.

"Will Deaf Clubs Survive Modern Times? How Is the Deaf Community Changing?" This is the theme of Lexington's eighth annual forum for leaders in the deaf community. Oscar has been organizing these forums since he became superintendent. Past topics have included racism, legislation, and technology and their effects on the deaf community. Perhaps none has seemed as devastatingly important as this year's.

The deaf community has come to a peculiar crossroads. On one hand, deaf culture may never have been stronger or more appreciated than it is today. On the other hand, it may never reach these heights again, as there are now indications on many different fronts that despite (indeed, partly because of) all the gains in recent years — the legislation, the media attention, the technological advances, the civil rights advances — deaf culture may be slipping into decline. It is losing its critical mass.

In 1963 and 1964, an epidemic of rubella, or German measles, infected people all over the United States. When the virus infects a woman in her first trimester of pregnancy, it can cause congenital defects in her baby. Thus an unusually high number of deaf children were born in the mid-1960s. Within the field, this swell in the deaf population is commonly referred to as the "rubella bulge." Around the same time, the research that proved ASL to be a legitimate language was becoming widely acknowledged and accepted. This began to affect educational philosophy. It also provided an important tool for deaf people in their demands for increased respect, recognition, and rights.

In the early 1970s, a series of lawsuits and acts of Congress granted deaf people new rights to access to public facilities. These culminated in 1975 with the passage of Public Law 94-142, the Education for All Handicapped Children Act. Within the deaf community, people printed up buttons that showed, beneath the legend "P.L. 94-142," two hands, palms down, fingertips meeting: the sign for *equal*.

By the mid-1980s, deaf people had gained considerable grassroots political power. In 1988, the Deaf President Now movement achieved its dramatic and well-publicized victory at Gallaudet. A year after that, five thousand people from deaf communities around the world gathered at Gallaudet for an international congress called the Deaf Way. And one year after that, Congress passed the Americans with Disabilities Act (ADA). The most sweeping legislation affecting deaf people to date, ADA ensures them the same protection from discrimination that ethnic minorities already have.

Deafness began to enter the realm of public consciousness as never before. Mark Medoff's play about deafness, *Children of a Lesser God*, became a hit on Broadway; its star, Phyllis Frelich, became the first deaf actor to receive a Tony Award. In 1987, the deaf actor Marlee Matlin received an Oscar for performing the same role in the movie version, and millions of television viewers around the world watched her sign her acceptance speech. Deaf actors appeared more regularly on television, in guest spots on weekly series and in TV movies such as the award-winning *Love Is Never Silent*; in the fall of 1991, *Reasonable Doubts* became the first series to star a deaf actor.

Schools and other institutions found that they could capitalize on the popularity, which heightened consciousness even further. Sign language classes proliferated, spawning jobs for deaf teachers and consultants to create standards and curricula. High schools and colleges began offering sign language courses and allowing students to use ASL to meet foreign language requirements. Public and private agencies began listing TDD numbers for hearing- and speech-impaired callers.

Meanwhile, advances in technology were changing what it meant to be deaf. Toll-free relay services began spreading through states across the nation. New signaling and communication devices, ever more compact and complex, appeared on the market. Listening devices became available in public spaces such as theaters and museums. Real-time captioning made it possible to project a speaker's words onto a large screen instantaneously at live lectures. More television shows and commercials were closed-captioned, and legislation was passed requiring that after June 1993, all televisions with screens larger than thirteen inches must come with built-in decoders. Deaf people could partake in society as never before.

Developments occurred in another arena as well, but here the accolades fade. This is the arena of medical technology, where developments have sparked a controversy that rivals, in the heat of its passion and the seriousness of its stakes, the great old oral-manual debate. The deaf community and hearing professionals are again at odds. In the old debate over language, deaf people fought for autonomy and dignity. Now they are fighting for the future of their culture.

The chief point of contention in this battle is the cochlear implant. To hearing professionals who have been trained to view deafness as a pathology, as a defect, the implant may look like a panacea. To hearing parents who have just learned that their child cannot hear, cannot communicate or understand them, the implant may look like salvation. But to members of the deaf community, who, without regrets or

· 272 ·

apologies, regard deafness as a culture, the implant is an indictment and a threat.

Imagine coming up with a "cure" for any other cultural minority or oppressed group — African Americans, say, or women, or Jewish people. Most hearing people find this analogy strained. After all, deafness is a handicap. No one could disagree that a person's life would be made easier if she could be cured of deafness. But couldn't we say the same thing about black people and women and Jews? In our society, isn't it more convenient to be white and male and Christian? Isn't life generally easier for members of the dominant culture? Yet we wouldn't dream of searching for ways to "cure" blackness or femaleness or Jewishness. Even if it were medically possible, it would be ethically abhorrent, a kind of cultural genocide. This is how many culturally deaf people view the efforts of the medical establishment to prevent, correct, and minimize the effects of hearing impairment.

While the National Association of the Deaf does oppose the use of cochlear implants in children on medical grounds, citing the potential dangers involved in the surgery, the crux of its argument relates to issues of culture and self-determination. Hearing professionals contend that the younger the candidate is, the more effective the implants can be. But deaf leaders point out that when children are implanted, it is hearing people — parents and doctors — who make the decision. They believe that children ought to be allowed to grow up with exposure to other deaf children and adults, to acquire and use ASL, to develop positive attitudes toward their own deafness and all of deaf culture, and then to choose for themselves whether to receive the implant or not. Deaf leaders maintain that few people who grow up with this kind of exposure would be likely to opt for the implant.

But the deaf community faces an extraordinary task in trying to persuade hearing parents and medical authorities, to whom the hope of "curing" deafness will always outweigh the benefits of promoting deaf culture. Deaf people have

been labeled for centuries as mentally deficient, socially naive, and incapable of sound moral judgment. Overcoming
these stigmas may take more time than the community
has left.

Already a newly refined cochlear implant, touted as far
more effective than those currently in use, is hitting the market. Scientists are now expecting a new infant vaccine to virtually wipe out meningitis, currently the leading cause of
deafness in children. As health care improves in general, less
deafness is being caused by illness and improper treatment.
At the same time, those who are already deaf are finding
themselves presented with more options, from implants to
telecommunications to mainstreaming to protective legislation, for gaining more access to the hearing world.

The deaf population is shrinking. That which remains is
further depleted by options that encourage migration into
hearing culture. As technology evolves, the pool will almost
certainly continue to shrink. How bittersweet that the technology that has so enabled deaf people may ultimately, in-
evitably, precipitate the community's demise.

Among many deaf people, the proposition of cultural demise is still almost unmentionable; in certain circles, speaking of it is a sort of sacrilege. There are those, however, who
are beginning to speculate and predict. And if it should happen, really, what will have been lost? If deaf culture should
recede into the past, eventually assuming only static existence in a few sign language dictionaries and ASL videotapes
on the shelf of a narrowly fabricated history, would any of
us be the poorer? If everyone could hear, if we could all
speak and listen, explain and understand in a single language, would we be somehow closer, better? Would there be
more hope for us as humans?

Unfortunately, being physically equipped to hear has little
to do with the predilection to listen. Sharing a common
tongue does not ensure earnest or successful communication. Missed connections occur among hearing people all the

time, splitting open countless minor chasms and yawning gulches, fissures that no vaccine or technological advance will ever be able to mend or prevent. That task will always fall to us.

It is a common language, the acquisition of language, that informs a cultural sensibility. Hearing people often remark in reverent, near-mystical tones about how beautiful sign language is, and to some extent this may be attributed to the inherent movements of the language itself. But the power of its beauty derives from what it symbolizes.

Its very existence is a testament to people's will to communicate. It pays tribute to our determination to make connections in the face of incredible odds. And although deaf culture as it exists today might come to an end, the potency of this symbol will never fade — nor will our need for it ever lessen.

My father may be on his way out. Deaf culture may be entering its decline. At the ragged ends of certain days, they seem headed down parallel gangplanks. On other days, that notion seems wildly implausible, like the sour stuff of nightmares reexamined in the light of the sun.

One day toward the end of spring, I went into the superintendent's office, heard my father on the phone in the next room, and remained in the outer chamber, opposite the desk of his indomitable assistant, Barbara Robinson. Barbara had the window open; a warm breeze ruffled her plants, and the sounds of recess cracked carelessly against the brick walls of the courtyard below. We grinned hello at each other and tussled briefly over whether or not I would accept a couple of homemade sugar cookies to which Barbara had fallen prey (yet another bake sale) and which she was now trying to foist on me. Eventually I reclined in one of the visitor's chairs, cookie in hand, trying not to get crumbs on my skirt. I had dressed up a little bit that day, having wrangled an invitation to join my father and Dr. Leo Connor for lunch.

Dr. Connor became Lexington's superintendent the year I was born and held that position until he retired twelve years later, when my father took the job. While our family lived at Lexington, Dr. Connor and his wife lived in the apartment above us; we were neighbors. I remembered Dr. Connor as extremely serious, with a precise, contained voice like the engine of a machine. His appearance was always neat and orderly; there was something almost courtly about him, which as a little girl I had found forbidding, and which had made my father's succeeding him seem incongruous — my father, the endless purveyor of jokes and stories, the signer, the ballplayer, the questioner, him with his Bronx teeth and solemn eyes and shirtsleeves.

About once a year, the two men meet for a meal. Dr. Connor remains executive director emeritus, an honorary position that does not entail maintaining contact with the daily workings of the school, but he likes to receive occasional briefings. And there is something my father likes about these meetings too, something valuable he derives from them. Something like history. A sense of place, of the changes wrought by the passage of time, and his relationship to it all. It has been a quarter of a century since the beginning of both my father's career and the deaf civil rights movement. Changes have occurred, and continue to occur, at a fantastic rate. I think lunches with Dr. Connor offer my father a kind of touchstone, an opportunity for reflection that becomes increasingly valuable and difficult to come by as deaf politics and Lexington politics grow more turbulent.

I was looking forward to the lunch with a nostalgic curiosity myself, and wished my father would finish up his telephone call. I became aware that his voice was projecting rather noticeably from behind the wall.

"Come down here and we'll show you!" he bellowed. And then again, up a notch: "Come down here and we'll show you!"

I cocked an eye at Barbara and asked with surprise

whether he was angry or just talking with a hard-of-hearing person. She gave me a shrewd look and answered quietly, "No, he's angry." He was on the phone with the school bus company responsible for picking up some of the emotionally disturbed students from Lexington's Special Education Unit; one of the drivers had been complaining about the students' erratic behavior.

"Don't use words like 'crazy' and 'hysterical,'" my father roared. "Don't talk about them that way!"

Barbara and I exchanged tight, queer smiles: it was so strange to hear him yell, so rare to see him lose his temper.

He emerged a few minutes later his usual self and sparred unsuccessfully with Barbara over whether he would accept the remaining cookie. Then he and I headed out to the parking lot, my father stooping to pick up litter in front of the main entrance, as was his custom. I thought he seemed tired. We drove slowly from the neighborhood, the sun kicking up spots all over the windshields of parked cars, tulips clustering upright around blue plaster lawn Madonnas, and crossed Astoria Boulevard. I was feeling that imperative to watch things closely, to notice stop signs and traffic lights, to look over my shoulder for oncoming cars when we made a turn, trying to share silently in the burden of getting us there.

Dr. Connor met us at the La Guardia Marriott. We sat behind a pillar, away from the glare of the picture windows, and Dr. Connor and my father mulled over changes in the field. During lunch, my father seemed to borrow some of his former boss's detachment; he seemed to lighten and relax, and he described Lexington's troubles with gentle irony. Dr. Connor congratulated him on becoming president-elect of the Conference of Educational Administrators Serving the Deaf, an old and influential national organization. (At the election, my father had been honored to learn that he was the candidate supported by the ad hoc caucus of deaf administrators; at the same time he had wondered, only half in jest, whether he could fulfill his presidential duties if he was ousted from Lexington.)

As I listened to the men talk, I thought how different from each other they were, in terms of background and style and educational philosophy, yet how amiable and mutually respectful. They shared the conviction that one of the things that makes Lexington a good place is its willingness to stand apart from popular trends. But Dr. Connor was always more of a traditionalist, whereas my father, after spending his entire adult life at the school, is perceived as a maverick by enough people to jeopardize his job. I knew that back when Dr. Connor was superintendent, the two did not always see eye to eye. Yet Dr. Connor chose my father as a protégé and subtly groomed him for the responsibility of directing the school.

My father may have been musing over this as well, because near the end of the meal, with sudden and frank curiosity, he asked the older man, "What did you see in me?"

With very little pause, Dr. Connor answered, "Intelligence and stubbornness."

Then I know my father must have been thinking the same thing I was, because he exclaimed, sounding dubious and pleased, "I was stubborn?"

"Yes," asserted Dr. Connor, this time with no pause at all. "You had steel in the backbone. Strong beliefs."

My father tucked his chin into his neck and frowned at his hands, folded on the edge of the tablecloth: he was extremely flattered.

Back outside, after lunch and goodbyes, the breeze had dropped. As my father and I drove back to Lex, the late afternoon unfurled, rich and mellow. A sunbather had dragged a lawn chair onto the field near the school; an ice cream truck blared hurdy-gurdy music out in front; people sat on the steps of the main entrance eating bananas and ice pops and signing. It had turned into one of those days when it was not possible to conceive of my father's leaving Lexington, nor of deaf culture's ever disappearing.

We left my father's office that day at the usual time, a little before six. He likes to claim that the usual is five; when pushed he will confess to five-fifteen, but in this he is sorely mistaken. All my life I have seen how difficult it can be to get him to leave.

When we emerged from the building, after a series of good evenings and *good evenings* to custodians and kids we met on the way out, the whole block was gilded by the clear slanting light of the June evening. My father stashed a five-inch stack of manila folders in the trunk of his car, then turned as he heard a car cruising slowly up to where we stood. Two alumni, both in their late twenties, both former wrestlers, idled a big gray van opposite him. He put his hands on his hips, and they all gazed at one another fondly for a minute.

"Did you work at the post office today?" my father asked the one who was driving.

I set down my bag and leaned against the car to wait out the small talk. There was no telling how long this might last.

"Tonight. I have an eight-hour shift, starting at eight."

My father grimaced. *"Do you sleep on the job?"*

"Most of the time," he was affably assured.

"That's my tax money!" my father protested. *"I bought you this van!"*

Everyone laughed. My father reached inside the window to yank down the brim of the driver's cap.

"You guys are funny," he pronounced, and they beamed.

When no one had anything left to say, they all stayed right where they were for just a little longer.

18

Graduation

At the last senior class meeting before graduation, everyone is edgy, and it's not just the heat, although undoubtedly that contributes a layer of tension, even here in the basement where it ought to be cool. The students are looking very sharp and self-conscious, with their hair scraped back or gelled or cut into fresh summer styles. The scent of cocoa butter intensifies with sweat, and bits of skin flash through their loosely crocheted vests, muscle shirts, and halters. They tip forward on metal folding chairs, angling themselves so they can see their class leaders, who have just jerked the light switch, calling the meeting to order.

James watches from the back of the room, focusing on the speakers intently. Amid the giddy anxiety of his classmates, he seems a well of stillness, soberly awaiting instructions about his last days at Lex. In the tilt of his chin, which he lifts now so he can see over heads, there resides a certain delicacy that makes him seem at once childlike and suddenly adult.

During the past month, however, James has not been without his own share of edginess, which has translated in turns into irritability (as supervisor of the bus room, he autocratically imposed a three-day ban on using the room as an afterschool hangout, in response to the unruly behavior of certain fellow students) and a kind of dopey sang-froid, which he uses to deflect serious thoughts about his future. In fact, the closer the future gets, the less he is able to envision himself in it, and he finds himself flirting with ways to stave it off.

Mostly, James has been thinking that Camden County College, whose summer program he is slated to begin next month, is really too far from home — after all, it's so far down the New Jersey Turnpike it's practically in Pennsylvania. James visited the campus on a school field trip this April, on a colorless day of tearing winds and insistent drizzle, and he maintained a critical eye throughout. The classroom divider walls were flimsy, cheap; the cafeteria portions were small; the buildings were too spread out. Worst of all, the campus apartments came unfurnished; students had to supply their own furniture.

"How?" James asked their campus guide, one of the deaf college students. He was still chewing on the wooden stick of an ice cream bar he had bought at lunch; a muscle flashed rhythmically at his temple.

"Borrow a car or rent a U-Haul," the guide explained with cheery helpfulness.

James considered the likelihood of being able to do either. *"We have to bring our own bed, even?"*

"That's right."

He stared at her for a moment, gnawing the ice cream stick in deliberate circles. Then he broke into a saucy mime, marching in place with a giant phantom bed hefted on one shoulder. This drew laughter from the Lex students standing around him, and James grinned, all dimples and chipped tooth, asserting his easy charm while diffusing any rebuke the student guide might have sensed. But inside, he felt shaken. The world now expected him to provide his own bed. It seemed unfairly, almost cruelly, abrupt.

Back at Lexington, he began mentioning to various friends that he might not choose to go to college right away. He toyed with the notion of staying in the Bronx instead and finding a job. Most of his older deaf friends were doing just that; some didn't even bother with the job, but managed to scrape by on their SSI checks alone.

And then, just last Thursday, James startled everyone by getting suspended. A dorm counselor charged that James had hit him while he was trying to encourage James to do his homework. James denied the story, said the counselor had been provoking him, annoying him, yanking at his arm; he had only shoved the counselor away. In either case, even the differences in the meaning of touch between deaf and hearing cultures could not have accounted for this behavior.

By reputation, James is nonconfrontational. He is one of the students most often called on by staff members to help break up fights. For the yearbook, he was voted "most easy-going." Even in his days of truancy and horseplay, James was never a fighter. The incident was grounds for a one-night suspension from the dorm as well as some concern, and the dorm supervisor took pains to assure Mrs. Taylor in his requisite note that James was usually pleasant and responsible, a dorm leader.

As for James, he took his punishment coolly, stretching the one-night suspension from the dorm into a three-day leave from all of Lexington. When he showed up again, he was his felicitous old self. But something seemed to be slightly altered. Perhaps the hiatus allowed him to discharge the anxiety over graduation. Now, his bearing at the class meeting seems somehow serene, quietly resolute. As he gives the speakers his sober attention, he appears every bit the college-bound man. His head in profile is round and neat, with a crisp diagonal part shaved into his short fade.

The rims of his eyeglasses frame his concentration like gold parentheses.

The class officers run through a long agenda, from the treasurer's report to prom tickets to senior luncheon to the class gift. The students act as podiums for each other, holding papers so presenters can read information and still have their hands free to sign. Two class advisers, both of them deaf, periodically interject comments and reminders.

"*All of you who are graduating*," explains one of them, informing the students about the upcoming alumni festival, "*you will all become alumni*."

James repeats the sign: *alumni*. It's new to him, similar to the sign for *graduate*. He tries it out on his own hands and nods.

At the front of the room, the class officers segue into a heated discussion about the class gift to the school. One faction is in favor of a television with a built-in decoder for the media department. Another advocates the purchase of books on deaf culture for the library. The students debate seriously; this will be their legacy.

Next to James, Paul Escobar is paying little attention. It won't be his legacy; he's not graduating. Twisting his head, he stamps his foot in an effort to solicit the attention of one of the class advisers, sitting four yards away. With all the bodies and commotion in the carpeted room, she doesn't feel the vibrations. Paul thrusts his arm sideways, jerks it once, twice, in what ought to be her peripheral vision, but the adviser is caught up in following the debate at the front of the room and does not turn.

"Yo, deaf!" Paul calls aloud, rudely, in his excellent speech. This fares no better, of course, but allows him to vent some frustration and at the same time to reassure himself of his superiority in at least one area: oral skills. At last he snatches off his baseball cap and throws it at her feet. She turns in his direction.

"*Can I buy a class T-shirt even though I'm not graduating?*"

he wants to know. But her gaze never lands on him; she has missed his question entirely, and now her attention goes back to the class officers. Paul gives up and sinks into a muscular slouch, barrel-legged dungarees shoved out before him. He sneaks a sideways glance at James, who is following the class meeting with such ardor that he hasn't even noticed Paul's antics. James, his old Bronx compatriot, his homeboy from first grade, his buddy in the Lex dorm — James is graduating without him, going off to college. Paul's eyelids droop.

James sits at the edge of his seat. It has just been announced that because this year's class is so large (nearly fifty students), everyone will be allowed only five tickets for graduation, and he is dismayed. Five is not nearly enough. Several students protest, and one of the advisers asks for a show of hands: *"How many people would want six tickets for graduation night?"*

James pumps both hands in the air, signing, *"Eight, eight!"* Even eight tickets would not be enough. He'd like nine. No, ten. The number of people he calls sister and cousin exceeds the parameters prescribed by biology. Up on Webster Avenue, a young man's graduation from high school is no small cause for celebration, and James knows all the family friends will be clamoring to attend.

The advisers promise to lobby for six tickets each. When the meeting is finished and the schoolday over, the seniors push back their chairs and weave to the front of the room. They have one last thing to tackle: figuring out the lineup for graduation. By tradition, the graduates process into the auditorium in order of height, so now they scrutinize one another, press back to back, lay palms flat across crowns. The girls tiptoe, pretending to wear pumps. The advisers survey the line, switching kids every so often. Someone notes the arrangement on a yellow legal pad.

The line begins with the shortest ones, who are standing under the clock. The middle-size girls find themselves in front of the chalkboard, which they automatically fill with hearts and flowers and their graffiti tags. The line continues, progressively more crowded and jostling, toward the exit. Other students — freshmen, sophomores, juniors — released from their last period classes, swarm around lockers just outside the door. Paul slips out, blending into the mass of those not graduating; James watches his friend recede down the hall. Then he commits himself to a place in line.

The buses have all left. James sits alone on the steps outside the student entrance. This spot is always shady in the afternoon; he can look out on the hot brilliance across the street and feel a pleasant chill from the metal banister against his spine. The litter gracing the steps below him reflects the time of year: a couple of peach pits, still glistening with strands of fruit; a pair of sunglasses with neon-bright frames, discarded or forgotten; the melted remains of an ice cream sandwich; a penny and a hearing aid battery, like twin charms, brown and silver.

He has been waiting here since dismissal, an hour and twenty minutes ago, for the arrival of his sisters, who want to attend his senior luncheon, which will be held in the Diamond Room at Shea Stadium this Sunday. Guest tickets are twenty-five dollars each, and the deadline to purchase them is today, so James has told his sisters that if they want to go they had better get themselves to Jackson Heights with cash before the day ends. He waits without impatience or worry, and is rewarded at last as five young women round the corner of the privet hedges and make their way toward him, laughing boisterously.

James does not budge, but smiles a private smile as he watches the approach of this delegation: his sisters, some by blood and some by name and all of them having made the complicated trip (two buses, two trains) to Jackson Heights. Maureen, the oldest and sassiest, was born in Jamaica but has the same father as James; Denise, whom James calls Neenee, is his full sister; Kisha and DeeDee are cousins; and Tina he describes as "my brother Joseph's baby's mother." As soon as the women spot him, their volume and mirth increase, and they cluster at the bottom of the steps, pointing to their mouths and stomachs.

"*Food*, James. We want to *eat*. We *hungry*." Maureen, wearing a pair of satiny hot orange shorts, goes pigeon-toed, does a little squat, and points at her crotch. "I got to go *bath*room, James." The others crack up and look over their shoulders to see if they are scandalizing anyone. The houses across the street look so sedate. Someone is slapping fresh paint onto his wrought iron railing. The lush branches of the towering plane trees in front of the school sway with the rushing sound of surf, then grow calm again. The women look back at James, Neenee jabbing a finger at her mouth to remind him.

"I don't have any food," he says. They are accustomed to his speech and recognize most of the words (although sometimes one must ask another to decipher something she has missed), just as James is accustomed to the movements of their lips. "You're too late," he announces boldly. "Go out to eat."

The women fall out again, bent over with laughter. "Snap! Did you hear what he say? He say we can go *out* to eat! Damn!" They eye him with glittering approval.

"Well, c'mon, James, I got to get to the *bath*room!" Maureen tosses her head; a hundred skinny braids tipped in gold foil beckon him, and James, descending like royalty among the women, leads them along the length of the school building to the main entrance, where they sign in as his visitors. He shows them to the bathroom; all five disappear inside.

James waits in the hall by the general office. On the stand to his left rests an old Lexington institution, the Black Book — a loose-leaf binder of community announcements that functions as a visual public address system. It is mostly used by staff and faculty, but now James flips idly through its contents. Lexington Annual BBQ, June 19th; Deaf Ministry Revival at the Beulah Church of God; Seido Karate for Deaf Adults; Job Opening at the New York Deaf Theatre; Sign Language Storytellers at the Queens Borough Public Library; Found Hearing Aid, Come to Health Services; Thank You to the Lexington AIDS Walk Team; Beautiful Room for Rent Near School; Third Annual Deaf Playwrights Competition; Deaf Purebreed Dalmatian Puppy for Adoption; the Latino Cable TV Station Will Film Lex's Hispanic Dance Club on Tuesday.

James's sisters could not have imagined all this activity, this extended network of supports and services, which is available to James whether he chooses to use it or not. This is the first time any of them have visited James here at Lexington, his home five days a week. Now, one by one, they emerge from the bathroom and proceed without pause to satisfy their next basic need.

"We can't get food, James?"

"I'm serious, I'm so hungry."

He shakes his head, turning up his palms and widening his eyes to impress them with the futility of their pleas. "You're too late," he tells them.

Maureen cracks open the bathroom door, sticks her head inside, and calls to the cousins, who are still fussing in front of the mirror, "Dang, he say we can't get the school hot lunch, we too late!"

The tiled chamber amplifies her voice back into the hall, and a stream of staff members, all pendulous briefcases and clicking heels, veers widely around the group without slowing down as they check their boxes in the general office on the way home. They look back over their shoulders with curiosity and caution, making rapid, instinctive judgments about the tenor and purpose of these strangers.

James waits all the while without visible discomfort or embarrassment, displaying impatience only when Tina, the last to come out of the bathroom, finally joins the others in the hall, and then it is only in fun. He leans against the wall and shakes his head in mock dismay. "Girls always take too long in the bathroom."

"What he say?"

"He say you take too long."

"I got to eat something."

"James, we hungry."

"Come on," he tells them, deciding to take them on a tour before he collects their money for the luncheon tickets.

The gracious chaperon, the perfect host, he conducts them to the residential wing with the easy dignity conferred by proprietorship, a claim he is entitled to make simply by virtue of being deaf. On these grounds, he is a native son. He seems to know everyone they pass, and to each teacher or maintenance worker he volunteers with muffled pride, "My sisters." He does not hear but seems to sense the fond editorializing that ensues behind his back: "I thought they were his girlfriends . . . Looks like a harem . . . James and his entourage." His place here is certain, blessed, and they make an impressive spectacle, the six of them sashaying down the main corridor.

At the elevator to the dorm, James swings to a halt and punches the green up arrow.

"You got a elevator?" cries Neenee.

The doors slide open in response. The women step inside, checking it out, exclaiming, "Oh! Oh! Uh-huh!" The tired old box heaves them hesitantly up to the second floor, where they spill out and trail after James, their attention fixed thirstily on the educational displays lining the hall, lengths of bulletin board checkered with construction paper backgrounds on which are mounted maps, drawings, diagrams, reports. Maureen can't help but read aloud the words cut from colored paper and stapled across the boards: "Our Neighborhood Communities . . . Our Field Trip . . . Seasons of the Year."

"This school is *baad*," Kisha praises.

"I wouldn't mind coming to a school like this."

Maureen pauses in front of a poster on which are mounted samples of real currency from assorted nations. "I like that one," she says slyly, tapping a long orange nail against a shakily attached dollar bill. The others laugh. They catch up with James.

He has taken a left into the dorm living room, which leads to the warren of laundry area, bedrooms, and modest kitchen, this last being their destination. Breakfasts and dinners are cooked here each day for the dorm residents; between meals they can help themselves. James takes clear plastic cups from a wooden cupboard and pours five cherry Kool-Aids from a pitcher in the fridge. "You pay me back for this," he says, ribbing the women coolly, sending them again into peals of laughter.

They drink and survey the place approvingly.

"You got a kitchen."

"This where you cook?"

"You got foods here!"

Maureen minces comically to a corner shelf and lifts the cover off a cake dish. "What's this?" she asks James, pointing a finger daringly close.

"Carrot cake," he replies, unfazed. "Left over from yesterday."

She pinches off an edge, speedily claps the lid back down, and makes a show of tasting the sample. The others laugh at her audacity, but James observes her with neither amusement nor indignation. His gaze is steady, lucid, almost musing. The sisters' presence here in the dorm kitchen, crowded against sink and stove and wooden cabinets, flashing their feisty spirits, their door-knocker earrings, their unabashed hunger — it is as if their filling up this kitchen has triggered in James a moment of self-reflection. With all the external excitement, his gaze seems inwardly trained, as if their presence permits him a certain awareness of his own favored, fortunate position here. With it comes an undeniable sense of loss, however, as the distance between his ease and his older sister's jittery bravado grows wrenchingly vast.

If Maureen feels the distance, she does not seem to register or mourn it. She grins and licks cake from her fingers with a smacking noise, tossing her head so that tiny darts of light bounce from the gold tips of her braids. James blinks. He gestures with his chin, addressing them all. "Come on, I'm going to show you my room."

"What he say?"

"His room, he say he going to show us his room."

They set their Kool-Aid cups by the sink and follow James farther along the narrow passages. When he unlocks his door and leads them across the threshold, his sisters whistle and hoot.

"Oh dang! Snap."

"This is fly."

"This your *room*?"

"When you graduate, you going to keep the bed?"

"This is my room. Don't touch anything," says James, but they know he is teasing and press past him, scouting out the closet, the bathroom, pulling open his wardrobe, his drawers, inspecting the posters on the walls, taking in every object: sneakers, books, flowered curtains, and a box of cheddar-flavored crackers, which Maureen seizes. She plunges her arm in up to the elbow. Kisha and Neenee directly follow suit, scattering cracker pollen in their wake.

"You clean my floor," says James.

"That's right. With a vacuum," Maureen cracks back.

"A broom," needles James.

"Boy!" Maureen stretches out on his bed, eating crackers one by one from her cupped palm, too content to play the dozens and rag back on James. "This is nice. I could stay here."

"They got a McDonald's around here?" wonders Neenee.

They pick over the contents of his room, desire and praise slipping wistfully from their lips.

"I wish I could go here."

"This is so nice."

"I'd like to go to a place like this."

"My school ain't no place you want to be."

James leans against the edge of his desk and watches them. Each one's conversation overlaps too quickly and randomly with that of the others for him to follow, and he does not try. He folds his arms and rests in the invisible web their voices spin, detached in their midst, an outsider even in his own room.

"You have to be deaf to go here?" asks Kisha in earnest.

"James not deaf. He hearing. He faking."

"Naw, he's deaf."

"Then how come when you call him real loud from the kitchen he turn around and come back real fast?"

"I know." Maureen speaks up grandly from the bed. "That's, see, he gets the vibrations, 'cause they bounce off the walls."

"Then how come when you call all the way from the other end of the apartment he can hear?" demands Neenee.

"'Cause he hearing." Maureen shrugs.

"That's what I'm saying."

"This room is snap!" Tina declares softly. Oblivious to the speculation over James's auditory abilities, she has been assessing the furnishings with a keen and loving eye, and now stops suddenly, brought up short by her own image. "It even got a mirror."

The others look. A ten-dollar full-length tacked to the wall reflects them all in its candid strip of glass: five wistful guests and one who belongs.

It isn't only that he has increased his gold (new ring, new medallion, new bracelet); this year James has gotten eyeglasses, had his wisdom teeth out, and, a week before graduation, received his new hearing aids. He has passed his Regents Competency Tests and his learner's permit test, made honor roll, and been accepted to college. He has taken care of business as never before, stalling nearly every inch of the way, falling one step back for every two steps forward, but he has got there nevertheless, so that now, like it or not, there is nothing left for him to do but leave.

He has packed up his dorm room bit by bit, removing small loads to the Bronx via subway every Friday for some weeks now. The last items he will clear out after graduation, when he says goodbye to the staff. He has watched a tree outside his dorm window grow choked with rosy buds; these will blossom after he has gone.

Graduation day brings rain and an odd chill, then turns muggy in late evening. The dinner before the ceremony is served under the flat fluorescent lights and air conditioning of the big cafeteria. Girls in sleeveless dresses show gooseflesh; boys lend their sport coats. They sit close together, the large graduating class and members of the faculty wedged tightly enough to impinge on signing, except that no one lets this happen; they rearrange place settings and push back chairs in order to chatter freely up and down the length of the tables, energy crackling from hand to eye. They bite their nails and lips. Of course they are nervous.

James wears a white sport shirt, a dark, narrow tie. To-night's supper is a strangely formal conclusion after all those shared meals up in the dorm. Just the other night, he filled a plate in the old familiar kitchen, scooping rice and peas and chicken off the stove and joining two other students at the big table in the next room, all of it as routine and unremarkable as if he would go on eating dinner there forever.

Pat Penn cooks the nightly meals, and often sits with them during dinner, her full white apron straining across her comfortable girth. Pat has a son who reminds her of James; James thinks of Pat as a second mother. Upon these impressions they have constructed a relationship that allows them to take special liberties with each other.

"Where were you yesterday?" she commenced the other night, badgering James with formidable devotion.

"Home," James answered, using speech, his eyes mischievously alert. He set his fork down and waited eagerly for her reaction. The two other students peered over their corn on the cob, expectant, amused.

"Why?" Pat snapped, moving her lips with concentrated purpose, her broad features fixed in a simulacrum of severity. She knows few signs but gestures widely to illustrate her points.

"I was sleeping." James answered her queries with a pretense of jaunty insolence but could not hide the delight with which he anticipated her retorts. He would not miss a moment of the woman's chiding; on the contrary, he seemed ravenous for it, his eyes dancing with naked gratification.

"Why?" Pat continued.

"I went out Saturday, woke up next day with a cold."

"That was Saturday. Why were you out yesterday?"

James laughed helplessly; Pat, the more experienced sparrer, concealed her smile and didn't let up.

"What did you do Sunday?"

James reestablished his facade. "Slept."

"So why weren't you here yesterday?"

"I told you, I was sick." He demonstrated with a sneeze.

Pat eyed him until he squirmed. "You think I just got off the boat yesterday," she said with a snort.

"What?"

She repeated herself, employing more emphatic gestures.

"Water?" ventured James, frowning. Pat tried again, but James was unfamiliar with the English expression, and the literal meaning made no sense. He assumed he was reading her lips incorrectly. "Forget it, I don't understand."

Pat would not relent. She stuck out her chin and challenged him further. "What are you going to do when you get to college?"

"No problem," said James, very cavalier. Then, seeing that he had gotten to her, he milked it. "No problem. College is different from high school. Don't worry about it."

For a moment it appeared that they had reached a stalemate. Then Pat played her trump. She lowered one lid in a sultry wink and blew him a kiss; James fell apart laughing, completely undone.

For two years Pat cooked him fried chicken and biscuits and collards, and, more important, badgered him and mothered him and understood his speech. Those dinners in the dorm are now over, and James will probably not find another Pat at Camden County College. He will have to live in an apartment, not a dorm, and fix his own suppers, and rouse himself for classes in the morning.

James has performed a delicate balancing act. Right up until the end he has cut school, procrastinated, relied on the nagging of Pat and other staff members. He charmed his way into their good graces when he first came to Lexington, and now he has charmed himself right out of their reach.

In the big cafeteria, the graduation dinner is over. James scrapes back his chair from the table. The seniors are all rising from their seats; the time has come for caps and gowns.

Upstairs, in the lobby of the auditorium, the graduates mill around, slow to get in line. An audiologist comes down the hall, searching through the thicket of blue-and-white gowns. "Where's James Taylor?" she asks no one in particular. "If anyone sees him, tell him he lost his hearing aid and I have it."

Parents and grandparents and siblings and friends pack the auditorium and keep on coming. Faculty ushers are carting more folding chairs into the huge room, setting up extra rows.

James takes his place in line. A couple of cafeteria workers wheel carts of juice and cookies into the gym for the reception that will follow the ceremony; they shake his hand as they go by. A dorm worker slaps his back and shakes his hand. Someone passes him his missing hearing aid; he twists it into his ear. A gowned teacher paces the line, examining mortarboards and tassels. James switches his tassel to match hers, then puffs out his chest for inspection, his stance so earnest that the teacher stops to giggle. She sets him straight: *"I already graduated! Mine's on the left! Have you graduated yet?"*

When at last all the tassels are properly aligned, the lights inside the auditorium dim. Teachers cue the students that "Pomp and Circumstance" has started. They file through the doorway, which is trimmed with baby's-breath and greens, march down the aisle, and fill the bleachers onstage. James sits in the highest row, looking regal in his sapphire gown, sage in his gilt-framed glasses. Somewhere in the darkness of the house sits his family: father, mother, mother's boyfriend, three sisters, cousin, two baby nieces. He knew he'd get the extra tickets somehow.

It is not enough to say that James has charmed his way through. Charm alone cannot account for the fact that he is graduating. Students come and go through these doors; some are able to receive help, some are not. Nor can James's achievements be credited to the special attentions given to him because of his deafness. His deafness is neither a talisman nor a curse, but something at once more prosaic and profound: an aspect of himself.

All around him on the bleachers sit classmates whose personal histories are mapped by their own struggles. Along lines of circumstance and lines of will, they have each navigated an individual path to this day. Some might look at these bleachers and see only deaf teenagers, set apart, united and dignified by the special struggles of deafness. But they are firmly linked to the others, those who sit in darkness just beyond the apron of the stage, an entire audience of lives mapped by individual struggles: hearing families, deaf families, teachers, ushers, interpreters, students. Although James cannot see or hear them, he senses their presence, their bodies and breath, and the occasional flashbulb popping blue in the corner of his eye.

When it comes time for the students to receive their diplomas, they rise as one but approach the dais individually, where they shake hands, kiss cheeks, and accept the documents cased in leatherette. Crossing center stage on the way back to the bleachers, many of them mug or pose or sign messages into the audience: *"Thank you all . . . I love you, Mom and Dad . . . See, Ma? I told you I'd graduate."* One student kneels, ducks his head, and points to the flat of his mortarboard, where he has used scraps of masking tape to spell I LUV LEX.

James goes next to last. He does not sign a message; the members of his family do not know sign language. He lifts his diploma high, the sleeve of his gown billowing down around his armpit, and executes a crisp bow. As he is straightening, a flashbulb goes off, and he spots his sisters, holding their babies in the air and cheering. The audience immediately goes black again, but now James knows just where his family is, and he smiles for a moment longer in that direction, as though he can really see them.

The last speaker of the evening, a hearing man, talks about deaf pride. "One of the wonderful things about any great social movement," he says, "is that we are *all* going to benefit from it." James watches the interpreter nearest him. Another is signing for the adults on the dais across the stage, a third for members of the audience. On waves of light and waves of sound, the message is sent forth to each person in the room, and there is comfort in the fact that it is meant for them all. The signs and words weave a kind of spell joining two houses, two families.

Later tonight, after the general reception in the gym, the dorm staff will throw James a private party. He knows that they have gotten him a sheet cake that says "Congratulations James" in yellow icing, and that the evening will end with all the Taylors going upstairs, where they will meet Pat and the other staff members and students, and everyone will have some cake. No one could question James's riches tonight: for the first time, both of his families under one roof.

Acknowledgments

I am very grateful to all of the people at Lexington whose generosity, patience, expertise, and trust made this book possible, especially Sofia Normatov and James Taylor and their families, teachers, and friends; also Barbara Robinson, and Pat McCormac (for the blueprints and treacle).

I would also like to thank Sam Freedman, Barney Karpfinger, Betsy Lerner, David Krajicek, Jim Evers, the Rochester Bureau, Dake Ackley, Reba, Andy, Michael, my father, and especially my mother, Sue.